As we enter what author Peter McAte(of the corporation, customers are dem: and practices, governments are passing regulations that are changing business operations, and activist investors are asking questions about business risk and factors like climate change.

How will your business respond to these demands? How quickly will you act and what effects will it have on the long-term health of your company? Most critically, how will you lead your organization to successfully implement these changes?

To create lasting change we need to take a hard look at several challenges:

- What is this concept we call "sustainability" and how do we describe it in actionable ways?
- How do new business models shape our behavior and create more positive results for people, society, and the environment?
- If we expect people and organizations to behave differently, what are the key capabilities and skills that we need to master?
- What best practices in talent development can we use to accelerate organization change for a better future?

In this groundbreaking book McAteer provides insights into solutions that leaders can adopt to make the right business case to their stakeholders and build a company that has sustainability at its core and brilliant innovations in its operations as a result.

Praise for *Sustainability Is the New Advantage*

McAteer has created a masterpiece on sustainability. He personalizes the sustainability agenda, then surrounds it with facts and offers guidance on how to grow the sustainability movement. He notes especially that planet, profit, and people can coexist and mutually reinforce each other to benefit all. Kudos for this great work.

DAVE ULRICH, Rensis Likert Professor, Ross School of Business, University of Michigan, and Partner, The RBL Group

Peter McAteer has written an extraordinary book. *Sustainability Is the New Advantage* is an all-in-one instructional manual that companies (of any size) can use to gain a clear competitive advantage by exploiting the opportunities offered by a commitment to sustainability. Every business school should be teaching at least one course based on this book. McAteer analyzes and illustrates the leadership required to meet a range of sustainability challenges, along with the new knowledge that will be needed, techniques for recruiting and developing the right talent, and strategies for providing continuous training.

LAWRENCE SUSSKIND, Ford Professor of Urban and Environmental Planning, Massachusetts Institute of Technology, and Director of the MIT Science Impact Collaborative

The book is really good. It's interesting. It's practical. And it displays great expertise. Drawing on his vast knowledge, McAteer's book is a masterly, practical synthesis showing what companies—and their leaders individually—need to do to build a more sustainable future. His comments about smaller businesses are spot on. Well done!

THOMAS A. STEWART, Executive Director, National Center for the Middle Market, Fisher College of Business, The Ohio State University

Combining practical tools and powerful stories, *Sustainability Is the New Advantage* is an indispensable guide to one of the most critical issues of our time.

SCOTT D. ANTHONY, Innosight Senior Partner and lead author of *Dual Transformation*

Sustainability Is the New Advantage opened up a whole new world for me as a leader. It challenged me to move from advocacy to action. Based on cutting edge insights, this is a game changing book and a "must read" for any leader.

SUSAN LANSING, Senior Vice President, Head of Learning and Development, Bank of the West

As dean of a European school with six campuses and a global student population, I am acutely aware of the fact that sustainability issues cross borders and require a collaborative sense of responsibility. McAteer's focus on current corporate leaders deals with a practical reality. If we are going to make progress on environmental and social challenges in the coming decades, the people currently working in organizations need to be re-trained to solve the problems. All business practitioners should read *Sustainability Is the New Advantage*. It is a stimulating book that invites readers not only to revisit their personal accountability on this topic but encourages everyone to take concrete actions. McAteer provides a practical path forward.

BERTRAND MOINGEON, Dean for Executive Education and Corporate Initiatives, ESCP Europe

Leaders urgently need new models and tools for doing business more sustainably. In this detailed yet pragmatic guide to adopting and driving sustainability practices, Peter McAteer shares a lifetime of hard won lessons and examples, providing valuable tools to help diverse teams and organizations to adapt to the essential challenge of our time.

DR. HAL MOVIUS, President, Movius Consulting and co-author of *Built to Win*

Sustainability Is the New Advantage taps into a topic of great relevance to everyone who cares about our planet and our local communities. McAteer offers examples from all over the world and adds personal insights that make the book inspiring.

S. HARIKUMAR, CEO and Managing Director, Origin Learning India

I've known Peter McAteer and his family for many years and have long respected their commitment to entrepreneurial business ideas, profit-ability, and values. Education was a force for change for Peter's fam-ily and advancing the acquisition of knowledge underpins all his career decisions. This new book has a personal touch and offers an argument that is deeply rooted in his family traditions and that interprets family as the global village to which we are all tied.

McAteer's vision for a sustainable business culture is one that individ-ual leaders and businesses large and small can incorporate in practical ways. McAteer writes in an accessible way while arguing with data and reason. He is able to tell stories of successful strategies that are engaging and scalable. As an educator preparing the current generation for lead-ership, I see this as a book that will engage and challenge.

SUSAN KING, Dean, UNC School of Media and Journalism

This book is a fresh call for action. A beautiful and necessary effort underpinned by the experience that comes from a long-standing pro-fessional career. McAteer puts the reader at the crossroads of the pri-vate and public sectors, of education and corporate life. At a time when discussions about sustainability seem entangled in politics, McAteer's book calls us back to the stage where human choice and motivation make a difference. His persuasive voice and creative use of research and stories encourages us to lead, learn, and collaborate.

ALFONS SAUQUET ROVIRA, Professor of Learning and Knowledge, ESADE, Chairperson, Academy of Business in Society (ABIS)

ANTHEM ENVIRONMENT AND SUSTAINABILITY INITIATIVE (AESI)

The *Anthem Environment and Sustainability Initiative (AESI)* seeks to push the frontiers of scholarship while simultaneously offering prescriptive and programmatic advice to policymakers and practitioners around the world. The programme publishes research monographs, professional and major reference works, upper-level textbooks and general interest titles. Professor Lawrence Susskind, as General Editor of AESI, oversees the below book series, each with its own series editor and an editorial board featuring scholars, practitioners and business experts keen to link theory and practice.

Strategies for Sustainable Development Series
Series Editor: Professor Lawrence Susskind (MIT)

Climate Change Science, Policy and Implementation
Series Editor: Dr. Brooke Hemming (US EPA)

Science Diplomacy: Managing Food, Energy and Water Sustainably
Series Editor: Professor Shafiqul Islam (Tufts University)

International Environmental Policy Series
Series Editor: Professor Saleem Ali (University of Delaware)

Big Data and Sustainable Cities Series
Series Editor: Professor Sarah Williams (MIT)

Climate Change and the Future of the North American City
Series Editor: Richardson Dilworth (Center for Public Policy, Drexel University, USA)

Included within the AESI is the *Anthem EnviroExperts Review.* Through this online micro-review site, Anthem Press seeks to build a community of practice involving scientists, policy analysts and activists committed to creating a clearer and deeper understanding of how ecological systems – at every level – operate, and how they have been damaged by unsustainable development. This site publishes short reviews of important books or reports in the environmental field, broadly defined. Visit the website: www.anthemenviroexperts.com.

Sustainability Is the New Advantage

LEADERSHIP, CHANGE AND THE FUTURE OF BUSINESS

PETER McATEER

ANTHEM PRESS

Anthem Press
An imprint of Wimbledon Publishing Company
www.anthempress.com

This edition first published in UK and USA 2021
by ANTHEM PRESS
75–76 Blackfriars Road, London SE1 8HA, UK
or PO Box 9779, London SW19 7ZG, UK
and
244 Madison Ave #116, New York, NY 10016, USA

First published in the UK and USA by Anthem Press 2019

Copyright © Peter McAteer 2021

The author asserts the moral right to be identified as the author of this work.

British Library Cataloguing-in-Publication Data
A catalogue record for this book is available from the British Library.

Library of Congress Control Number: 2020949906

ISBN-13: 978-1-78527-691-0 (Pbk)
ISBN-10: 1-78527-691-3 (Pbk)

Editorial and design development by LifeTree Media Limited
Editor: Don Loney
Design: Greg Tabor
Cover image: Kit8

This title is also available as an e-book.

CONTENTS

LIST OF ILLUSTRATIONS

Figures

Tables

FOREWORD

When I was asked to write the foreword to this book, I took a moment to ponder the fundamental question that underlies its purpose: Is sustainability good for business? Although many in academia or professional practice might answer yes, one look at the percentage of products sold that fully comply with sustainability principles suggests that the answer is hardly certain or universal. As with many difficult tasks, faster progress often requires a good storyteller to make a compelling case and offer a path forward. I am happy to say that Peter has achieved that goal with this book.

For the better part of four decades, I've worked with local, national, and international public-sector organizations to improve the quality of government services and the health of our communities. A hallmark of this effort is supporting urban parks around the United States and throughout the world to improve their quality, accessibility, and financial stability, often through cross-sector partnerships. To me, this is the goal of sustainability—financially stable, vibrant communities that support innovative industries and schools that are a joy to live in. Although many people share this aspiration, the journey has been a challenging one.

Through my work with Columbia University's School of International and Public Affairs, I have engaged with public servants from Brazil to Hong Kong and developed customized programs for public and private organizations on every continent. Although the sustainability challenges and degree of difficulty may vary among countries and organizations, two things are clear. The desire to support the United Nations

Sustainable Development Goals is very strong, and so is the need for a blueprint that allows more organizations to participate and generate results.

I have known Peter McAteer since his days at the United Nations Development Program as a dedicated teacher, problem solver, and innovator. Today, in addition to being a successful entrepreneur, he is one of the thought leaders in the business world who recognize that sustainable business practices are not only essential to preserving our planet, but also good for business.

In this important new book, Peter builds a very effective logic model, beginning with a detailed examination of what sustainability is, how the field is evolving, and why all of us should embrace a personal commitment to the success of this methodology. He takes the time to translate the general principles of sustainability into sound and beneficial business practices, and also explains how the practice of business sustainability can vary based on an organization's size, location, and the nature of its business. In essence, he lays out a blueprint to get started.

Throughout the book, Peter weaves a narrative that highlights the twin values of new business models and public–private partnerships. They serve as the source of new knowledge and innovation and offer benefits for a broader range of shareholders. As someone who has worked for decades on public–private partnerships, I am in complete agreement. When done well, the Sustainable Development Goals and the idea of a triple bottom line provide the value bridge that can not only make it easier for corporations to improve their results, but also connect them more effectively to the communities where they live. Increasingly, this is also supported by research.

During the past several years, Columbia graduate students have helped document numerous case studies in Asia, sub-Saharan Africa, and Latin America that emphasize the importance of social value investing as well as business solutions for challenges that were once the focus of development aid. Businesses are often a source of innovation and a continuing source of capital and great ideas. Social value becomes paired with economic value. Our research shows that communities gain the most from the type of investment that yields self-sustaining benefits—that creates jobs and strengthens local ownership. Forging a generation of business professionals who embrace this concept is one of the core messages of this book.

One additional factor Peter describes in great detail is how the practice of sustainability will be different in smaller organizations. Again, my experience bears this out. Smaller organizations and small businesses are often the heartbeat of a community and the key to almost all social challenges. Unfortunately, they are also often the orphans of new business practice: too small to control their supply chains, too limited in their talent base, and frequently undercapitalized. However, in many parts of the world, smaller businesses are the dominant employer, so finding ways to engage smaller businesses in sustainable solutions is perhaps the best way to create safe and healthy communities. Although some of the themes Peter highlights are familiar—emphasizing communication, connecting commitment to measurable social outcomes, and encouraging innovation—what is new and inspiring is how Peter combines purpose, passion, and performance measurement into a recipe for small business success.

Businesses striving to be sustainable face challenges similar to those confronted by the management practice total quality management in its early stages several decades ago, and Peter recognizes the equal need for such businesses to develop operating practices that transform high-level concepts into day-to-day activities. He presents a number of useful techniques to help make sustainability and standard operating procedures one and the same. As is often the case in both private- and public-sector transformations, a small number of key practices, done exceptionally well, often provide the quickest and most consistent results.

The final chapters of the book focus on creating a learning culture conducive to the spread of sustainability knowledge throughout the organization. Of particular importance is the connection Peter makes between sustainability and the evolving nature of organizational design: a sustainable learning culture now applies not only to the traditional organizational structure, but also to partnerships, ecosystems, and value chains. Again, Peter provides a step-by-step guide to recruiting people who are most likely to embrace the business and social values of sustainability, and who will keep that spirit alive every day in an extended workplace. As an expert in training and development, Peter presents his wisdom in those areas tailored to fit the challenges of sustainability.

I highly recommend this book as a great read and an invaluable resource guide that you will use over and over again as you lead and as you pursue your quest to create a truly sustainable business.

William B. Eimicke
Professor of Practice, Columbia University's Graduate School of International and Public Affairs
Co-author (with Howard Buffet) of *Social Value Investing: A Management Framework for Effective Partnerships*

INTRODUCTION

"The greatest threat to our planet is the belief that someone else will save it." ROBERT SWAN

I wrote this book to bring attention to the damage we are doing to our planet and to present a plan for change agents to create sustainable business outcomes. Sustainability is the issue of our times and reflects collective, long-term, damaging behavior that needs our immediate attention. Mass immigration challenges speak to inequality, oceans filled with plastics to unsustainable consumption, and unusually strong weather events to climate change. Poverty remains endemic even in the wealthiest of nations, and the lack of clean water and sanitation is a growing challenge for millions. Yet these issues are not new. They have been with us for generations, and the warning signs were visible if you chose to look. So, why has progress been so slow? Why have we chosen to continue behaving in ways that are clearly harmful? In some instances, despite overwhelming information, we continue to make matters worse.

In order to accelerate change, our effort must be a united one. We need to help everyone in our organizations develop a heightened degree of awareness about both the problems and the opportunities. How can we generate positive economic results while solving the problems of polluted oceans, unpotable water, and unsafe working conditions? We need to come up with new ideas, scale solutions, and develop the talent to operate sustainable businesses. I generally have faith that people have good intentions, which is why I believe these challenges are solvable. I do not believe most business leaders or government officials deliberately seek to destroy the environment, operate sweatshops, or ruin the communities in which they live. The problem lies in the way we have been trained to behave, the incentives that encourage similar behavior, and the business practices that keep us going down the same path.

I have been an advocate for "conscious capitalism," or responsible growth, for a long time. However, even making that statement is something of an excuse. While I may profess advocacy, I have also happily driven gas and diesel cars for forty years and racked up several million frequent flyer miles in aircraft. My lifestyle and consumption patterns were not intended to harm, but they have clearly been part of the problem. I would ask every reader to make the same reflection. I have good friends in India who routinely forego business appointments because of the horrible traffic congestion or miss flights because the air pollution is so bad. The pristine beaches near my brother's home in Florida are repeatedly choked with red tide—a normal phenomenon made substantially worse by warming ocean currents and excess nutrient pollution.

No matter where you sit as you read this book, there are likely changes you can see around you. My fiancée's family is from Thailand, and she can remember when almost every beach was a pristine oasis where one could escape the summer heat. The famed beaches of Krabi and Phuket, with their towering limestone cliffs and powdery sand, are rightly featured in many films for their breathtaking beauty. Yet the famed Maya Beach in Krabi, scene of the 2000 Leonardo DiCaprio movie *The Beach*, has been closed to tourists this year because of environmental damage. The same thing happened in the Philippines when the government shut down the popular tourist island of Boracay for six months.

The great city of Rio de Janeiro in Brazil hosted the 2016 Olympics. If you have visited the city, you will have experienced its rich culture, exquisite food, and welcoming people. Yet the water pollution in Guanabara Bay was so bad that sailing athletes were advised to avoid being immersed in the water. Major urban areas around the world suffer similar problems of unhealthy air and water quality. These challenges were not created overnight and are never the result of one person or one set of actions. Yet the answer rests with each of us taking responsibility—consistently, repeatedly, and collectively with others.

Much of the social success we've enjoyed over the past twenty to thirty years addressing poverty, for example, is due to new job creation, particularly in India and China. During a four-year period of rapid growth in Asian economies (2002–2006), I worked at the United Nations, and we spent billions of dollars per year in economic development. It had an impact, but the real leverage was obtained when there was both strong business and active civil society participation. We collectively made positive reductions in poverty, improved standards of living, and increased health-care outcomes for many. At the same time, we have a long way to go in improving unsafe working conditions, expanding opportunities for women, and building communities able to maintain basic services.

The simple questions we all need to ask are, Can our business be an engine for economic growth *and* social good? Can we have both strong investment returns *and* healthier communities, or will it always be a choice of one or the other? To get higher profits, do we need to sacrifice something like land, air, or water quality? If that is the unalterable reality, then why is this so?

The starting point in this discussion on change begins with some self-reflection. The more we think of problems like hunger or access to clean water as a problem not of our making or a matter of self-interest, the more we deflect accountability and any sense of urgency. As long as I am okay, or my business seems okay, then why should I care? However, since I believe the data says that issues of sustainability are getting worse, it seems reasonable to ask the questions, What have I done to contribute to these problems? How do I learn new ways of behaving to improve on the status quo? As Nelson Mandela once said, "Education is the most powerful weapon which you can use to change the world." To that end, creating change is a process of education and business transformation.

My personal reflections have caused me to take action. In some ways they open a new door on the opportunities presented by our challenges. Planet Earth could care less about us. But we humans do need to care about one another, and that requires change. Why? Because we will all benefit from healthier communities and an economy based on sustainable advantages. Specifically, we must be the drivers of change within our organizations, because they are the drivers of economic value and often linked to excess consumption or negative social outcomes. As much as we say that businesses compete, the reality is that they do not; rather, people compete, as individuals, teams, and leaders. To create sustainable organizations, innovation must be married to the goal of creating a better future. We must see sustainability as the opportunity, not the problem; as the source of new value, not a constraint. Putting a plan into action requires change agents—people like you who become curious about what they can do and how they can create meaningful change. Or, as several interviewees for the book have put it, those who refocus attention on creating a "sustainability advantage."

Our New Learning Journey

To create lasting change we need to take a hard look at several challenges and give people the tools to succeed. To meet that challenge, I have divided the book into three parts. The goal is to take you on a learning journey that enables you to take action.

The first part of that journey is an education process to understand this concept we call sustainability. I begin with a bit of family history to present some perspective. Since I have asked you, the reader, to reflect on how you behave, I have tried to do the same thing. I am hoping you will enjoy my travels through history and see some parallels in your own family tree. I start by asking simple questions about the origins of sustainability and querying at what point we began to make choices that have led us to where we are now.

The first goal for this part is to build core foundational knowledge. Do we have a common definition for sustainability, and how did we arrive at that definition? What new business models can shape our behavior and create more positive results for people, society, and the environment? Can the business models work the same for both large and small companies or are there differences?

I consider the answers to these questions the launching point for change. They allow you as a change agent to ask open-ended questions of others to get them to make personal reflections. They allow you to flip the conversation from a view of organizational risk to one of new opportunity. Developing a compelling case for change is the first step on a common journey. Your ability to articulate a business case, in your own words, is how you create followership and is part of the value you bring to your organization.

A second goal for the first part of the book is to communicate that the definition of sustainability is not static but dynamic, and therein lies a key challenge when discussing economic and social value creation, as well as business transformation. This means that change agents must be open to continuous learning and new opportunities for innovation. Inevitably, you need a broader systems perspective to understand how our behavior (and your behavior) has downstream impact and which set of business models will work in a given situation. You need a passionate commitment to sustainability, but also an ongoing curiosity for new knowledge discovery and sharing. I will offer examples of new business models, their desired outcomes, and examples of organizations that use them. But you need to use that foundation as a jumping-off point to build your own network of knowledge discovery and information sharing. All change agents, regardless of level or function, must be constantly engaged in learning about new models and evolving practices. The latter parts of the book are designed to address the tools and techniques needed to support your learning journey.

Part Two of the book is about creating and leading the sustainability agenda. If you've ever done a lot of research, you know the feeling when you see patterns emerge. For this book, three important patterns developed: the central role of the one committed leader, the need for sustainability to be part of your business's DNA, and the related practice of embedding sustainability in how you engage in everyday practices like problem-solving. Those three points recurred many times in the course of my research for the book, so I have given them prominence in Part Two.

The final part of the book is all about building a better toolbox for change. What new practices can we use to accelerate organizational change? What existing techniques and practices can be adapted to serve a better future? How do I use these resources to scale my sustainable business? In any business, there is typically a tension between reducing variability, because that allows better efficiency, and introducing new variability, because that is the essence of innovation and change. In your new sustainable business model, the balance in tension shifts towards introducing variability, because so much will be new. That reflects both the risk (and discomfort you may feel) and the new potential. Your role as a change agent is to unlock those opportunities and use the bounty of new experiences as part of your talent development tool kit. New practice areas may not be well understood, but they can be unique opportunities as knowledge-creating or discovery assignments.

The book closes with a review of the seventeen United Nations Sustainable Development Goals (SDGs, covered in depth in chapter 2) and an overview of resources for the sustainability champion—hopefully you. I also come back to my personal story in the afterword, reinforcing the idea that the challenge of sustainability has emerged over many generations and will only be solved when we anchor new mental models not only in our companies but also in our educational institutions, families, and communities that continue this legacy. Through all of what we may consider the modern era, each generation has desired a good job, happiness, peace, and security. Each succeeding generation has inherited a world of greater economic prosperity and knowledge, although the benefits have not always been evenly distributed. Our goal as champions of sustainability is to shift the paradigm so that each succeeding generation carries forward a healthier planet, stronger communities, and the expanding benefits of social value creation.

PART ONE

SUSTAINABILITY AND THE EVOLUTION OF BUSINESS

Chapter 1

A JOURNEY OF SELF-DISCOVERY

"There is no discovery without risk and what you risk reveals what you value." JEANETTE WINTERSON

My first ancestor to arrive in the United States was my great-grandfather, Matthew McAteer. He was born in Northern Ireland in 1856 and arrived in New Jersey through the port of Jersey City in 1882. Other relatives would arrive later though Castle Garden in lower Manhattan, the gateway to America before Ellis Island opened a decade later. Matthew would have sailed in steerage class on a coal-fired steamer for a fare of approximately four British pounds, the equivalent of almost 340 British pounds today.[1] He was among the more than 1 million Irish who had come to the United States in the preceding fifty years to escape the great Irish potato famines. The famines were the direct result of unsustainable agriculture practices and a dangerous dependence on monoculture farming. Matthew settled in the New York City area. At that time, the world's population was approximately 1.2 billion people. New York City had grown to approximately 1.2 million people. What would follow Matthew to New York and to the country generally were a range of unsustainable practices already creating negative social outcomes around the world.

I doubt that when Matthew arrived in the US he had concerns about his carbon footprint. Although I can count six generations of McAteers since his arrival in the US, I do not recall a family conversation in which we openly discussed being complicit in pollution, inequality, or climate change. I'm sure most families would say the same thing. However, the signs were there if you wanted to look:

- major European cities had experienced air and water pollution for hundreds of years;
- London experienced deadly fogs in the 1800s, when still air trapped a lethal combination of industrial pollution and gases from wood- and coal-burning stoves;
- most of the great European rivers passing through major cities or industrial zones were heavily polluted in the 1800s;
- by the late 1800s, the lung disease bronchitis[2] had become the leading cause of death in Great Britain;
- the American bison, once numbering in the tens of millions, was almost wiped out by the late 19th century;
- the US census of 1870 found that one in eight children aged ten to fifteen was already formally employed. That number reached one in five by 1900;[3] and
- by the middle of the 19th century, authors such as Charles Dickens were writing extensively about inequality, children's rights, and social reforms that would become part of the sustainability agenda in the 21st century.

Matthew's birth in the 1850s is a notable event for my family in the United States, but it also coincides with a milestone in the history of business. The first phase of the "age of the corporation," when organizations like the Dutch East India Company reigned, was winding down. The world was still dominated by colonial powers, sailing ships still plied the seas, and forced labor practices were common. However, the middle of the 19th century marks the transition to the second phase of the age of the corporation, an era characterized by industrial innovation and great migrations from farm to city.

Although the corporation has been with us for over four hundred years, industrial activity prior to 1850 did not contribute any meaningful change in global greenhouse gases. In the middle of the 19th century, atmospheric CO_2 stood at approximately 270ppm. However, after 1850, "the world generally experienced a constant growth of emissions"[4] as well as constant growth in economic activity. Figure 1.1 illustrates the enormous changes that happened from that point forward.[5] The three variables on the graph are not directly comparable since they use different scales, but the trend pattern is unmistakable. As populations and economic development increased, so too did consumption and the production of greenhouse gases.

More people to feed generated higher demand for agricultural output. Farmers responded by increasing productivity by an average of 2 to 3 percent per year for over a century and a half.[6] During that same time period, according to the World Wildlife Fund, "half of the topsoil on the

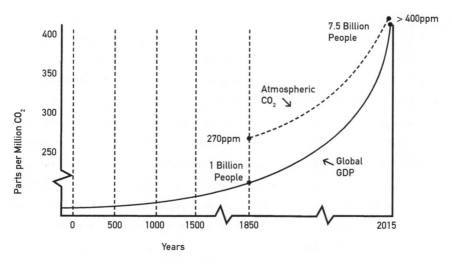

Figure 1.1: Population, GDP Growth, and CO_2

planet [was] lost."[7] We planted crops that degraded the soil, reduced soil nutrients, and created longer-term changes in soil salinity. But bigger yields meant more customers and more economic growth. The year 1850 marks the beginning of a clear shift to a world with ever-expanding wealth and consumption.

This era of economic activity strengthens the narrative that the purpose of the corporation is to deliver value to shareholders. Reliance on coal and then oil, and the emergence of the steam engine, revolutionized industrial activity with little thought to either labor regulations or the respectful treatment of the environment. Environmental impact tended to be local, and there was a lack of consciousness about how local events might connect to global patterns.[8] Although there were protests about clean air and water, the science was in its infancy and the new economic value being created outweighed the social concerns. According to author Jim Morrison, writing in *Smithsonian*, "Laws were passed in Britain, the United States and Germany, but with little teeth. They called for 'best practice' solutions—an easy out—levied insignificant fines and contained numerous exemptions. Coal remained cheap. No one was willing to slow the industrial engine."[9]

One of the outcomes of early industrial development was a growing recognition that science could spur new innovation and that the right talent could generate enormous value. Talent development and professional education led to the creation of powerful craft societies and guilds. For the next fifty years, the primary tool for talent development remained the apprenticeship, with access often determined by your status and position in society. At the same time, a growing need for both research and professional managers contributed to the evolution of the university system and a general expansion of research and development.

The first modern-era assessment of greenhouse gases happened during Matthew's lifetime, attributed to Swedish scientist Svante Arrhenius in 1896.[10] However, the general feeling of the day was that global warming would take thousands of years to occur and might indeed have positive consequences. He and other scientists were trying to understand climate by researching the causes of variance in the earth's temperature, or what triggers an ice age. He understood that increasing CO_2 (called carbonic acid at the time) might increase global temperatures. He elaborated on his thoughts in 1908: "By the influence of the increasing percentage of carbonic acid in the atmosphere, we may hope to enjoy ages with more equable and better climates, especially as regards the colder regions of the earth, ages when the earth will bring forth much more abundant crops than at present, for the benefit of rapidly propagating mankind."[11] These remarks were influenced by research that pointed to periods in the earth's geologic record when higher temperatures and higher oxygen levels led to a great diversity of large plants and animals. Scientists were not yet making the connection to rising oceans, acidification, and other problems.

From Migrants to Citizens

My mother's parents arrived in the US prior to World War 1 from Eastern Europe. My grandmother grew up in Poland on a family farm; my grandfather was born in Lithuania, also on a farm. My mother's family lived in a small house without indoor plumbing and had a side yard where my grandmother grew vegetables. I remember my grandmother's love of her cherry and apple trees and can recall stories of how my grandfather would use his car to bring home baskets of manure to fertilize her vegetable crops. Grandma, like all farmers of her era, was an organic farmer, as a fragrant ride in the car would attest. Although cow manure and decaying farm refuse contributed to greenhouse gases, they were offset (at the time) by a proportionately smaller population and larger global forest cover. I'll give grandma and grandpa a pass since they planted trees, used an outhouse, and generally had a very small carbon footprint.

Between the world wars, one grandfather worked as a railroad engineer while the other worked in a Ford car assembly plant. Both the railroads and the automobile industry were significant contributors to carbon dioxide emissions and chemical waste. They also contributed greatly to the idea of a national (if not yet global) supply chain. My father was trained as a refrigeration engineer and was employed by commercial heating, ventilating, and air conditioning (HVAC) companies. Innovations in all manufacturing and construction industries relied heavily on carbon fuels and toxic chemicals. When my father was born, in 1921, carbon emissions in the US were already 1421 metric tons of CO_2.[12] Global emissions of carbon at the time of my father's birth were already three times higher in the US than when my grandfather was born, and fifteen times higher than when my great-grandfather was born. I'm sure neither gave much thought to global warming, although local water pollution was garnering attention.

The year I was born, 1956, the world population stood at 2.8 billion people[13] and atmospheric CO_2 had risen to over 300ppm. In October of that year, *The New York Times* published an article titled "Warmer Climate on the Earth May Be Due to More Carbon Dioxide in the Air."[14] Although there was not yet scientific consensus, the evidence was beginning to build that humans have a substantial impact on the environment. In December of 1956, the British Parliament passed the Clean Air Act[15] in response to "Great Smog" events in London that had killed thousands. In 1958, Charles Keeling of the Scripps Institution of Oceanography (US) started recording daily CO_2 levels at Hawaii's Mauna Loa Observatory. The atmospheric CO_2 benchmarks used today in the United Nations global climate studies incorporate the Keeling Curve, which graphically represents historical data on climate change.[16]

My paternal grandparents grew up in the city of Paterson, New Jersey, home to the second largest waterfall on the United States east coast after Niagara Falls. Paterson was originally developed with funds raised by Alexander Hamilton and the Society for Establishing Useful Manufactures[17] to take advantage of waterpower from the Passaic River. By the late 19th century, Paterson was a hub of manufacturing, including railroad cars and silk, and was one of the most important cities of the early American industrial era. Unfortunately, Paterson also became known for child labor abuses, poor worker safety, and pollution. By the time

I was a teenager in the 1970s, the manufacturing industries had all but abandoned Paterson, and by the 1980s areas of the great Passaic River were declared toxic Superfund sites by the US Environmental Protection Agency (EPA),[18] which meant that they were identified as being among the most polluted rivers in the US. The great river and falls were abandoned by the very companies that polluted them. It was cheaper for companies to go bankrupt or move rather than fix the environmental degradation they created.

When I entered elementary school, Rachel Carson published her landmark book *Silent Spring*, in 1962.[19] Although I remember one of my older siblings reading the book, I recall the 1960s more for the Vietnam War, rock music, and long hair. My uncle Bill, who lived in California, would report the problem of "smog," but California was a long way off. My older brothers and sisters were in high school, and the environmental movement was just beginning to enter the public square. News coverage and the consequent impact were decidedly local until the formal declaration of Earth Day on April 22, 1970, when the topic became one for family discussion. By then, my mother was an avid recycler: we had a compost pile for our garden and my father began to recycle copper and brass. At the same time, we routinely threw out batteries, changed our own motor oil, and disposed of the oil as well as greasy rags in the garbage. Although we were conscious of the dangers of pollution on one level, we still engaged in behaviors that clearly contributed to the problem.

The world's population would increase by another billion people by my sophomore year in high school (1972) and would reach 5 billion by my thirtieth birthday. The 1980s gave rise to the personal computer revolution and a massive increase in electronic waste. We solved the problem of e-waste in the United States and Europe not by improving recycling or changing product design, but by exporting much of the waste to less-developed countries in Africa as well as China and India. Extracting valuable metals like palladium, copper, and gold employed thousands of workers, but it also exposed them to toxic chemicals and simply moved the waste stream from one country to another. This solution also added to the pollution problem by creating a larger carbon footprint through shipping the waste halfway across the world. *That such a solution made sense suggests a fundamental problem with the business and financial models that enabled it.*

Today, global e-waste is estimated to be 44.7 million metric tons, according to the International Solid Waste Association (ISWA).[20] Of equal concern is that solid e-waste is rising on a per capita basis, now 6.1 kilograms per person, and is estimated to grow to 52.2 metric tons of total e-waste by 2021. *The Global E-waste Monitor* estimates that we have no documentation on fully 76 percent of all e-waste, noting, "This is likely dumped, traded, or recycled under inferior conditions."[21]

I spent many of my middle adult years based in the Boston area, historically known for its great cod fishery. The Massachusetts State House in Boston is home to the "sacred cod," a five-foot-long wooden statue of the fish that represented a historical path to wealth creation since colonial times. The port of Boston's very existence was in part due to its proximity to the great fishing grounds of the Grand Banks and George's Bank, as well as the bays of New England.

As I mentioned above, we massacred the bison to the point of extinction, and another tragic massacre was taking place offshore. According to the Atlantic Cod Fishery website, "In 1994, it was found that only 2,000 tons of spawning stock biomass, or the dry weight of all fish in a species that can reproduce, were still in the Grand Banks, less than 1% of the historical biomass."[22] Fishermen had reported smaller fish and smaller catches for decades, but overfishing by massive trawlers went unchallenged for almost too long. The partial or full closure of commercial fishing grounds by both the Canadian and US governments in the 1990s was "a brutal shock to the people who made a living catching fish in waters once so thick with cod it was said you could leave your boat and walk to shore on their backs."[23] In 2000, the World Wildlife

Fund (WWF) placed cod on its endangered species list. It remains on the WWF's priority species list to this day.[24]

The Fundamental Dilemma

Humans have been changing their environment for thousands of years. Ancient practices of controlled burns transformed forest into grasslands. Hunting of selected species has changed the balance of predator and prey. Overfishing has changed what we eat and clear-cutting of forests has changed wildlife habitats. From afar, each of these decisions seems acutely short-sighted. When you have already cleared 95 percent of the old-growth forests, how can you argue for cutting the last few? When you have already depleted a fishery by 90 percent, how can you argue for continued fishing?

Yet to the businessperson who needs to pay bills and support a family, denial is part of self-interest. For the business owner trying to get a return on investment or the community seeking jobs, the situation is similar. Consider that in the decades between the mid-1930s, when my father was a teenager, and the time I collected my graduate degree in 1980, 90 percent of American workers received 70 percent of the income growth. More recently, from the time of my graduation until the time my oldest son received his bachelor's degree, 1980 to 2015, 10 percent of the American population got 100 percent of the income growth. The bottom 90 percent got nothing.[25]

When it is your job, your community, and your life, continued incremental damage seems okay. For over 150 years we have consistently believed that economic value creation is the only role for a business, and that the collective commons of air, land, and water have little comparative value.

In the year 2017, with strong climate change data and with increasing investment in alternative energy, we still consider opening vast new coal mines. The Abbot Point Mine in Australia is one such example.[26] Despite the drop in worldwide coal consumption from 2016 to 2017, this coal shipping port located only twelve miles from the Great Barrier Reef is being expanded. The focus is still on the purported thousands of jobs to be gained instead of on the environmental damage. The estimated environmental impact locally is minimized by the fact that producing countries typically do not count greenhouse gas emissions for any of the raw materials they sell internationally. The emission increases are credited to the consumers who often live in a different country. As such, the investment in the Abbot Point Mine results in a dichotomy: "Australia has pledged to reduce its greenhouse gas emissions to 26 percent to 28 percent below 2005 levels by 2030, but the coal it sells to India and other countries would not be counted in its total."[27] Environmental impact assessments also tend to look more at the direct impact of the expanded operation instead of the aggregate changes happening in the environment. This is particularly challenging, since the Great Barrier Reef experienced some of the worst bleaching events in history in 2016 and 2017. More than two thirds of the reef suffered extensive damage. Additional stress on this ecosystem from increased burning of coal, shipping damage, or silt in the waterways may have long-term consequences.

One of the greatest challenges related to sustainability is that the need for change is happening during a period of increasing inequality. According to Jack Ma, co-founder and executive chairman of Alibaba, "In the next 30 years, the world will see much more pain than happiness." Ma was speaking about job and business disruptions caused by the Internet and artificial intelligence, and added, "Social conflicts in the next three decades will have an impact on all sorts of industries and walks of life."[28] Job losses from automation may increase and inequality may grow worse. Even in developed countries like the United States, many people feel that they have not benefited from globalization or innovation. And even if economic activity increases, the will to become sustainable may take a back seat to more local, social problems.

For the better part of 150 years, as economic activity has increased, so have global carbon emissions, the exploitation of resources, and pollution.[29] The goal was to produce shareholder value. If social good was created, it was an unintended side benefit of growth and was often dispensed with if the business was not generating sufficient profits. However, the environmental impact often remained. The current amount of global atmospheric CO_2 has reached levels not seen in eight hundred thousand years! Although the full extent of human impact is not completely understood, most climate scientists surveyed agree that "climate-warming trends over the past century are extremely likely due to human activities."[30] And consider that the UN Population Division estimates there are 7.5 billion people in the world today and this number may grow to 8.5 billion by 2030 and 9.7 billion by 2050.[31] Carbon dioxide levels in the atmosphere have increased to over 410ppm[32] and continue to trend upwards. With global economic development and pollution increasing every decade, there will be more demand for consumer products as well as energy and clean water and air.

Author Elizabeth Kolbert has called the current era the Sixth Extinction[33] to draw attention to the mind-numbing loss of biological diversity caused by humans in fewer than two hundred years. We, as a human race, are on the verge of doing something once the purview of deadly asteroids, pandemic plagues, and super volcanoes.

The great human dilemma is that the business and policy models that efficiently produce valued products—including cheap clothing, smartphones, and flat-screen TVs—are the same ones creating pollution, inequality, and global warming. Technology innovation has increased wealth and productivity in virtually every profession, from farming and fishing to finance. Our choice has been to see the benefits of this innovation, without considering the downstream or long-term costs.

So, Where Are We Today?

Having demanded your attention to this point, I encourage you to take a deep breath. It is a lot to take in. In a little more than a few pages, I have compressed 150 years of history and highlighted some pretty startling facts. You may have heard many such facts before, but it seems more compelling when you link the history and time line together. You may be thinking of your own ancestors and your unique family tree. Our personal histories often revolve around major events like births, wedding, and jobs, or world events like wars, elections, or crises of the last century. For many, the way we retell our personal history reveals something about who we are and what we value. However, what I have tried to do and what I suggest each reader do for him- or herself is retell that history against a background of sustainable or unsustainable practices. Where were you or your father or grandmother at each historical stage I described? What industries did everyone work in? Were air and water pollution or the challenges of poverty or global warming a dinner conversation at your house when you were growing up? Did any of those conversations lead to different actions?

Although there is some recognition among large and small businesses of the importance of changing behavior, old-economy practices and especially political pressure are in conflict with forward-thinking sustainable business practices. Progress is frustratingly slow. For example,

- British Petroleum is still paying for the Deepwater Horizon oil spill in 2010, one of the most costly environmental disasters in history. Yet six years later, politicians are debating the relaxation of the very rules designed to prevent a new disaster from happening.
- When California had its worst sustained drought in the past century (2012–2017), the city of Los Angeles reduced water consumption by 20 percent.[34] Despite ample evidence that long-term weather patterns will reduce the water supply, water consumption is now back on the rise after one good winter of above-average precipitation.
- The United Nations Food and Agriculture Organization (FAO) estimates that 52 percent of global fish stocks are fully exploited, 77 percent are overexploited, and a further 7 percent are fully depleted.[35]
- Our ability to naturally respond to increases in greenhouse gases has been highly compromised. Eighty percent of global forest cover has been lost since pre-industrial times.[36]

- According to the World Bank, global access to clean drinking water, clean air, affordable energy, hygienic waste management, and adequate food production are all under threat.[37]
- Today, the equivalent of a truck-size load of plastic is dumped into our oceans every minute. The oceans already contain almost one ton of plastic for every three tons of commercial fish. By 2050, if such abuse continues, the oceans may contain more plastic by weight than commercial fish.[38]
- A CNN report stated that "the average square kilometer of ocean contains around 20,000 microplastic pieces."[39]

In 2018, the high courts for the city of Mumbai, India, enacted a ban on many types of common plastics, including shopping bags, cups, and straws. The courts were responding to the mounting pollution of land and water in the metropolitan area of over 22 million people that disposes of more than 1100 tons of plastic per day,[40] often dumped illegally into landfills and waterways. This is a story less about sustainable change or a strategic choice and more about a crisis response to an increasingly common problem. Proponents claim it is a necessary response to combat poor sanitation, disease, and destruction of the environment. Opponents claim that the act will destroy many companies and eliminate fifty thousand jobs.

The difficulty for politicians in choosing a crisis path is that it aligns winners and losers in opposing camps. Regardless of the actions taken in Mumbai, the nature and frequency of these problems will not go away. Many of the problems are the direct consequence of business models that value economic gain over all else. From a leadership perspective, I think this leaves us two paths, which I outline in later chapters. The first is an incremental change strategy in an era when societal issues and potential distrust of corporate partners is mounting. This suggests you are listening, adapting, and looking for a better path, however slowly. It often involves a focus on a sustainability project that saves the business money. The second option is the choice to be a market leader that others will follow. This requires changing your products and services and seeking new opportunities for value creation. Both paths require changes in how people behave, although the techniques and investments in talent development can vary substantially. Over the last 150 years, one issue remains consistently valid: the right talent, focused on the right priorities, can produce the sought-after outcomes, no matter how challenging.

Reader Reflection

IMAGINE for a moment that you live in one of the fifty-nine countries in the world rated by Freedom House (2017) as only partly free or one of the forty-nine countries rated as not free. That means your country does not hold free elections or that its elections have a predetermined outcome. If you are particularly unlucky, perhaps you also live in one of the dozen countries experiencing war or major conflict. You may have direct experience with refugees fleeing war, persecution, or economic hardship. My US ancestors were not extraordinary in choosing to leave the land of their birth for a better opportunity. But "migration" may take on a new meaning in the coming years.

Experts published in a variety of studies have concluded that unsustainable practices may accelerate climate change. According to a UN assessment, "One-quarter of the world's population resides within 100 km distance and 100 m elevation of the coastline."[41] There is a high probability that our near-term future will be filled with more migration challenges than ever before. Low-lying coastal areas may be affected by rising sea levels; farming regions may become less productive due to changing weather patterns; and water resources may become less secure due to melting glaciers, seawater intrusion, and competition among densely populated areas. Imagine that, through no fault of your own, you were born in one of the areas that will experience such changes.

What would it be like to have no job, no say in how you may live from day to day, or no hope for your family's future? Would you consider moving to another country? Would you pay someone to help make it happen? Would you migrate illegally?

Consider how living in an area under threat would influence your view of sustainable challenges like climate change or clean energy.

If this reflection has you wondering about what you would do, that was the point. There is no absolute answer to many of the dilemmas I will pose throughout the book. However, there are skill sets you can develop that will guide you to an appropriate solution for your situation and stakeholders. The sustainability advantage is derived from a change in your mental model that allows you to consider new perspectives based on changing boundary conditions and the need for both economic and social outcomes. The ability of an organization to scale such an advantage is what talent development and leading change is all about. To resolve a dilemma similar to the one posed in this reflection, you need a problem-solving process that allows you to consider multiple issues and multiple perspectives.

Changing your stakeholder analysis based on the change in context— be that weather events driven by global warming or a new legislative agenda—is an important aspect of the solution. Getting the right people into a dialog can offer qualitative insights that turn a problem into an opportunity. As famed management guru Peter Drucker once observed, "Every single social and global issue of our day is a business opportunity in disguise." Group problem-solving can also be important because it reduces the impact of individual biases and helps you focus on principles instead of positions. We'll cover this idea in greater depth in chapter 6.

TAKEAWAY: Accept Personal Accountability

When I was a young boy, we traveled to the New Jersey beaches in the summer. During one particularly memorable summer, I was on a hot streak at the boardwalk and won a transistor radio in a game of chance. For those not old enough to remember, transistors and portable radios were big things in the 1960s and the Seaside Heights boardwalk was filled with games where you bet on a number or threw darts to win a prize. Unfortunately, my new radio lived a hard life at the beach and eventually found its way into the trash. The sad fact is that my 1960s plastic radio was likely made of non-biodegradable ingredients like ethylene and propylene. I don't know which landfill became its final resting place, but it is likely still there in some form.

Accepting personal accountability means accepting responsibility for the thousands of individual actions we take (like disposing of a plastic radio) and for using our voice to influence the actions of others. Our challenge is to repurpose and redirect economic activity and its growth in ways that address our common interests in a sustainable world. To quote Walt Kelly's cartoon character Pogo in the first Earth Day poster, "We have met the enemy and he is us."[42] As we think about the issue of "common interests," we may also consider the dilemma described in the reader reflection, above. Local issues tend to get people's attention. Issues at a greater distance do not. The overwhelming evidence is that the problem is our behavior, not a lack of technology or capital. Our activities are also more interconnected than we might understand, and sustainable business practices can have an impact near and far. An individual and collective commitment to change will allow us to rethink how we build businesses and both local and global communities that are sustainable.

Most businesses pursue an advantage naturally. The fact that they act in ways that are unsustainable means that most leaders do not see sustainability as a viable business advantage. To create meaningful change, we need to change that dynamic and show that it is not only possible but preferable and profitable. Before we can begin the change process, we need to clarify the definition of sustainability, the first step in helping the change leader reflect on how to build the sustainable organization.

Chapter 2

CONNECTING SUSTAINABILITY TO YOUR LIFE EXPERIENCE

"You cannot get through a single day without having an impact on the world around you. What you do makes a difference, and you have to decide what kind of difference you want to make." JANE GOODALL

In 2002, I was recruited to join the United Nations Development Programme (UNDP). UNDP was founded in 1965 to "eradicate poverty and reduce inequalities through the sustainable development of nations." When founded, UNDP was one of only a few global development players, and its mandate was to fund development programs in emerging and post-crisis economies. By 2002, the world had changed and new players like the Gates Foundation and hundreds of large nongovernmental organizations (NGOs) were now offering services. I was asked to restructure the training and development and knowledge-management functions so that UNDP could operate as a more modern advisory services organization in the business of global development.

I was not hired for my grip on global poverty, the environment, or post-crisis development challenges, but rather for my experience with organizational learning and knowledge-based organizations. Mark Malloch Brown, then head of UNDP, was attempting to transform the organization from a funding agency to an advisory and professional services firm specializing in development. The United Nations had recently passed the Millennium Development Goals (MDGs) that served as the new development framework. For the first time, most countries in the world agreed to a broad-based and common development agenda with goals, desired outcomes, and time lines.

To support the MDG effort, we restructured UNDP (leading change was something I was familiar with) to focus on six key practice areas:

- sustainable energy and environment;
- poverty reduction;
- democratic governance;
- HIV/AIDS;
- information and communication technology (ICT) for development; and
- crisis prevention and recovery.

The largest of the practice areas was sustainable energy and the environment, which had an investment of over US$10 billion in the decade prior to my joining.[1] All of these practice areas and the original MDGs form the heart of what we now call the "global sustainability agenda."

As I started my new job, I tasked myself with building greater foundation knowledge in our core practice areas. Prior to building a talent development plan or starting a consulting assignment, the internal change agent (and the external consultant) needs to have a strong sense of the organization's mission and competitive differentiation. Talent development decisions are anchored in a strategy that provides everyone with a shared sense of purpose. I started my process by discovering more about UNDP, the UN system, and how we arrived at this challenge called sustainability. I also wanted to know how we were different from other UN agencies like UNICEF (children), UNFPA (population activities), FAO (food and agriculture), or the World Bank (a UN affiliate focused on lending). I wanted to understand not only the challenge of global development, but also who had unique capabilities to contribute.

What Is Sustainability?

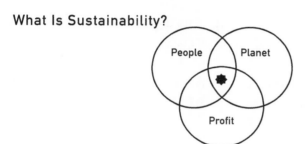

Sustainability is viewed as the intersection of three principles: society, the environment, and the economy. Or simply put, people, planet, and profit. The simplicity of the definition is enhanced by the graphic of intersecting circles shown above, because it suggests the ongoing interaction between the three areas. Creating balance between these three issues addresses the "what we want to achieve" of sustainability.

For a business to be sustainable, its goal should be to act in ways that have a net positive effect on (1) shareholders; (2) employees and the communities in which we work; and (3) the environment. Such a business, theoretically, could last indefinitely. At a minimum, economic gains should not degrade the environment or violate key agreements on human rights. A more generous definition suggests that value creation should be positive for all three principles.

In the early 1970s, the chief economist for the World Bank, Herman Daly, set out a series of conditions, now called the Daly Rules,[2] for environmental sustainability. I was not familiar with them when they were first released, but they became one of my favorite talking points. They are simply stated and offer an easy-to-communicate framework:

1. Renewable resources such as fish, soil, and groundwater must be used no faster than the rate at which they regenerate.
2. Nonrenewable resources such as minerals and fossil fuels must be used no faster than renewable substitutes for them can be put into place.
3. Pollution and waste must be emitted no faster than natural systems can absorb them, recycle them, or render them harmless.

The importance of the Daly Rules are that they begin to address more of the "how we behave" component of sustainability and that they encourage thinking about the circular nature of economic development. The Daly Rules place a greater emphasis on systems thinking.

In the 1980s, the United Nations established the World Commission on Environment and Development and published its main reference report, *Our Common Future*, in 1987. The report emphasized the importance of "development that meets the needs of the present without compromising the ability of future generations to meet their own needs."[3] The definition of sustainability underwent further refinement in the 1990s and 2000s with the UN Conference on the Environment and Development (1992), the United Nations Framework Convention on Climate Change (UNFCCC, 1992), the Kyoto Protocol (1997), and the Environmental Performance Index (1999).

The eight Millennium Development Goals passed by the UN member states in the year 2000 marked a change in the global development agenda. Until then, development problems were often organized individually, funded by different agencies and addressed separately. One report or agreement would focus on the environment and another on child security and poverty or inequality. For the first time, the objective was to demonstrate that very significant challenges such as global warming, poverty, and inequality are interconnected. Describing the goals from a systemic perspective was helpful in changing public consciousness and also in driving better collaboration in the public and private sectors. These changes were reflected in the UNDP Regional Human Development Reports (HDRs) published for each of the five main regions of the world where it offered services. The reports provided a summary of activities within each region, such as the Arab States, that connected a range of issues like poverty, women's rights, and democratic governance.

The UN Global Compact was started in 2000 to connect private and public partnerships in support of the new MDGs. This led to the first UN Global Leaders meetings in 2004 and the first Private Sector Forum in 2008. The latter was specifically tied to the MDGs and creating solutions for food sustainability. Another Private Sector Forum was held in 2009 and focused on the MDGs and climate change.[4] Although the initial efforts in the public- and private-sector partnerships focused on raising funds for UN activities, the shift over time has been towards a better understanding of sustainable markets and business models. This change in perspective is also key to a later recommendation of the importance of systems and design thinking as core skill areas in a sustainable business.

In my four years at UNDP, I found the MDG framework helpful for high-level discussion. It offered a focal point for collaboration as well as some amount of definition on specific goals. At the same time, feedback from business and industry suggested it was difficult to translate these high-level frameworks into daily business practices. The interest was there, but even powerful CEOs felt constrained by the pressure to prioritize revenue growth and profitability.

Fifteen years later (2015), the MDGs evolved into the United Nations Sustainable Development Goals (SDGs) (Table 2.1).[5] These goals were established in the action plan *Transforming Our World: The 2030 Agenda for Sustainable Development*.[6] The SDGs expanded the MDGs from eight goals to seventeen and offered much more detail on potential targets, with 169 measures.

Table 2.1: United Nations Sustainable Development Goals[a]

1. No Poverty	6. Clean Water and Sanitation	11. Sustainable Cities and Communities	16. Peace, Justice, and Strong Institutions
2. Zero Hunger	7. Affordable and Clean Energy	12. Responsible Consumption and Communities	17. Partnerships for the Goals
3. Good Health and Well-Being	8. Decent Work and Economic Growth	13. Climate Action	
4. Quality Education	9. Industry, Innovation, and Infrastructure	14. Life Below Water	
5. Gender Equality	10. Reduced Inequalities	15. Life on Land	

a "Sustainable Development Goals," United Nations Development Programme, accessed June 20, 2018, http://www.undp.org/content/undp/en/home/sustainable-development-goals.html.

To support the adoption of these goals, the United Nations modified and enhanced its voluntary membership organization, the UN Global Compact. The Global Compact (Table 2.2) asks businesses and civil society organizations to align their strategies with ten principles linked to four larger themes, and to take action to support the seventeen SDGs. Unfortunately, the themes and principles do not evenly align with the SDGs and they leave out a range of key challenges, such as,

- How do I do this profitably?
- What do I do if key stakeholders do not agree?
- How do small or medium-size businesses participate?
- How do I respond if my competitors do not act in a similar fashion?

Table 2.2: United Nations Global Compact Principles[a]

UN Global Compact Theme	UN Global Compact Principles
Human Rights	Businesses should: • support and respect the protection of internationally proclaimed human rights; and • make sure that they are not complicit in human rights abuses.
Labor	Businesses should: • recognize the freedom of association and the the right to collective bargaining; • eliminate all forms of forced and compulsory labor; • abolish child labor; and • eliminate discrimination in respect of employment and occupation.
Environment	Businesses should: • support a precautionary approach to environmental challenges; • undertake initiatives to promote greater environmental responsibility; and • encourage the development and diffusion of environmentally friendly technologies.
Anti-corruption	• Businesses should work against corruption in all its forms, including extortion and bribery.

a "The Ten Principles of the UN Global Compact," United Nations Global Compact, accessed July 3, 2018, https://www.unglobalcompact.org/what-is-gc/mission/principles.

To help resolve the conflicts in definitions and goals, a number of organizations such as Dow Jones,[7] B Labs, and Corporate Knights[8] have created sustainability indexes, certification programs, and awards that attempt to benchmark corporate behavior. These benchmarks use some combination of key themes such as people, planet, economy (profit), and governance, as well as the UN SDG definitions and a weighting formula to judge an organization's relative sustainability or its progress as a sustainable organization (for comparison, see Table 2.3).

Table 2.3: United Nations Sustainability Models Defined

Sustainability Model	Explanation
17 UN Sustainable Development Goals (SDGs) with 169 measures	The "what we want" list of sustainability, as defined by representatives from 193 governments around the world.
UN Global Compact Principles	The principles link the SDGs to key themes and international agreements on topics like corruption and human rights.
SDG themes of people, planet, prosperity, peace, and partnership Global Compact themes of human rights, labor, anti-corruption, and environment Sample themes from corporate benchmarking groups like Dow Jones or nonprofits like B Labs: society, planet, economy, and governance	The themes offer an organizing framework that can be adapted for industry–specific purposes.

The importance of these definitions to business transformation cannot be understated. If I am in the entertainment business, how do I adjust my behavior? What am I responsible for now that I wasn't responsible for yesterday or a year ago? If I look to the SDGs or any other definition of sustainability, do they help me answer these questions? If I am in the banking industry, where do we draw the boundaries for accountability and opportunity? Am I now responsible for the labor practices in companies I lend money to? How about lending to areas at risk for climate change events? How do changes in "boundaries" change the way I hire, develop, and reward talent?

Evolving Definitions of Sustainability

All effective consulting engagements start by trying to define and refine the problem. This process begins by answering the question, What do we know and not know, and how can that lead us to action? At conferences,

I begin the conversation around sustainability by presenting a few short quizzes. Table 2.4 provides an example (see Table 2.6 for the answers).

After discussing the questions and answers, I ask for a show of hands on several questions: Do you feel your company is responsible for addressing a problem like child labor or access to clean water? Do you feel this is part of your job? Many people do not make a direct connection between these challenges and their work, job, or lifestyle, yet they still feel the problem exists and is important. Therein lies a key challenge when discussing economic and social value creation, as well as business transformation.

Table 2.4: Sustainability Quiz

	How Much Do You Know About Sustainability?	A	B	C	D
1	What percentage of global fish stocks are fully exploited?	38%	52%	64%	77%
2	The average square kilometer of ocean has how many micro pieces of plastic?	5,000	12,000	20,000	40,000
3	How many children aged 5 to 17 are trapped in child labor?	75 million	112 million	152 million	221 million
4	What percentage of the global population live in extreme poverty?	5%	11%	15%	27%
5	How many megacities have populations of over 10 million?	12	22	31	40
6	When was the last time that the earth had this much CO_2 in the atmosphere?	800,000 years ago	12,000 years ago	1492	1850
7	How many millions of people do not have access to clean water?	277 million	540 million	780 million	1.2 billion
8	How many millions of people do not have access to clean sanitation?	500 million	800 million	1.2 billion	2.5 billion
9	How much of the world's topsoil has been lost in the last 150 years?	18%	32%	50%	67%
10	How many Sustainable Development Goals (SDGs) were adopted by 193 nations in 2015?	10	14	17	24

The sustainability challenge must be translated into the life experience of the people you work with. The more each person feels both a sense of accountability and the ability to take action, the more successful you will be. The easier we make the journey for business partners, the more we have willing travelers.

In my experience, three fairly simple issues hold companies back from taking action. The first is a lack of a common "business" definition that helps provide a point of focus for a company. Any business definition for sustainability must be actionable at the strategic level, but also operational at the lowest level of an organization. A point of focus is essential for providing clarity of vision and purpose. The second is what is called the "boundary problem." Boundaries define the business you are in, the customers you seek, or the accountability you accept for sustainability. How broad, how long, and how interconnected are your accountabilities? The third is the idea that a business is only responsible for economic value creation, or a "profit is the only thing that matters" mentality.

Let's start with the issue of definitions. For many years, the term "sustainability" was the domain of the environmental and international development communities. Having worked in a variety of industries since the 1980s, the word "sustainability," as broadly defined, was rarely mentioned in a regular strategy session. Companies were consumed with terms such as "downsizing," "rightsizing," "globalization," "reengineering," "disruption," and "offshoring." Sustainability in my "corporate" world was a small footnote or a side conversation.

I like to think of the SDGs as a starting point from which more specific definitions and frameworks can develop. Organizations such as the Indian Apparel Industry Association have developed specific programs to engage members in the use of sustainability as a driver of innovation. According to Ashok Rajani, chair of the Apparel Export Promotion Council (AEPC), "There is a strong emergence of Sustainability requirements as an important competitiveness tool. It is a great opportunity for us to differentiate ourselves in the global market and offer a sustainable value chain."[9] Similar activities can be seen in industries ranging from packaging[10] to events management.[11] In some cases, groups of like-minded businesses collaborate to adopt standards that can influence their specific industry segment. An example is the Cement Sustainability Initiative[12] under the auspices of the World Business Council for Sustainable Development. The twenty-four partner companies account for over 30 percent of global cement production and serve as a coordinating body for regional cement trade associations and the development of a "Getting the Numbers Right Database" on CO_2 emissions and energy standards.[13] These more specific frameworks take into account unique sustainability challenges.

One of the more interesting models for sustainability is called the Gapframe, which takes the seventeen SDGs and converts them into twentyfour measures aligned with four categories and sixty-eight indicators. At face value, this would seem to make the definition more complex, but in some ways it makes it easier to understand and manage. Certain SDGs, such as sustainable consumption and production, are divided into two goals, which makes the objectives more discrete. Others are simply reworded to make them easier to understand. The four categories also match well with the simplest definition of people, planet, and profit with the addition of a governance category. I find those categories easier to explain to business leaders than the four themes and ten principles from the UN Global Compact or the seventeen SDGs.

The Gapframe measurement system is the result of an initiative by the Swiss Sustainability Hub that included a number of universities such as the University of St. Galen and Business School Lausanne with participation from a number of Swiss and European government agencies and companies. The version in Table 2.5 is based on Gapframe 1.0 (version 2.0 is under development).

Table 2.5: Gapframe 1.0

Planet	Society	Economy	Governance
1. Biodiversity	9. Health	15. Employment	20. Public Finance
2. Carbon Quotient	10. Equal Opportunity	16. Resource Use	21. Structural Resilience
3. Oceans	11. Education	17. Sustainable Consumption	22. Peace and Cooperation
4. Land and Forests	12. Living Conditions	18. Sustainable Production	23. Business Integrity
5. Clean Air	13. Social Integration	19. Innovation	24. Transparency
6. Water	14. Quality of Life		
7. Clean Energy			
8. Waste Management			

The similarities and differences of the models can be seen when you bring the models together, side by side, as I have done in Figure 2.1. I have highlighted the United Nations 2030 Agenda for Sustainable Development (the document that describes the seventeen SDGs) in the center since this is the "official" government-sponsored version. Although I like models to be simple, in many ways I find the Gapframe model, with its twenty-four goals developed by a small team of business schools and corporate participants, the easiest to use.

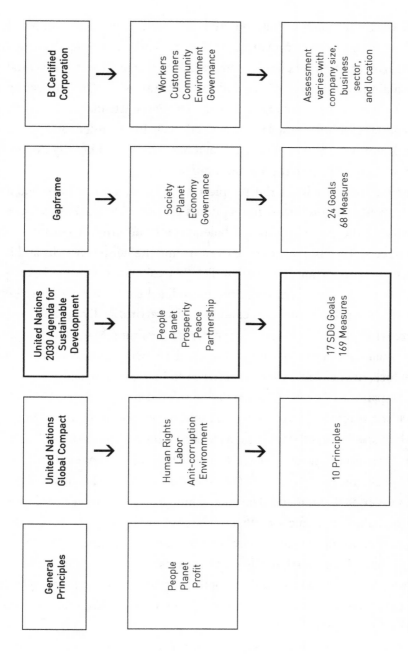

Figure 2.1: Comparison of the Five Models

Reader Reflection

IMAGINE for a moment that you are senior policy officer for an NGO working with the government of the Faroe Islands. These small islands are heavily affected by climate change and ocean health. It is essential they maintain their economies and local culture while also mitigating the effects of non-sustainable practices. The Faroe Islands are governed by Denmark, although the Islanders are fiercely independent and proud of their heritage. The economy is small but strong, and heavily dependent on resources from the surrounding ocean.

For hundreds of years the people of the Faroe Islands have eaten whale meat and conducted annual hunts for pilot whales. Pilot whales are among the more common whale species and are not considered endangered. Locals consume the meat during the winter months and it is seen as an important part of their diet. The excess is considered excellent bait for fishing. Some countries consider the hunt for whales to be unethical, but that position is challenged by territories like the Faroes, where whaling has long been part of the local culture. Many locals consider whaling a perfectly sustainable practice, using local resources to meet local needs. Some even want to see an increase in whaling.

An expansion of whaling is generally considered in opposition to SDG 14, which stipulates that we conserve and sustainably use the oceans. Almost all whale species breed slowly and have been reduced from historical numbers. There is also strong scientific evidence that whale meat contains high levels of chemicals such as PCBs (polychlorinated biphenyl compounds).

However, SDG 2 is focused on ending hunger, SDG 8 on the promotion of sustainable economic growth, and SDG 12 on the sustainable production and consumption of resources. Will banning whaling in the Faroe Islands have disproportionately negative consequences for the Islanders in order to address a problem largely the purview of countries far away? Are the SDGs in conflict? Is this more about imposing the values of one country on another?

What will you do? Your NGO is under pressure from people who fund your organization to take a very public stand. They are demanding action.

This sort of dilemma presents a difficult challenge. A substantive argument can be made that the whale meat is unhealthy given the high levels of toxic chemicals. However, strong emotional and cultural arguments often trump hard science when the argument is seen as an infringement on local sovereignty or heritage rights. The collaborative problem-solving frameworks you will explore in chapter 6 (which I suggested would be helpful in chapter 1's reader reflection) are part of the solution. Can we preserve historical rights while satisfying the intent of sustainable practices? This type of dilemma is often resolved by first reaching agreement on longer-term principles and then balancing short-term competing interests against long-term progress. The leadership development challenge is to build a knowledge base of the cultural, religious, and national identity issues that allow you to be a trusted broker in any dialog with local stakeholders. You will surface conflicts between different SDGs as you resolve legacy issues that may involve water rights, facility location issues, worker conflicts based on national identity, trade disputes, or issues of inequality. Remember always that you will reap benefits from background and historical knowledge that allows you to be respectful of the issues while guiding the problem-solving process.

TAKEAWAY: A Sustainability Agenda Needs a Fluid Framework

Sustainable development goals and their models can provide the change leader with a baseline from which to build an agenda for his or her organization. Definitions bring clarity, but as this chapter points out, our definitions and goals have evolved over time and will continue to do so. The sheer number of SDGs and measures can also seem overwhelming. As the dilemma above illustrates, different SDGs may appear to be in conflict and cultural dimensions can lead to different interpretations. However, working within a framework is the essential starting point and leads to a discussion of change within the business, which is the focus of Chapter 3. Later chapters discuss the skill sets needed to address the evolving nature of the sustainability challenge.

Table 2.6: Sustainability Quiz Answers

	How Much Do You Know About Sustainability?	Answer
1	What percentage of global fish stocks are fully exploited?	According to the United Nations Food and Agriculture Organization (FAO), 52% of global fish stocks are fully exploited, 77% are over exploited, and a further 7% are fully depleted.[a]
2	The average square kilometer of ocean has how many micro pieces of plastic?	According to reporting in 2018 done by CNN in coordination with the Woods Hole Oceanographic Institution, "The average square kilometer of ocean contains around 20,000 micro plastic pieces."[b]
3	How many children aged 5 to 17 are trapped in child labor?	According to the International Labour Organization (ILO), 152 million children ages 5 to 17 are still trapped in child labor (2017).[c]
4	What percentage of the global population live in extreme poverty?	According to World Bank estimates (2013), approximately 11% of the global population, or 763 million people, were living in extreme poverty, defined as less than US$1.90 measured in 2011 purchasing power parity.[d]
5	How many megacities have populations of over 10 million?	According to United Nations data, there were 31 megacities of over 10 million in the world in 2016.[e] Other reports using a broader definition of metropolitan areas suggest there were 47 metropolitan areas with more than 10 million in 2017.
6	When was the last time that the earth had this much CO_2 in the atmosphere?	Carbon dioxide levels in the atmosphere have increased to over 410ppm in 2016. According to ice core data, atmospheric CO_2 has not been that high for almost 800,000 years.[f]
7	How many millions of people do not have access to clean water?	The US Center for Disease Control cites statistics showing that 780 million people do not have access to reliable clean water.[g]

Table 2.6: (Continued)

8	How many millions of people do not have access to clean sanitation?	The US Center for Disease Control cites statistics showing that 2.5 billion people do not have access to clean sanitation.[h]
9	How much of the world's topsoil has been lost in the last 150 years?	According to the World Wildlife Fund, half of the topsoil on the planet has been lost in the last 150 years.[i]
10	How many Sustainable Development Goals (SDGs) were adopted by 193 nations in 2015?	Seventeen United Nations Sustainable Development Goals (SDGs) were agreed to by 193 member states in 2015. The goals are part of *Transforming Our World: The 2030 Agenda for Sustainable Development*.[j]

a United Nations Food and Agriculture Organization (FAO), *General Situation of World Fish Stocks*, accessed September 5, 2018, http://www.fao.org/newsroom/common/ecg/1000505/en/stocks.pdf.

b Zeena Saifi, Victoria Brown, and Tom Page, "Start-up Devours Pollution with New Plastic Recycling Method," *CNN*, March 9, 2018, https://edition.cnn.com/2018/03/09/world/miranda-wang-tomorrows-hero/index.html.

c "40 Million in Modern Slavery and 152 Million in Child Labour around the World," International Labour Organization, September 19, 2017, http://www.ilo.org/global/about-the-ilo/newsroom/news/WCMS_574717/lang--en/index.htm.

d "Understanding Poverty," World Bank, accessed July 20, 2018, http://www.worldbank.org/en/understanding-poverty.

e United Nations Department of Economic and Social Affairs, Population Division, *The World's Cities in 2016—Data Booklet*, 2016, http://www.un.org/en/development/desa/population/publications/pdf/urbanization/the_worlds_cities_in_2016_data_booklet.pdf.

f "Scientific Consensus: Earth's Climate Is Warming," NASA: Global Climate Change: Vital Signs for the Planet, accessed July 30, 2018, https://climate.nasa.gov/scientific-consensus.

g "Global WASH Fast Facts," Centers for Disease Control and Prevention, accessed July 28, 2018, https://www.cdc.gov/healthywater/global/wash_statistics.html.

h Ibid.

i "Threats: Soil Erosion and Degradation," World Wildlife Fund, accessed June 20, 2018, https://www.worldwildlife.org/threats/soil-erosion-and-degradation.

j "Transforming Our World: The 2030 Agenda for Sustainable Development," United Nations Sustainable Development Goals Knowledge Platform, October 21, 2015, https://sustainabledevelopment.un.org/post2015/transformingourworld.

Chapter 3

SUSTAINABILITY AND EMERGING BUSINESS MODELS

"You never change something by fighting the existing reality. To change something, build a new model that makes the existing model obsolete." BUCKMINSTER FULLER

W ith a definition of sustainability in hand that aligns with your business, the next goal is to consider how your business model may change. There are two important considerations: First, how bold is your change in strategy? And second, what capabilities do you have to support that strategy?

For a bold few, sustainability offers the opportunity to reinvent their business. Early adopters validate the market opportunity and help establish the ground rules that others follow. Market leaders tend to fit into several categories:

- First are companies that are already well aligned with sustainability. This includes companies like outdoor apparel company Patagonia that has established itself as a market-leading benefit corporation. Patagonia has long been a champion of environmental and social causes that align well with its core customer base. Many of the early adopters of different models were already aligned with key sustainability values. The new definitions and models gave them the opportunity to codify their value propositions and offered membership in a larger community of like-minded organizations.

- Second are companies where the major shareholders, owners, or founders drive change because of their vision and values. W.S. Badger (health and beauty), Tesla (energy and transportation), and Galaxy Entertainment (hotels and casinos) are all examples of companies in which the wishes and support of the founder and majority shareholders have enormous influence.
- Third are companies making the economic argument that sustainability is the "land of opportunity." Some are new startups like NooTrees, a Singapore-based company that makes paper products from sustainable bamboo sources and is tapping into the growing interest in alternative "green" products. Others, like CropEnergies of the Südzucker Group in Germany, make biofuels that reduce greenhouse gases by substantial amounts over traditional fuel sources. Changing economics in the energy sector in particular have made moves into wind and solar energy a smart bet for investors.

To accelerate sustainable change, we need a fourth category of "bold companies"—large and small businesses that make everyday products. In every sector, from appliances to clothing and food, we need market leaders to help make the business case and drive competition. They become the example for others to follow. Such leaders need clarity of purpose, strong support from their board and advisors, and a business plan that promises big things.

Unilever, the large UK conglomerate, is an example of the type of company that needs to become more sustainable. Over 2.5 billion customers use one or more of Unilever's four hundred branded prod-ucts every day. The company employs 170,000 employees worldwide and has an annual revenue of US$80 billion.[1] Most importantly for this discussion, the company is not led by a single controlling shareholder or founder. Its decision to become more sustainable will be evaluated by traditional competitive standards. Substantial change for a company of this size involves considerable costs and risks.

Unilever was a company in turmoil in the early 2000s. It was per-ceived as inefficient; growth had slowed and profits were disappoint-ing; and the company was losing market share to key rivals. The appointment of Patrick Cescau as CEO in 2004 started Unilever on a revised "Path to Growth" strategy[2] that reduced or eliminated some products and brands and reduced global employment. After four years under Cescau, Unilever hired a new CEO, Paul Polman, in 2009. This was a surprising move because the company was known for its practice of hiring from within.[3] Polman was with competitor Procter and Gamble. Hiring an "outsider" communicated a need for change at Unilever.

Polman's job was to remake Unilever with his Sustainable Living Plan,[4] launched in 2010. He had to convince his board that the way to separate Unilever from competitors was to fully embrace the idea of sustainability and to align the company with broader social goals in the minds of customers, investors, and employees. As a reminder of how bold this plan was, fully 37 percent of executives in a UN Global Com-pact survey reported they could not directly connect sustainability to business results in the year Polman launched his plan.

In 2013, with Unilever stock only moderately higher since Polman's promotion, the UN survey reported that most CEOs felt that their "responsibilities to the more traditional fundamentals of business suc-cess, and to the expectations of markets and stakeholders, are prevent-ing greater scale, speed and impact [on sustainability]."[5] So Polman's Sustainable Living Plan was one of conviction. Unilever posted the fol-lowing on its website: "The Unilever *Sustainable Living Plan* (USLP) is our blueprint for achieving our vision to grow our business, whilst decoupling our environmental footprint from our growth and increasing our positive social impact."[6]

Several years after launching his plan, Polman is one of the few long-serving CEOs who have managed to redirect a large publicly traded company towards alignment with the SDGs. He has done it while delivering both good business results and meaningful progress on social goals. In 2016, Unilever reported the following results:

- revenue growth: +3.7%;
- net profit: +5.8%; and
- return on assets: 17.9%.[7]

These results were positive, and compared well versus the competition. Although you could argue that performance could be better, the key line in the annual report was that "Sustainable Living Brands grew 50% faster than the rest of the business."[8] That suggests the move away from traditional products and processes not only is good for business but probably should be accelerated. During Polman's tenure, shareholder value increased slowly during the first few years of his plan. That means he had to excel at communicating future value and demonstrate clear indicators of progress he hoped to scale. Polman's success was due in part to his abilities as an authentic communicator who actively worked to remove barriers to change. He is noted for developing and promoting staff who excelled at creating new sustainable value. Overall, shareholder value increased approximately 80 percent in his first seven years as CEO, with much of that increase occurring in the last two years as the new Sustainable Living Brands performed better.[9]

In addition to the strong top- and bottom-line numbers, Unilever has a diverse scorecard of other value indicators (2016):

- 46 percent of managers are women (an increase from 38.2 percent at the end of 2010);
- over six hundred Unilever sites were sending zero non-hazardous waste to landfills; and

- Unilever is the #1 Fast Moving Consumer Goods (FMCG) graduate employer of choice in thirty-four of the sixty countries where it recruits.[10]

Polman has managed the leadership equivalent of the high-wire act: delivering positive short-term results and providing evidence of long-term high growth in new investment areas, while engaging employees, shareholders, and customers in a positive narrative about saving the planet. The Unilever brand is well on its way to becoming synonymous with sustainable living.

Old Thinking and New Thinking

Preparing for a bold approach requires a hard look at new sources of competitive differentiation. This involves rethinking how a business is defined, measured, and held accountable. The corporate design and the management paradigms that served us for 150 years need to change.

Much of what we think of business strategy today can be traced to a series of thought leaders in the post–World War 2 era, including Bill Henderson (Boston Consulting Group), Bill Bain (Bain & Company), Fred Gluck (McKinsey), Gary Hamel and C.K. Prahalad, Roland Christensen, Kenneth Andrews, Clay Christensen, and Michael Porter. They collectively wield great influence on our thinking about competition, competitiveness, strategy, and innovation. Our fundamental beliefs about organizations that design products, create demand, and maximize shareholder value are based on their contributions.

As we emerged from the 1970s and 1980s in the heat of technology innovation and globalization, we began to see changes in business thought that paralleled the international development discussion on the environment and sustainability:

- C.K. Prahalad's (with Stuart L. Hart) *The Fortune at the Bottom of the Pyramid*,[11] originally published as an article in 2002 and later as a book in 2004, started the conversation about the big business opportunities to be derived from solving key development issues such as reducing poverty or solving hunger problems. Essentially, you can do good and make profits! As a reminder, Prahalad's work comes on the heels of the UN's Kyoto Protocol (1997) and the Millennium Development Goals (2000).

- Major consulting firms such as McKinsey have built sustainability practices and conducted annual surveys to provide insights and best practices to clients.[12] McKinsey and Accenture have also partnered on the development of new business models like the Circular Economy in partnership with leading nonprofit groups like the Ellen MacArthur Foundation.

- Gary Hamel, visiting professor of strategic and international management at the London Business School, has stated that "it is time to reinvent management." His Management Innovation eXchange is an "online community where the world's most progressive business leaders share their ideas on how to build organizations that are fit for the future and fit for human beings."

- Michael Porter (with Mark R. Kramer) has proposed a new business model for creating shared value.[13] "Companies could bring business and society back together if they redefined their purpose as creating 'shared value,' generating economic value in a way that also produces value for society by addressing its challenges." According to Porter, "This will drive the next wave of innovation and productivity growth in the global economy."[14]

Green Growth

Proponents of what may be called "green growth" emphasize business decisions that follow the Daly Rules. For example, green growth businesses would not invest in any carbon energy project, but would invest in a wind or solar power project. "Clean capitalism" or "conscious capitalism"[15] are alternatives that look more broadly at business to provide a balance of economic and social impact. All three of these ideas are more concept than pure business model and generally imply that a business should not invest in products or businesses that have negative consequences for inequality or the environment.

Shared Social Value

Michael Porter weighed in on the business model debate with his *Harvard Business Review* article in 2011. Michael's status as perhaps the world's foremost strategy thought leader added considerable weight to the argument. His perspective, called the Shared Value Initiative (SVI), encourages businesses to see opportunity in the development of social good. Companies like Kirin Brewing Company in Japan (an SVI partner) have created new non-alcoholic product lines. They make use of their brewing skills and capability, but create products that are accretive to their top and bottom lines while addressing a social problem like impaired driving. In a similar vein, companies like Mercure Hotels have created concepts such as "positive hospitality,"[16] which involves working with guests to reduce the consumption of water through unnecessary cleaning of towels and bed linens. These programs increase revenue or reduce costs while communicating to customers that the organization cares about the environment. If ideas like "clean capitalism" are conceptual guideposts, the Shared Value Initiative is an evolutionary model that promises positive incremental or net positive gains.

Although many judge these as good initiatives, some view them as ineffective in the long term. Proponents of "de-growth" point to the Jevons paradox, first described in 1865 regarding the use of coal.[17] The paradox states that as technology increases availability and lowers cost, total consumption increases. So business growth always means we consume more and more. The logic would follow that as concepts like shared value produce new positive social and economic gains in one side of the business, another business may continue with negative outcomes—at lower costs to the consumer—potentially increasing the total amount of negative outcomes. This also characterizes a "net benefit" or "offset" strategy where the total positive benefits are said to balance the negative.

Decoupled Growth

One answer to the Jevons paradox is a concept called "decoupled growth," proposed by the United Nations Environment Programme. This requires an organization to "use fewer resources per unit of economic output and reduce the environmental impact of any resources that are used."[18] Unilever is one of the foremost champions of this practice. At a recent (2017) Academy of Business in Society (ABIS) conference in Brussels, Belgium, Unilever described the company's goal to double revenue by 2020 while reducing its impact on the planet by 50 percent.[19] It remains to be seen if these type of business models have natural limits or can be scaled across different industries.

The Circular Economy Model

Whereas many traditional business models focus on the design, production, and selling of products, a different model has emerged that asks a company to include post-sale recycling and waste recovery. Frequently called the "circular economy model," it suggests that if you make it and sell it, you have to accept it back and recycle it. Expanding the business model in this way may cause companies to rethink product design, since the value chain has a new set of costs that was previously outside the bounds of corporate responsibility (the boundary problem).

This idea gained great traction in 2014 with the publication of the report *Towards the Circular Economy* by the Ellen MacArthur Foundation and McKinsey & Company.[20] The Platform for Accelerating the Circular Economy (PACE) program was introduced in 2017 to accelerate interest in the circular economy model and is hosted by the World Economic Forum.[21] Estimates are that this would greatly increase employment in countries where products are consumed and reduce consumption of key resources.

The Benefit Corporation

In at least two countries, the United States and Italy, there is now legislation to offer an alternative to the traditional corporate structure, the benefit corporation. If you recall my earlier comment about three issues holding companies back—business definitions, boundaries, and a profit-only mentality—benefit corporations are designed to address the last of these. This change in legal structure allows a company to formalize its social commitments and provides the CEO and board support for a more balanced business plan. The key features of a benefit corporation are threefold:

- First is the registration of a new company or the amendment of an existing company. This typically requires the preparation of articles of incorporation that outline the public benefits the company will create. In most locations, the articles also must include a specific statement that the company is a benefit corporation. In some instances, the benefit corporation legend must also appear on stock certificates. There must be both board and shareholder approval.
- Second is the generation of an annual report to satisfy the transparency requirement of the legislation. That generally includes a public display of an annual report on the company website as well as reporting on both general and specific social outcomes.
- Third, in most areas, is the requirement to use an independent benchmarking service to offer some level of validation on the company's claims of social good.

Danone North America, a major food company,[22] is the largest benefit corporation in the world as of 2017. More than four thousand other corporations, partnerships, and sole proprietorships have registered as benefit corporations in the US since legislation first passed in 2010. The benefit corporation is now a legal entity in thirty-three US states and Puerto Rico,[23] although reporting requirements and conditions vary slightly from state to state. Italy passed its legislation in December 2015, and a small number of companies have registered as benefit corporations.[24] Many of the companies that have pursued this registration, such as King Arthur Flour and Plum Organics, appear to be well aligned with the environmental or social movements. No Fortune 500 company has yet made the transition.

The legal model grew out of a lobbying effort from a number of law firms and concerned citizens, including the B Labs certification organization. B Labs is an independent nonprofit third-party benchmarking organization that is often used to satisfy the benchmarking requirement of benefit corporation legislation, although companies may choose a more industry-specific approach.

B Certified Corporation

The B certified corporation (B Corp) is often confused with the benefit corporation, because of the similarities in names. However, they are distinct and separate. B certified companies are asked to take a B Impact Assessment (BIA) and then sign a pledge to "compete to be the best in the world, while being the best for the world."[25] The B certification process is designed to inform consumers about how a company is run and its commitment to deliver product or service value as well as environmental and social good. The B certification does not confer legal status like a benefit corporation, but it provides both transparency to customers and a benchmarking comparison for the company.

The B certified corporation process is used by thousands of mostly small to medium-size companies in over fifty countries.[26] In 2015, *Corporate Knights* magazine published a report[27] on the "best of the best" B certified companies by creating a list of the top one hundred. Thirteen percent were sole proprietorships, 35 percent were micro businesses, 34 percent were small businesses, and 13 percent were medium-size companies. The B Impact Assessment has two primary steps:

- First, a company completes the B Impact Assessment, which rates each participating company on environmental, worker, customer, community, and governance practices. If a company achieves an overall score higher than eighty out of two hundred points, it is eligible to become a B certified corporation.

• Second, a company is directed to take certain actions to amend its legal documents to offer protection for executives and board members. The suggested legal steps include amending a company's articles of incorporation to be brought into alignment with the sample legislative models adopted in some US states and Italy as actual legislation. The B Impact Assessment offers a gap analysis and recommendations on how to improve.

Patagonia, based in California, is an example of a benefit corporation that is also a B certified corporation. It registered as a benefit corporation soon after the legislation passed in 2012. Its annual reports describe progress on "six specific benefit purposes" of the company. In general, a benefit corporation designation does not change the accounting rules or tax structure. The "official" change to a company's governance structure is designed to communicate and support a more balanced approach to people, planet, and profit.

Although Patagonia is also a B certified corporation, it sees value in additional links with specialized partners and benchmarking efforts. Patagonia also works with the Fair Labor Association[28] (FLA), the Fair Factories Clearinghouse[29] (FFC), the Conservation Alliance,[30] and the Sustainable Apparel Coalition,[31] among others, to improve or assess specific parts of their operations. This expanded use of functional business definitions for sustainability will be key to designing talent development plans.

A summary of business model ideas is listed in Table 3.1 with sample companies that have explored the benefits of each.

Table 3.1: New Business Models Defined

New Business Models	Explanation	Representative Organization or Authors
Net Benefit or Offset Strategy	A value-balancing paradigm in which negative impacts are offset by positive contributions. Some companies use a definition that includes only the company's contributions, while others include their suppliers.	British Telecom (Net-Good Program) IKEA
Shared Value	Requires a business to identify opportunities where they can leverage their resources to identify socially beneficial outcomes or make contributions as a percentage of profits derived from a community.	GlaxoSmithKline Kirin Brewing (Japan) Michael Porter
Natural Capital	Requires the pricing of resources from the collective commons such as water, forests, estuaries, etc. This requires "pricing" of the impact of any pollution or the reduction in other resources as a result of business activity.	Dow Chemical in partnership with the Nature Conservancy Veolia (True Cost of Water Program)
Circular Economy	A company that manufactures a product must also handle customer returns and recycling. The concept may also apply to value-added resellers and retailers in addition to manufacturers.	Mostly experiments by companies such as Steelcase, Michelin Tires, and Grundfos[32]
Clean Capitalism	These are very broad concepts and are similar to shared value. Variations include green capitalism, conscious capitalism, and green growth.	Corporate Knights (publisher of a self-described magazine of clean capitalism)
Benefit Corporation	A legal designation in the US and Italy that allows you to declare your business purpose as having both economic and social goals.	Patagonia (US) Badger (US)

Table 3.1: (Continued)

New Business Models	Explanation	Representative Organization or Authors
B Certification	A benchmarking process versus recognized standards for sustainability. Variations include Dow Jones and other sustainability indexes, as well as industry-specific certification programs like Green Seal, WaterSense, Rainforest Alliance, and Fair Trade. Each offers some form of benchmarking, standard, or award indicating that a company meets or exceeds certain standards.	Natura (Brazil) Oliberté (Canada) ¡Échale a tu casa! (Mexico) EcoZoom (Kenya)
De-carbonization	Requires the movement away from fossil fuels largely in construction, transportation, and energy production.	City of Paris (cars), UK (cars), China (electric utilities), Tesla (cars and solar energy)
De-growth	Requires a company or country to accept that growth is not inevitable and that a company will have cycles of growth, decline, and stable revenues. The focus shifts to reliable revenues and changes in productivity to match.	More of a concept used in international negotiations
Decoupled growth	Suggests that a company can have higher productivity and revenue growth with declining negative social and environmental impacts.	Unilever

The Link between Business Models and Talent Development

So, what do all of these models mean for talent development? The choice of a sustainable business model is an opportunity to engage staff in a discussion about changes to markets, products, customers, and capabilities. The dialog can be a major source of learning and can be used to jump-start a series of new initiatives.

Consider the challenge of calculating the carbon footprint of the recent Winter Olympics in South Korea. Calculating your carbon footprint is aligned with Global Compact Principle 8 (undertake initiatives to promote greater environmental responsibility) and Sustainable Development Goals 12 (Responsible Consumption and Production) and 13 (Climate Action). The Olympics involved almost 3000 athletes in 102 sporting events, as well as thousands of additional support staff, spectators, and production crews.

According to the official PyeongChang 2018 Winter Olympics website, the Games were estimated to produce 1.59 million metric tons of carbon.[33] In support of the Games, organizers purchased certified emission reduction credits (CERs) that are internationally recognized and traded and are certified to meet the definition of a metric ton of carbon as defined by the Kyoto Protocol.[34] This might be characterized as an "offset or net benefit" strategy. This illustrates how a business might try to calculate and offset its carbon emissions. However, the calculation is all about where you draw the line (or boundary).

Most of the 1.59 million tons of carbon production calculated for the Olympics comes from travel and energy use at the Olympic village. But does it count the manufacturing of the skis, skates, and bobsleds competitors bring to the Games? Does it include the manufacture of food and utensils used, or the preparation activities before the Games, or the activities of the country Olympic committees in the years preceding the Games? The answer seems to be no.

If we were to plan a future Olympic Games with a focus on the seventeen SDGs, we might start with a new idea like de-carbonization or a circular economy model and rely more on renewable energy sources, thus eliminating the need for so many carbon offset credits. We might keep the Olympic village in one location to avoid having to build new facilities every four years, and instead repurpose the funds for sustainable infrastructure. That strategy would also facilitate the circular economy by creating opportunities for reuse, recycling, and remanufacture of Olympic equipment. By redesigning the Olympic experience from scratch, we might change athlete preparation, venue construction, equipment use, resource sourcing, transportation needs, and perhaps the customer viewing experience. If we want to create positive social impact across all seventeen SDGs, then we change almost everything.

This example illustrates how definitions, business models, and boundaries collectively influence what you want to accomplish. To redesign the Olympics, we would need to start with two things:

1. A business model that allows us to plan and forecast both economic and social impact for the Games that takes into account not only areas of direct impact like energy use and environmental degradation but also indirect impacts from preparation and life-cycle costs that involve people in ninety-two countries.

2. A clear definition of sustainability that provides boundaries for the different people and businesses involved. The deeper you go into individual business practices, the more you realize that the SDGs lose value as a guidebook. They are much too high-level. The missing links are functional or industry definitions that allow us to figure out how we apply sustainability practices to the manufacture of a pair of skis or a restaurant business trying to avoid food waste.

A new business model and a solid definition of sustainability provide clarity of purpose, but there are still at least three missing pieces. The first is a new mental model for the leaders who organize the Games, for athletes and coaches, and for the entire business ecosystem that allows the Games to happen. What framework or set of business processes will encourage them to think and behave differently? Second, what new skills must be learned to maximize sustainability outcomes? Finally, transformational change always starts with one committed leader who can combine clarity of purpose with passion for the work and the ability to encourage great performance. We'll address these points later in this book.

Reader Reflection

IMAGINE for a moment that you are part of a design team that just evaluated all of your company's products using a new sustainability test. The CEO has suggested she is considering a change in the company's registration to benefit corporation status, but she wants a general assessment of where the company stands before the decision is made. Your product assessment as well as other process reviews indicate the company would receive a relatively low B Impact Assessment score unless it accelerates the change process. Your team assesses your company's products for alignment with sustainability goals and each product is judged for toxicity of ingredients and manufacturing processes, the ease of service and repair, and the ability of the product to be recycled when it is disposed of. Your best-selling products, which account for 60 percent of your revenue, rate poorly. Redesigning these products will bring them into closer alignment with your company's sustainability principles and may even give you a competitive edge in the marketplace. However, doing so will be expensive and there is no guarantee that customers will see the value in redesigned products.

Your design team could act immediately, but committing the necessary resources will reduce gross profits. Analysts and investors may question the company's direction. You could wait another year, but you would have to restock the old designs in the meantime and keep non-sustainable products in circulation for several years. You could move gradually and redesign one product at a time, but maintaining inventory of old products while investing in new products potentially has a multiyear negative effect on gross margins, until all product redesigns are in the market. The messaging may also be confusing to both customers and suppliers.

Alternatively, you could move more slowly and wait until the market demands greater change or the local government forces your hand with new regulations. However, that choice would likely kill the company's decision to register as a benefit corporation.

What would you do? Which of the sustainable goals are affected? How important is changing the company registration to a benefit corporation? How would you approach the situation and what recommendations would you make?

Part of the value of building foundation knowledge that includes the history of sustainability, the sustainable business goals, and emerging business models is to improve the quality of the dialog in your organization. As you read the first few chapters of this book, were you surprised by the scope and challenge of sustainability? The more knowledgeable your leadership team, the better your sustainability plan and the fewer missteps. That's why organizations often start with demonstration projects involving energy efficiency, recycling, or packaging optimization, for example. If you do that in conjunction with an assessment of your products, you may find that you can create financial benefits that serve your short-term goals while making investments that pay off down the road with a more balanced set of social and financial outcomes. As we point out later in the book, leaders need to act with authenticity. Several case examples we present in the coming chapters illustrate leaders who have successfully navigated the multiyear transition process, balancing both short- and long-term value creation with strong stakeholder communication.

TAKEAWAY: You Need a Broad Systems Perspective, Multiple Models, and Benchmarks

As we have seen, defining what we mean by sustainability is an evolving process, and one definition does not fit all types of organizations and industries. Inevitably, a broader systems perspective is needed to understand how our behavior has downstream impact and which set of models will work for our specific situation. This perspective is crucial to the idea of sustainability as a competitive advantage. Engaging in activities that increase energy efficiency, improve recycling, or reduce your carbon footprint can be viewed as projects that save money. However, they do not fundamentally change your business purpose or products and approach to the market. That requires a new business model that conveys an advantage based on your approach to sustainability. The early adopters among sustainable organizations tend to share several characteristics:

- they use the big SDG definitions as a general guide;
- they construct a common, easy-to-understand narrative of how sustainability connects to their business model as a statement of purpose;
- they use industry, geographic, or functional models and assessments to translate sustainable business opportunities into goals, projects, and jobs;
- they tend to be more integrated across business functions and to use business assessments and reporting to bring individual actions back into a systems-wide perspective on economic and social value creation; and
- their clarity of purpose sends clear messages to the business ecosystem and potential partners, as well as to the talent and investment markets.

Early adopters of sustainability have used benchmarks and models as a valuable guide to building sustainability practices in their organization. The broad recommendations I have just described apply mostly to large or multinational organizations with specialized staff functions. In chapter 4, I will discuss business models for the small and medium-size organization and tell the stories of a number of diverse and innovative businesses from different parts of the world.

Chapter 4

SMALLER COMPANIES NEED A DIFFERENT SOLUTION

"Creativity involves breaking out of established patterns in order to look at things in a different way." EDWARD DE BONO

I f you are a leader in a smaller organization, you will have recognized that much of what I have discussed to this point applies to larger companies. The largest firms may employ tens of thousands of people, have multiple locations, and have a substantial impact on waste, water, and energy use. They also have a disproportionate impact on local employment and community development because of larger contributions to the local tax base and more sophisticated infrastructure. In many cases, large global businesses have a dedicated chief sustainability officer (CSO) or a senior executive with a similar mandate. These companies will generally publish an annual report on corporate social responsibility and have a dedicated HR function. Typically, they will also have specialized functions and budgets for recruiting, talent development, and training. The question becomes, Does a sustainability advantage accrue only to the largest of companies, and do smaller businesses just become followers of a larger trend?

However, the importance of small to medium-size enterprises (SMEs) cannot be overstated. If your organization is in this category, then you should know that according to the Organisation for Economic Co-operation and Development (OECD), SMEs account for 70 percent of employment among the thirty-six OECD countries. They account for 45 percent of employment and one third of GDP in emerging economies.[1] In addition, they are less likely to move than a big firm and a larger percentage of the capital they invest stays in the local community. Small to medium-size businesses are also important in times of post-recessionary recovery. According to Thomas Stewart, executive director for the National Center for the Middle Market at Ohio State University,[2] "SMEs created almost two-thirds of all new jobs in the United States since the end of the great recession in 2007–2008."[3]

Small to medium-size enterprises are generally defined in the United States as companies with fewer than five hundred employees,[4] but this is one definition among many. In the European Union (EU), the standard definition is 250 employees with revenue less than 50 million euros.[5] The common EU definition offers three categories of SMEs (based on head count, turnover, and asset classifications), while the US Department of Labor has seven categories of SMEs (0 to 499 employees). The Asia Development Bank[6] distinguishes SMEs by different income levels (four categories from low-income to high-income economies) and by number of employees, which varies by country and industry from two hundred to one thousand employees. In the ten-country Association of Southeast Asian Nations (ASEAN) trading bloc, the definition of an SME generally includes a business that employs fewer than three hundred employees, and accounts for 89 percent to 99 percent of all companies and between 52 percent and 97 percent of all employment, depending on the country.[7] They may also contribute between 40 percent and 70 percent of the pollution waste stream.[8]

To paint a big picture of the potential impact of SMEs on sustainability goals, consider that there are over 27 million SME businesses in the United States alone.[9] The World Bank estimates that there are 70 to 100 million formal micro to small and medium-size enterprises in emerging markets, and as many as 285 million if informal micro businesses are included.[10] As the global population continues to increase, the World Bank estimates that we'll need 600 million new jobs over the next fifteen years to maintain progress in reducing poverty and hunger.[11]

The common characteristic of SMEs is the smaller the company, the more limited the human resource department and training budget. They may not employ a separate CSO staff or file a corporate social responsibility (CSR) report. They also tend to have less bargaining power with suppliers, limited capital, and a leadership team that is not as specialized as their big-company counterparts. At the same time, SMEs are where entrepreneurs live, new ideas find investment, and risk takers emerge to start new social enterprises. Given the potential impact of SMEs on meeting global sustainability targets, they must become part of the global solution.

SMEs may be retail stores, restaurants, small professional services firms, and local manufacturers. They may be interested in "doing good," but the focus is often on capital and cash flow. Investing in your own research and development (R&D) is difficult, auditing suppliers is challenging, and doing anything that raises costs is often deadly. My experience as co-founder of several SMEs and advisor to many more is that only a small percentage of SME companies are focused on sustainability. Many more would participate if barriers could be reduced and resources made available, which is particularly true in emerging markets. But hundreds of company success stories prove that, despite difficulties, it can be done.

In larger markets like the US, you find companies like the W.S. Badger Company, a second-generation family-owned company that is a benefit corporation and recipient of B Corp certification. Meeting these standards is not a small commitment, since it almost always involves the same small team of people that are also leading product development, sales, and operations. It takes considerable focus and effort to do the assessments, and to complete the reporting and support the audit requirements. As discussed in past chapters, a highly engaged founder is critically important. For Badger, that individual is Bill Whyte, a.k.a. Badger Bill. The company goes to great lengths to report on its electricity and water usage; its goals to increase the use of post-consumer packaging; and its waste production and recycling efforts. One thing that distinguishes Badger from many other sustainable businesses is its success in transitioning from the first-generation founders to a second generation of leadership. At Badger, it's all in the family.

W.S. Badger's Green Team

Founded in 1995, the W.S. Badger Company is based in New Hampshire (United States). It remains family owned and operated, with Badger Bill Whyte as CEO; his wife, Katie, as chief operating officer; his daughter, Emily Schwerin-Whyte, as VP of sales and marketing; and Rebecca Hamilton as VP of innovation and sustainability. It manufactures organic skin care products and has grown to exceed ninety employees as of time of writing. It is also part of the growing certified B Corp movement, having passed its first assessment in 2011. Badger conducts regular B Impact Assessments (BIAs) and consistently scores higher than the median industry average. It emphasizes its family-friendly policies, offsets 100 percent of its electricity usage with renewable energy credits (RECs), and measures trash production, recycling, and CO_2 emissions. The company reports using only post-consumer recycled paper in 98 percent of its paperboard packaging.[12]

Badger is also committed to developing its employees and reports that internal candidates fill 64 percent of open positions. It also makes use of monthly meetings for stakeholder engagement and has started a train-the-trainer program to ensure development across departments. Badger's community involvement, responsiveness to environmental challenges, and family-friendly practices have always been part of its value system. As we've seen with larger companies, it helps to have a founding vision with strong core values! These values and social awareness were embedded in the company, leading to B certification, which has given the company membership in a larger like-minded community and a way to communicate, measure, and benchmark its efforts.

I spoke to Rebecca Hamilton about Badger's path to sustainability. She recounted a story of working on an employment commission for the state of New Hampshire. The commission was set up as a working group to help address the challenge that businesses have of finding or developing talented employees. New Hampshire has an unemployment rate of 2.7 percent,[13] which effectively means full employment. According to Rebecca, "I may have been the only person to say we don't have a problem finding employees. Whenever we're hiring, we have plenty of people who apply, especially millennials. We also have very low attrition."[14]

Badger did not start out with an explicit strategy to become the employer of choice; it started as a mission-driven company with family values. At each stage of growth, it had concerns about losing that vision if the company grew too fast. As they wrestled with those challenges, Rebecca says they "sought out the B certification process as a way to give them a road map. The goal was to give more structure to who we are so we could scale while deepening our mission."

Badger is known as a company that stays true to its values and pays well and has good benefits. As importantly, it is known for leadership behavior that Rebecca describes as "kind and respectful," noting, "We want to make money, but we view money as our fuel to do good, not our goal."[15] At Badger, they do what they call mission-based hiring. It involves everything from the application to the phone screening to the interviews. The final interviews always involve one of the four owners from the founding family. The key questions seem to be, Is the potential hire talented? and Will he or she be inspired by what they do?

Badger developed a biannual strategy that involves a board-level review that is followed by a discussion among the leadership team and then a company-wide review. The strategy encompasses a longer-term environmental impact strategy Rebecca refers to as the company's "North Star." A key part of Badger's goals are annual training programs to deepen its staff's understanding of sustainability and to build a sustainability Green Team that takes on big global issues and brings them home by defining a local connection.

This year, the Green Team identified both immigration and drug abuse as key national social issues. It gathered data and made the connection to local concerns, including New Hampshire's drug addiction rate, which is second highest among US states. It organized volunteer efforts to help with addiction support and adapted company hiring and benefit policies to be more supportive. Badger stated in a company report, "Our first step was to engage a recovery advocate who presented a picture of how businesses and individuals can come together to create a supportive environment for those in active addiction and recovery."[16]

It also translated the national immigration debate into local immigration challenges and decided to help newcomers to the state get acclimatized. New Hampshire has become home to more than 3500 refugees since 2010, with recent émigrés from Iraq, Bhutan, and the Congo settling primarily in the towns of Manchester and Concord.[17] The company participated in community programs to help with housing, job, and transportation issues. Badger employees also hosted fifty refugees to make a more personal connection. Each Badger employee is given sixteen hours of paid time off to pursue volunteer activities they feel are important, and employees often report on those efforts in company impact assessments and blogs. Badger has become an employer of choice in part by translating big national sustainability issues that drive change into local actions that bring the company's values to life.

Jana Small Finance Bank: Focused on the Urban Poor

Another illuminating success story is Jana Small Finance Bank in India. Although Jana is not an SME any longer, the vast majority of its customers remain micro businesses or individuals who collectively sign off on loans for each other. For many community SMEs in India, Jana is the SME mothership. The company traces its roots to the Sanghamitra Urban Program that made its first micro finance loan in 1999. It was renamed Janalakshmi in 2006 and received its Royal Bank of India (RBI) license in 2008 as Janalakshmi Financial Services. It became Jana Small Finance Bank in 2018. Today, Jana Small Finance Bank has 550 offices and 15,000 employees in India who serve millions of sole proprietors and small businesses. Approximately 25 percent of its bank branches reach what are called "unbanked" rural areas.

Founder Ramesh Ramanathan has focused his efforts on creating an organization that addresses the problems of the urban poor. Part of that vision is the idea of "financial inclusion" as a mechanism to improve job creation and promote higher incomes among rural families. His focus has been on helping "the tea shop owner, the street vendor, and the small family business."[18]

Ramesh is co-author of the book *Urban Poverty Alleviation*.[19] According-ing to Ramesh, "Very few companies, from a DNA standpoint, are socially conscious. However, being financially viable is a huge asset in attracting people and attracting investment." He emphasized the impor-tance of the promoter in helping to define the business agenda and man-age the tension between the social and economic goals. "In a socially focused, financially viable business, the promoter must be a lighthouse for the enterprise. Genuineness must shine from within. The promoter helps define the agenda, maintains communication over time and main-tains the sense of purpose."[20]

I have worked with Gautam Bhushan, executive vice president at Jana Bank, in several different companies over the past twenty years. Although Gautam is now a regional leader for the bank, he was for-merly head of training and development for several companies in India. Gautam described moving to Jana as a decision to join an organization where "people are there to make a difference." He participated in the creation of several pilot education programs when he first came to the bank, one of which involved voluntary education programs to teach the children of customers about financial literacy skills. Another involved street theater to help break some stereotypes and informally educate the community. Both Ramesh's and Gautam's comments reinforce the importance of a healthy and viable ecosystem to support sustainable development among small businesses.

Rype Office Ltd: Matching Mission to Government Policy

The story of Rype Office Ltd in the United Kingdom reinforces the importance of SME success tied to a viable ecosystem and smart public policy on sustainability. Founder Greg Lavery describes the opportunity: "If you believe that sustainability creates real value, you have three choices. You can go into consulting, you can invest in a sustainable business or, if you identify an opportunity that you think is great, you can do it yourself." Greg chose the latter.

The UK government first introduced a landfill tax in 1996 to improve waste management and encourage recycling. In its 2010 budget, the government announced that the tax would increase eight pounds sterling per ton, per year, until the tax was eighty pounds sterling per ton, and would remain at that level from 2014 through 2020.[21] The importance of this policy is that it created a very predictable model for estimating the cost of waste disposal and made heavy items like office furniture prohibitively expensive to toss in the trash. Enter Greg Lavery and the birth of Rype Office.

Rype Office offers to remove office furniture from companies so they avoid the disposal costs. Rype also buys overstock items that might otherwise be disposed of. The company then refreshes, refurbishes, or remanufactures the furniture and offers it to local businesses at varying grades (A+ to B) at substantial discounts off new furniture prices. Buyers may also receive Building Research Establishment Environmental Assessment Method (BREEAM) or Leadership in Energy and Environmental Design (LEED) credits for the furniture. According to Greg, "Government policy created the opportunity and the kind of predictability a small business needs to build a plan, attract investment, and market to customers. We can reduce the waste stream through remanufacturing by as much as 95 percent on some items. Remanufactured furniture looks great and offers real cost savings."

Rype Office also makes the type of decisions that suggest it focuses on more than just the economics of remanufactured furniture. When I asked Greg what Rype did to create a culture of sustainability, he offered the following insights:

- The number-one hiring criteria is a passion for creating a better world. He has hired people without much job experience but with a "real passion for sustainability." He described such people as not constrained by what they think they can do.
- He calls remanufacturing "problem-solving at the micro level with lots of repetition." He asks people to focus on what is the most sustainable way of doing things.
- When Rype Office gets larger projects, they take on disadvantaged staff or work with partners who support the long-term or chronically unemployed.[22]

W.S. Badger has benefited from a more mature ecosystem of suppliers as well as from holding on to the strength of a founder's vision. Rype Office has benefited from both good government policy and an ecosystem of partners to enhance its brand and long-term viability. Jana Small Finance Bank became a powerhouse within a micro finance ecosystem that has been operating in India for over three decades. That maturity allows Jana to be more innovative in supporting rural communities, in helping innovators to share stories, and in improving the literacy of communities. Jana also benefits greatly from having an active promoter at the helm. It is equally illustrative to look at situations where the story is more challenging.

Fishing in East Africa: Local Challenges Are Complex[23]
In the East African country of Kenya, the fishing industry around Lake Victoria provides tens of thousands of jobs. Most are small businesses in

fishing, fish processing, food service, sales, or transportation. The population of Kenya has more than doubled in the past thirty years, while commercial fish landings at Lake Victoria ports have declined by over 60 percent. Illegal overfishing is hard to control. Complicating matters is the availability of frozen fish from other countries, which is often cheaper to purchase than local fresh fish.

For the consumer, lower costs mean they buy more imported fish, but that leads to greater poverty among fishermen, who must land more fish to make the same money. Continued overfishing puts greater stress on the resources. Commercial fish farms can help address supply issues, but they can cause environmental problems and they generally benefit a smaller number of people. One solution would be improving the ability of local fishermen to refrigerate, store, and transport their fish, or what is called a "cold supply chain." But building the cold supply chain is difficult for any single fisherman or SME, so it doesn't get done. SME contributions to sustainability can be greatly enhanced with the participation of industry associations, NGOs, and good government policy. Otherwise, the cycle of unsustainable behavior can be difficult to break.

SME Investment Challenges in Brazil

The challenges of ecosystem maturity are particularly acute in developing markets and during economic downturns. Since global economic activity has cyclical periods of growth and recession, preparing for these events can prevent a pullback from sustainable business practices. Brazil has experienced a deep financial crisis since 2014, suffering several consecutive years of declining GDP. Such a recession has not occurred in the country since 1931.

I have previously worked with an innovative Brazilian education company called MindQuest, known for its global education partnerships and creative programs. I asked CEO Mauricio Wendling Lopes about the impact of the recession on sustainability practices and SMEs. He observed, "The smaller businesses are focused on survival. The last four years have been very intense and difficult. Anything that takes time away from profitability and innovation is often considered a waste of time. They focus on efficiency and maximizing sales from a sense of survival. Sustainability tends to remain strong in larger companies, where strong ownership tends to make investments on a much longer time horizon. For them, it is already embedded in who they are. They effectively create their own ecosystems. For the SMEs, it is a very challenging environment."[24]

> Whenever we find a barrier to our goals, it is inevitably part of a specific business practice such as marketing, manufacturing, packaging, or shipping. The startup experience itself is the crucible for learning. It is the collaborative processes and a common mental model that helps develop sustainable best practices both individually and for the teams. For the small business owner, it's about embedding the sustainability mindset into everything you do and linking with a broader community of like-minded people. Simple business practices done exceptionally well, with repetition and shared insights, are the general model.

The Four Sustainability Promises of KPPM Global

In 2016, I co-founded a business called KPPM Global, based in Thailand. The company makes health and beauty products and was the brainchild of my fiancée Krittiyanee "Kriss" Prompaeng and several colleagues, including Sawai NaNakorn and Saruda Purivittayatera. The health and beauty market has global annual sales of over US$300 billion and represents a category that touches the daily lives of people around the world. It is also a growing category in Asia, home to 40 percent of the world's population with the fastest-growing middle class. It was the perfect demonstration project to test our ideas on sustainability. Kriss would serve as the chief creative officer and I would focus on sustainable strategy and business development.

I shared with our team the Daly Rules, many of the business models described earlier, and several annual reports from benefit corporations. We borrowed best practices from SME company development by emphasizing transparency and engagement and by discussing both general and specific public good. We started by leveraging our network of contacts to identify manufacturers and suppliers who already had a track record of developing more sustainable products so we could learn from their experience. We made some trade-offs in the early going, particularly with global suppliers, so we could develop our own expertise by working within successful networks. Over time, our goal is to bring that expertise back to local suppliers and communities.

As a team, the high-level SDGs were helpful only as a definition of sustainability. We decided to simplify our business focus as four promises:

- **For Customers:** A commitment to build and innovate new products and services that are good for people and good for the environment. That means a constant focus on designing, marketing, and selling the best possible products and services in environmentally and socially appropriate ways.
- **For Shareholders:** A rigorous focus on long-term value creation. That means balancing the needs of customers, employees, partners, and communities with the desire to provide strong long-term shareholder returns. We want to build a business based on sustainable practices that add value to both current AND future generations.
- **For Employees and Partners:** A sustained effort to promote economic and social gains for every person or organization that contributes to our business success.
- **For Communities:** A commitment that our activities will be a net benefit to the communities where we work and where we sell our products and services. Wherever possible, we will use a decision-making process that respects local needs, cultures, and challenges.

Although I keep copies of the SDGs and the Gapframe on the wall, the four promises are a more common reference point. It's simply easier to use the promises in day-to-day discussion. Much like Rype Office, the keys for us are the weekly meetings and problem-solving sessions that allow us to think about how we can do what we do better. In a small business, daily problem-solving is the engine of organizational learning from which the business design evolves. Those who consistently help solve problems become the mentors for those who follow. As such, they must also be your early sustainability champions.

Reader Reflection

IMAGINE for a moment that you live in a country experiencing a deep financial crisis. You have a small business that manufactures packaging for stores and food vendors. You offer plastic bags, food wrap, and single-use products for restaurants. Just before the crisis, you invested heavily in new equipment and the bank loans are a strain. You are forced to reduce your staff and work longer hours just to make ends meet. Many of your best customers are struggling, too. Average people have lost most of their savings due to inflation; many have lost their jobs. They do not shop as often or eat out, and that affects your business. Everyone is looking for favors: your customers want credit terms and your suppliers expect only cash payments. Life is difficult.

In the news, officials from both your country and neighboring countries talk about the importance of policies aligned to sustainable development goals. You generally support the goals and the idea of having sustainable jobs and healthy communities. You would not disagree that forests are under threat, big cities and coastal areas have serious pollution problems, and corruption seems like an unsolvable problem. Crime rates are a growing concern for you, your family, and neighbors. The officials talk about banning plastics in major cities. If the talk becomes law, you stand to lose your business. Your competitors and suppliers will go out of business, too. Job losses will mean even more hardship.

How do you respond to this challenge? Do you fight the impending legislation? Do you protest in the streets? Do you accept the changes as better for all and move on (if you can)?

If you are in any unsustainable business, or a business with high negative social outcomes, this reflection points to the value of acting now. The dilemma in particular is currently being acted out across the world. Local and national governments are responding to public demand that the problem of single-use plastics clogging landfills and public waterways be addressed. If you wait for the market to catch up with your unsustainable practices, then you will find yourself in a position with few supporters and very little leverage. That is why we need to see more businesses acting proactively to explore alternative products and product systems. Sustainability challenges can be seen as opportunities if they are engaged early. That was the lesson of Rype Office, which created an entirely new business from the intersection of changing public policy and new market demand. The value of a sustainability "green team," as illustrated by W.S. Badger Company, would also be helpful in this situation, particularly if the team started investigating options a year or two before the change was forced upon your business. The answer is not to resist the change but to get out front and transform your business.

TAKEAWAY: SMEs Need to Excel at a Few Key Practices and Build a Robust Ecosystem

To create a sustainability advantage in the SME market, we need to simplify the message by creating clear business value propositions and statements that drive product development, sales, and marketing decisions.

- Certification standards like the B Impact Assessment, although sometimes time consuming to undertake, offer three values: (1) they serve as a road map for sustainability actions; (2) they provide good development assignments for those who work to satisfy the standards; and (3) they deliver brand identity by positioning you within the sustainability community.

- The founder or promoter role is essential for small businesses with a focus on sustainability. Active participation and support sends clear market signals, which are important for the ecosystem, for other investors, and for senior talent.

- Staff training and development can be a big issue since there are few low-cost training programs on sustainable business practices. Action learning is the key, as is networking within communities of practice and leaders serving as teachers. Designating a "green team," as the W.S. Badger Company has done, can help focus energies and priorities.

- Hiring for passion often provides entry-level staff with high energy and senior-level staff with strong experience.

- Hiring a few key senior staff with excellent experience provides the basis for a leader-as-teacher program. Senior leaders often leave bigger companies for the chance to do something that really makes a difference. They often bring the skills that need to be taught across the organization.

- A strong ecosystem is critical to creating sustainable advantage for SMEs. Government and industry associations, committed vendors, and colleagues often fill the education gaps.

In this chapter, we focused on the small to medium-size business as a global force in the sustainability movement and the challenges SMEs face to first thrive and then implement strategies for sustainability. The reader reflection illustrated the threat posed by economic and political uncertainty. The businesses discussed in this chapter all had champions who saw ways to innovate through a sustainability lens. Embedding sustainable innovation practices in a business culture helps ensure that a business can thrive during economic downturns. That theme continues in chapter 5, in which I offer a six-step model for the onboarding of sustainable practices, including design thinking and systems thinking. I also discuss the business case that moves your organization from sustainability projects to sustainability as a competitive advantage.

PART TWO

LEADING THE SUSTAINABILITY AGENDA

Chapter 5

IT ALWAYS STARTS WITH ONE COMMITTED LEADER

"Knowing what's right doesn't mean much unless you do what's right." THEODORE ROOSEVELT

It is a truism that effecting change starts with a great leader. INSEAD professor Manfred Kets de Vries describes effective leaders as having two key roles. The first is the role of "architect" to design an organization with the right strategy and structure. The second is a "charismatic role" to communicate clarity of purpose and empower others to achieve success.[1]

If I use a consulting metaphor, a new engagement is often framed with two points: determining a "point of focus," or where the organization wants to be in the future, and the "point of entry," the activity that will be our first project. Both are important and indicative of the scale of the challenge, the resources available, and the tolerance for risk. Inevitably, the goal of the consulting engagement is to help drive business transformation (Figure 5.1). The potential scale of the impact on the business and the inherent degree of risk will determine who runs it. It either becomes the direct project of the CEO or

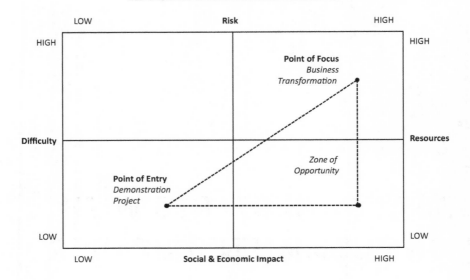

Figure 5.1: Risk and Impact Scale of Business Transformation

a handpicked senior leader deemed capable of driving change. These kinds of assignments are highly developmental and often transformational for personal careers.

Where Change Can Begin: The Demonstration Project

For many companies, the point of entry for a sustainability leader will be a demonstration project, which is generally an opportunity to test ideas and build both political and social capital within the organization. The choice of a demonstration project as the first step in a transformation process is supported by data. For example, in a 2016 McKinsey survey, more than half of 2400 companies surveyed had made investments in energy-efficient equipment and one-third of those were making use of renewable sources of energy.[2] These types of efficiency goals are often the first attempts at sustainability undertaken by large companies, because they offer a well-understood return on investment. However, that same survey indicated that only 29 percent of companies managed their business portfolio so as to capitalize on trends in sustainability. The takeaway here is that changing your business portfolio carries too much risk to be a starting point. Creating a demonstration project allows you to experiment in a more controlled environment.

Greg Lavery, introduced earlier as the founder of Rype Office, is a former Booz consultant and was co-founder of the UK sustainability consulting firm Lavery/Pennell.[3] He calls the typical first projects "non-labor resource efficiencies" that involve "energy efficiency, waste reduction, material efficiency, packaging optimization, transport efficiency, and recycling or remanufacturing."[4] Initial demonstration projects often are lower risk with a direct cost savings payback and can reinforce the idea that supporting a sustainability agenda is good for business. They can also provide some sense of current capabilities and gaps that form the basis for a broader change strategy. However, the downside of selecting efficiency projects is that they do not always offer evidence to support a new business model or validate new market opportunities.

To summarize current market tendencies, I have organized the sustainable company journey into a four-phase model (Figure 5.2).

No matter which phase your company is in, each leader or sustainability advocate can take six specific steps to add value.

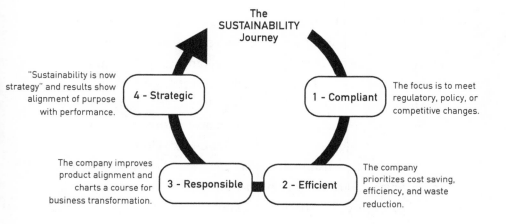

Figure 5.2: The Sustainability Journey

Six Steps Every Sustainability Leader Can Take

Step 1: Rethink Your Role as Leader

Sustainability is an issue that can carry with it strong emotions, and the transformational leader can tap into those emotions for better results. During my time at the United Nations, I helped train and develop teams that worked on the BAM earthquake in Iran in 2003, health-care epidemics in sub-Saharan Africa, and the terrible tsunami that struck near Banda Aceh, Indonesia, in 2004. Although these are extreme examples, the clear impact of these events on people and communities motivated people to work exceptionally hard. As a business owner, your new social and economic goals are an opportunity to make new connections between your team and people in your communities that will be the beneficiaries of your focus on sustainable outcomes. The more you focus on clear and strong social outcomes, I think you will be surprised at how motivated people are to achieve levels of excellence. Your business will benefit from better team dynamics, improved employee and customer satisfaction, and an improved triple bottom line: people (social value), profit (economic value), and planet (environmental value).

In my experience, most transformational leaders share several key characteristics and perform the following roles:

- **Authentic Communicator:** The advantage of embracing sustainability is that you can wrap the company's purpose in the mantle of global or local good. Your messages become more powerful when your bond with stakeholders is built on trust. To do this effectively, you must communicate honestly, openly, and frequently with both clarity of purpose and ongoing evidence of positive progress.
- **Key Talent Developer:** No one can drive change alone, so it is imperative that transformational leaders spend considerable time recruiting and developing key talent to build team and organizational capability. To grow a sustainability agenda to organizational scale requires leaders across the organization to serve as teachers or discussion leaders, with considerable time devoted to coaching

and providing feedback. Transformational leaders need to be highly visible in the talent development process.

- **Change Enabler:** Sustainable business practices will require investments in key practices, new technology, and partnerships. Senior leaders must remove barriers to change, respond to market volatility, and catalyze innovation.
- **Innovation Investor:** One of the most important roles for a transformational leader is to look for investment options where employees have identified new opportunities for value creation. If leaders view their role as supporting a portfolio of innovations, they are continuously looking for the bright idea, the serial innovator, the opportunity for scale, and ways to create leverage and speed. The goal is to build a healthy innovation portfolio within the business.

Step 2: Communicate New Business Goals

A key step for most leaders is to engage employees in a discussion about new sustainability goals. Changing the boundaries of business accountability can encourage entirely new discussions and generate a variety of opportunities for innovation. Table 5.1 illustrates how certain boundary characteristics can lead to new business discussions based on new and insightful questions. For example, some banks have started to look at models for global warming and are asking how this might affect their loan portfolio. Such high-level discussions have then been converted into specific metrics on the number of customers or projects (loans) at risk. Similar conversations are occurring in different parts of the world at insurance firms that are rethinking risk models for hurricanes, floods, and other weather events that may involve trillions of dollars in potential claims.[5] These are examples of how a change in boundary conditions can lead to broader or new accountabilities. The key is to translate high-level discussions into functional, team, or individual goals that connect everyone back to the new value proposition.

Table 5.1: Boundary Characteristics and Changes

Sample Boundary Characteristic	Potential Changes in Boundary Definition
Natural Systems	Are you using a resource like water, air, or energy at a rate that exceeds the natural capacity of an aquifer or reservoir to replenish itself? For example, are you sourcing textiles from arid areas that are water intensive?
Inputs	This may include taking extra responsibility for both where and how your raw materials are sourced. For example: Were they harvested from sustainable forests? Did they involve child labor? Were workers paid a living wage? Are your input processes (yours or your suppliers) damaging to communities or the environment?
Cradle to Grave	Are you assuming responsibility for your product from design and creation to use, reuse, and recycling back to base materials?
Accountability	Do you take responsibility for how your products are used? Are they harmful if used incorrectly or for purposes other than originally intended? Do you accept the return of products for recycling after their useful life?
Relationships	Do you assume responsibility for the working conditions at your tier 1 suppliers? How about the tier 2 suppliers?

A variety of leading companies are experimenting with new forms of measurement tied to the Sustainable Development Goals (SDGs). These can be formal goals or simply a discussion framework used as a challenge to the organization. Solvay, a European chemistry company, created a scorecard that lists the company's product operating vulnerability versus market alignment with the SDGs. Each product area is classified on a five-point scale, from low alignment to high alignment with the SDGs. Each product is cross-referenced to look at the potential monetized impact.[6]

I have amended that framework here as an exercise so you can see the impact of both a rating scale and different boundary conditions on your company (Table 5.2). You can perform this exercise with products, services, or key processes.

Table 5.2: Sustainability Scoring Exercise

Sustainability Alignment (higher is better)	Definition	Boundary Conditions		
		Narrow	Intermediate	Broad
1. High Negative	High economic value but low social value and/or net negative environmental impact.	Definition is constrained to impact on direct company resources and assets.	Definition is extended to include all current and anticipated tier 1 business relationships.	Definition is extended to include all current and anticipated tier 1 and tier 2 business relationships.
2. Net Negative	Some positive and negative attributes, but overall net negative for social and environmental considerations.			
3. Neutral	Economic, social, and environmental values balance out.			
4. Net Positive	Overall net positive attributes for social and environmental considerations.			
5. High Positive	No negative attributes. High positive attributes for all three triple-bottom-line considerations.			

This type of exercise is a way to provide clarity on where the business currently operates and offers an opportunity to discuss possible changes before making concrete plans and commitments. Even if you choose to make only incremental changes, the fact that you provide transparency on alignment tends to create pressure to do something. A competitive advantage may also result from new business goals for business teams looking to align innovative solutions with customer needs.

The global health and consumer products firm Philips has adopted a series of new metrics to align with the SDGs, including an internal metric to help improve the lives of 3 billion people by 2025. This is not a standard metric, but it offers an aspirational element to company activities. Philips has also offered more specific metrics tied to different business model ideas:

- 15 percent of revenues will be from circular economy solutions, and
- 70 percent of revenues from green solutions.

Those metrics are hard to compare from company to company and may lack the details of traditional scorecards, but you have to start somewhere. Part of the value in creating these new metrics is the discussion that ensues. BASF, a company that produces chemicals, plastics, pesticides, and oil and gas products, has developed a "value to society scorecard" that seeks to assign monetary values to company activities and now has multiyear longitudinal data to offer comparisons.

Some companies, like Dutch global financial giant ING, have developed both direct and indirect measures that partly address the boundary question. Direct measures concern the way we typically think about a company's performance, which is the collective impact of things done by employees. Indirect measures account for an expanded definition that includes partners and customers. For example,

- ING has been quoted as saying that the company is "directly" carbon neutral in the forty-one countries in which it operates; and
- indirectly, the company recognizes its impact through financing with research that suggests that 50 percent of its lending is in climate risk areas, and 50 percent of its customers in thirteen markets are at risk of losing their jobs or may change jobs in the next five years.[7]

ING specifically targets SDGs, including Goal 12 (Responsible Production and Consumption) and Goal 8 (Decent Work and Economic Growth), areas in which it believes it can produce the largest impact.

Step 3: Communicate a New Commitment to Social Outcomes

Companies of all sizes have created engagement programs that directly communicate their interest in creating social good or solving social problems. As the following examples indicate, the variety of programs can be significant, and it is easy to find communities in need of help:

- WhiteWave, whose brands include Horizon and Wallaby organic yogurt, earned a 100 percent rating in 2016 from the Human Rights Campaign Equality Index[8] for its LGBT (lesbian, gay, bisexual, and transgender) policies, including workplace nondiscrimination, inclusive health-care policies, and workplace protections. WhiteWave introduced Values in Action (VIA), a program that enables staff to volunteer over eleven thousand hours to nonprofit organizations.
- GlaxoSmithKline has reserved 20 percent of profits in certain developing markets to help train local health-care professionals.[9] The goal is to help improve local health-care delivery and the local "last mile" supply chain.
- Sony Corporation offered more than seventy public science program workshops that attracted over three thousand participants.[10]
- Patagonia, a leading company in corporate social responsibility, audits both its tier 1 and tier 2 textile suppliers to ensure the safety and application of employment standards for migrant workers in overseas factories.
- Thailand-based construction conglomerate SCG Corporation provided for the employment of more than three hundred disabled individuals in forty-one provinces in Thailand.[11]

Step 4: Train Everyone on the Basics of the Sustainable Development Goals

Although many companies produce a corporate sustainability report that references the SDGs, I find it rare that staff are taught the foundational concepts for each goal and are engaged in a discussion about their relevance to business and society. I have helped companies build their corporate universities for more than a dozen years, and the inclusion of workshops, conferences, and e-learning that address topics like sustainable energy, poverty, or migrant worker rights are the exception. Teaching the foundational concepts and their relevance is an effective way to help educate staff and stakeholders on goals of social concern and possible innovation opportunities.

The more aggressive a company wants to be in addressing sustainability goals, the deeper the education and training can be. Consider the following three goal statements:

1. Reduce supply chain carbon footprint by 20 percent year over year.
2. Develop a sourcing standard for textiles that minimizes the harmful effects of animal grazing while supporting standards of animal welfare.
3. Eliminate any fees paid by migrant workers applying for jobs in tier 2 supplier factories.

Each goal statement defines a very different set of goal boundaries. Put yourself in the position of a supply chain manager:

- How would you define the outcome measures for each? What activities are included or excluded in your goal definition?
- Who are the new stakeholders?
- Have you ever done anything like this before? Has your supply chain team?
- Does your team have the skills to meet these new challenges?
- How much control do you have over the key variables or business processes?
- Are you prepared to have your compensation based on successful completion of these goals?

Now, let's say you are the talent development manager trying to offer support:

- What types of skills and capabilities are needed to successfully execute on these goals? Do gaps exist?
- Is there a requirement to hire new capability or train existing staff?
- What resources are available to help?

The more unique these types of goals, the more you need an iterative problem-solving process to clarify key questions. A new "workout process" is covered in the next chapter.

Step 5: Enable People to Innovate in Your Value Chain

As enablers of change, leaders can teach innovation practices and define for each level of the organization how employees and stakeholders are able to participate. If your organization has engaged in a process to evaluate the sustainability alignment of your core products and processes, you can then assign teams to work on solutions to improve results. Table 5.3 highlights some of the types of innovation as well as areas of impact and the potential scale of output. The key is to align the types of innovation training with the individuals or groups that can be empowered to make the changes. As an illustration, you can look for breakthrough ideas in business models using either an open or closed innovation model. The distinguishing factor, particularly in larger businesses, is who can act on the desired innovation output.

Table 5.3: Types of Innovation and Impact

Type of Innovation	**Open Innovation:** This includes ideas like co-creation; the wisdom of teams; collective genius; the Creative Commons; open source innovation; public incubators and accelerators; hackathons; and innovation tournaments.
	Closed Innovation: This includes proprietary activities; patent and copyright filing; secret programs like "skunkworks" or private R&D shops; and closed prototyping labs.
Area of Impact	**Innovations:** These can occur in almost every facet of a business to include new agreement structures; brand definitions or sub-brand innovations; changes to business models; new marketing and sales channels; how you communicate; the customer or employee experience; innovations in information flows or information management; legal structures or contracts; measurement systems and scorecards; business, customer or supplier networks; different types of partnerships; changes in how you define social or economic performance; key process changes, products or product systems; service design; social values; or organization structure or technology (to name just a few).

Table 5.3: (Continued)

Scale of Innovation	**Business or Organizational Level:** The scale of innovation can be business wide and involve disruptive innovation; radical innovation; new business startups or entrepreneurial groups; reengineering; or blue ocean designs.
	Team-Level Innovation: Team-level innovations can involve continuous improvement; Kaizen concepts; total quality programs; six sigma programs; or reverse engineering activities (again, to name just a few).

Table 5.4: Examples of Innovation Impact

Roles	Examples of Innovation Impact (from Table 5.3)
Executives as well as business, functional, and geographic leaders	Business models; social value; organizational structure; the business brand; performance values; communications
Marketing	Brand; channel; product; product system; customer experience
Human resources	Employee experience; social value; performance
Finance	Measurements; business model; integrated reporting; communications
Technology	Enabling technology; process; information; network
Key individual contributors	Process; performance; network; communications

You can begin the process by teaching the tools of innovation and then focus on efforts where people have the greatest likelihood of improving activities within their own or neighboring value chains (Table 5.4). That taps into local knowledge and makes it easier to share part of the value creation with the people making it happen. Depending on the size and scale of your organization, you may be able to make improvements in dozens of different key products, processes, or systems within a new sustainable business models.

Simply put, you can take a functional area, offer employees essential training on several techniques for both open and closed innovation, allow them to self-select areas where they want greater training, and then target specific sustainability impact areas where they have both the ability and opportunity to create change.

Step 6: Offer Specialized Development

Each functional area will benefit from specialized development to enhance innovation output. Several skill areas will be relevant to everyone in the organization:

- stakeholder engagement (everyone);
- systems thinking (everyone);
- design thinking (everyone); and
- change leadership (all executives, senior leaders, and team leaders).

Sustainability touches every aspect of the organization, so every job level and area of accountability can be involved. One challenge is to encourage key staff to take time to rethink activities that have become second nature. Stakeholder engagement is a well-developed process, but it will be necessary to have key staff revisit their assumptions with newer expectations for community involvement, social goals, and different commitments to governments, suppliers, and partners. Effective stakeholder assessment is critical since new sustainable business models can put additional stakeholder groups on par with shareholders. Giving voice to these stakeholders can be an effective tool in balancing social and economic priorities. Effective stakeholder analysis typically has several key features:

- identifying individuals with the direct ability to influence or block success;

- identifying individuals with the ability to serve as advocates or allies; and
- identifying relationships between individuals.

Depending on your new business model, boundary definitions may change for key roles or activities that add new stakeholders or open up new stakeholder relationships. Even if a skill set or technique like systems thinking or stakeholder analysis is already in use, it can change greatly when applied to expanded boundaries and new stakeholders. It may also be true that the direction of influence or the strength of the influence (both positive and negative) in stakeholder relationships may change, even for stakeholders with longstanding relationships. Taking the time to understand these changes is often best done as a group exercise where old assumptions can be tested with newer definitions and experience.

Systems-thinking tools such as causal modeling and systems mapping are excellent tools for exploring how things work (discovery), for codifying new heuristics and emerging practices (rules of thumb), and for identifying new relationships. As sustainable business models expand our view of accountability, these tools will help inform a business about new resource relationships and connectedness. That will affect how social outcomes are monetized and how we price or assess environmental impact. Systems-thinking and design-thinking tools help provide the visual evidence that leaders need to make a strong business case, convince stakeholders of a new plan, and evolve product lines for better alignment with sustainable goals.

Design thinking is generally described as a mindset for reflecting on people and their needs. The concept of "human-" or "user-"centered design needs to expand to take into account social outcomes and products with broader boundary restrictions (e.g., impact on customers, suppliers, communities, and the environment). However, current design-thinking tools like prototyping and linear regression analysis are highly valuable, regardless of your business strategy. Prototyping skills are essential for creating business experiments that test assumptions. Linear regression is a simple tool to establish the relationship between one business action and an outcome. Both are valuable for any business strategy and can also be applied to social value creation.

Above all, as I implied in the title of this chapter, it is committed leadership that is required to make change stick. Organizations walk a hard road when it comes to change. Nitin Nohria and Michael Beer at Harvard Business School reported that 70 percent of companies fail to achieve their change goals.[12] Their colleague, Professor Emeritus John Kotter, reported in *Harvard Business Review* that "60% to 90% of all change efforts fail."[13]

The keys to success involve a substantial commitment of leadership time, investments in key staff development, active prototyping and experimentation, active communication, and effective reporting. Any transition to a new sustainable business model will require such commitment and investment from a business leadership team. Table 5.5 illustrates how select practice and development areas can be changed in consideration of new sustainable business opportunities. These can easily be adapted for a geographic or function unit as an experiment, and they largely represent foundation knowledge areas that are well understood.

Table 5.5: Impact of Practices within New Sustainable Business Models

Focus	Sample Development Content
Improve your understanding of the Sustainable Development Goals.	Provide staff with specific training on selective SDGs to improve common understanding. For example, • safe and sustainable cities • gender equality • poverty and hunger • water and sanitation • climate change • conserving marine resources and special ecosystems
Examine how your leadership role can support sustainable change.	Adapt management and leadership training sessions to focus on the four key roles that support sustainability: • authentic communicator • key talent developer • change enabler • innovation investor

Table 5.5: (Continued)

Apply design thinking to consider how new sustainable business models may change the way you structure the business.	Conduct group sessions to reframe the concepts of "customer-centric" or "human-centered" to consider new social outcomes: • define new business "boundaries" to expand areas of accountability • explore how prototyping can be used to model sustainable changes • make use of techniques like linear regression analysis to examine how changes in certain variables affect outcomes
Explore how key innovation practices can be used to improve both economic and social outcomes.	Conduct action learning sessions and innovation tournaments, and include a review of key innovation practices: • specific techniques for both continuous and breakthrough innovation • tips for organizing innovation teams • techniques for accelerating innovation activity like innovation tournaments and hackathons • managing the innovation process, including imagination or ideation and continuous improvement and scaling of innovations across an enterprise
Discuss a change leadership strategy that would start with team or functional experiments.	Create team assignments for high-potential staff to build the case for change and where to start: • creating a change leadership team • designing successful pilots • communicating results • dealing with resistance • aligning incentives with new behavior • anchoring changes in the corporate culture
Apply systems-thinking strategies to test boundary definition challenges.	Conduct action learning sessions that reframe new business opportunities and key challenges: • explore connectedness with new stakeholders • use causal modeling and feedback loops to establish relationship strength and influence direction • map new systems to create clarity of impact • create proposals for new business "experiments"
Conduct a fresh look at key stakeholders and stakeholder engagement strategies.	Relook at workflows with integrated team sessions to re-ask the question, Who are my stakeholders? • How does sustainability change my understanding of stakeholder needs and positions? • How does their relative influence and persuasion ability change with new goals? • How does each contribute to social value creation (e.g., to economic value creation)?

Reader Reflection

IMAGINE for a moment that you are CEO of a health and beauty company in a developing market with over two hundred employees. Business has been good for several years, although the industry is highly competitive. You notice that more and more people are interested in organic products and that natural ingredients are very popular. You speak to your leadership team about creating a new vision for the business based on sustainable business practices and all-natural products. Everyone is enthusiastic but looking to you for guidance!

You arrange meetings with your key suppliers. You do not manufacture the products yourself but rely on a group of local subcontractors. You are not the biggest company your suppliers deal with, but you have been a good customer for years and consider many of them to be both professional colleagues and friends. You speak to them about your new vision for sustainability and ask them to redesign your products using organic ingredients and no preservatives, biodegradable packaging, plant-based inks for printing, and post-consumer recycled paper for the shipping boxes. Your suppliers tell you that few customers are asking for such changes, but to expect proposals and pricing.

You receive the proposals in two weeks. Your overall costs will increase by at least 20 percent and you will need to sell more products before you realize any cost breaks. The proposals state that the pricing is the best your suppliers can do given the limited number of orders they have for such products. If you agree to move forward, finding the necessary capital may mean reducing your marketing and sales budgets or your gross margins.

What will you do? Do you raise prices to accommodate the higher costs? Do you break ties with current suppliers and look for cost efficiencies with new ones? Do you make compromises on how closely you adhere to your new vision? If you make compromises, how do you explain the choices to your leadership team that is looking to you for guidance?

As the founder of several small businesses, I can sympathize with this challenge. You are too small to dictate changes and you can't grow unless you differentiate your business. The path to success with this challenge combines the lessons from the last two chapters, on leadership and small business solutions. With a smaller business, the challenge may not be the enthusiasm of your employees but rather the willingness of your ecosystem to support you. It can be a strong limiting factor in your growth. As I illustrated in Table 5.5, there are a variety of practices, from design thinking to innovation, that will be helpful. Conducting a fresh look at key stakeholders and stakeholder engagement strategies may allow you to discover suppliers willing to partner under a new set of risk and investment parameters. If you win, you both find new sources of growth. My reflection on this dilemma is that it illustrates the danger of compromising on your vision. Your belief in the strength of your vision provides motivation to your team to find new and innovative practices that limit risk while helping you make positive forward progress. A strong team can help educate your partners on the new value propositions. The process of exploration, based on conviction and need, tends to lead you to like-minded individuals and companies with a similar passion.

TAKEAWAY: Transformational Change Requires Leaders With Equal Parts Purpose, Passion, and Performance

- Your first sustainability leader is your de facto chief sustainability officer (CSO).
- A committed leader helps create the initial sustainability projects (almost always about efficiency and cost savings).
- Unless the leader is also a founder and major shareholder, then the more strategic view of where you want to go evolves later as success provides social and political capital for change.
- The first leader/advocate must have passion but also the ability to drive high performance, particularly on efficiency issues like energy usage, waste, and process improvement.

- Leaders serve as discussion enablers to further translate the narrative into stories, problems to be solved, and new practices.

In this chapter, I have highlighted the vision of the leader or change agent as central to the drive to become more sustainable. Plans, strategies, and models come into play, as does daily problem-solving. In the next chapter, I am going to take a look at long-term communities whose sustainable practices meant prosperity for many generations. Perhaps there are some lessons to be learned.

Chapter 6

DAY-TO-DAY PROBLEM-SOLVING ACCELERATES CHANGE

"We do not inherit the earth from our ancestors—we borrow it from our children." NATIVE AMERICAN PROVERB

I began this book with a look back to the midpoint of the 1800s. Despite my focus on a century and a half of modern industrial life, it is but a small slice of the global human experience. All long-lived civilizations, from the Native American tribes to the continuously occupied cities of Beirut, Damascus, and Beijing, have one thing in common: they managed to maintain some semblance of balance with the environment and society for an extended period of time. Some communities, such as the Aksumite Empire of Ethiopia, lasted for more than one thousand years. The Carthaginian Empire lasted for more than four hundred years, and the kingdoms of ancient Egypt lasted for over five hundred years. What can these civilizations teach us in our search for a more sustainable world?

I recently returned from a trip to Vietnam, which has several excellent examples of long-lived communities. The Tan Le Commune in Thái

Binh Province has been making straw mats for five hundred years, and more than 80 percent of the households are still involved in the straw mat trade today.[1] Similarly, near present-day Hanoi is the village of Cu Da, a time capsule of preserved architecture that is also the center of traditional glass noodle manufacturing and has been for over seventy years. Today, the villagers typically sell fifteen to eighteen tons of noodles per day.[2] In both cases, the businesses of straw mats and glass noodles cannot be separated from the communities where they are produced. The education process of teaching future generations, the social and economic value that accrues to the communities, and the community commitment to sustain the traditions offer us an example of how daily business challenges are handled in support of larger community interests.

Ancient Practices

Let's step back and consider what it would be like to live in such a community. Imagine you are a member of a Native American tribe called the Ho-Chunk in what is now Green Bay, Wisconsin, in the United States. It is a warm evening in the summer of 1450 and you are meeting with a tribal elder to resolve a problem. Over several days there are discussions with members of your family as well as other elders and tribal members with status. The key is to reach consensus with the various parties on what is good for the tribe.[3] What is good for the tribe is best for you!

A successful tribal leader is often described as someone who can look into the future to determine direction and make decisions. In fact, many Native American peoples have a "vision quest" process that leaders use to look for signs of what is best for their people. "They saw how the buffalo gave itself to the people, how the grass gave itself to the buffalo, how the rain gave itself to the grass [and] how the people gave themselves back to the vast plains that sustained them."[4] In other words, their view of life is the circular, sustainable economy and community.

Various other Native American traditions call for what we would describe as a role-play exercise tied to what is known as the Seventh

Generation Principle. A group of tribal members with the most status—chief, warrior, medicine man, or elder—would meet to consider any major action. Their meeting would involve praying to their ancestors as well as assuming the role of different members of the tribe to think holistically about the future. The key question is not, What is the best decision? but, How will a decision affect the current generation, then our children and grandchildren, and on for seven generations? The entire goal is the sustainability of the tribe and the environment that nurtures its prosperity. The great law of the Iroquois Nation states it as follows:

> Look and listen for the welfare of the whole people and have always in view
> not only the present but also the coming generations, even those whose faces
> are yet beneath the surface of the ground—the unborn of the future Nation.[5]

Around the world, different communities have developed variations on this theme. The *loya jirga* (grand assembly) practiced by the Pashtun peoples of Pakistan and Afghanistan is a decision-making process adapted for a tribal culture that has lasted for a thousand years. The first *jirga* of record dates to 977.[6] In this culture, decision-making is for the most part highly decentralized and handled locally. Every so often there are issues such as conflict or social change that require a more consensus-oriented process. Thousands of representatives gather and subdivide into groups for discussions and presentations. Summaries of the various presentations are collated into draft decisions and then put to a vote. Kings and supreme leaders have ruled Afghanistan for generations, yet the *jirga* has survived, not as a legal vote but as the "will of the people."

In Botswana, there is a traditional process called the *Kgotla* (or *Hotla'*). It combines aspects of the role-playing and forward-thinking exercise of Native American tribes with the open community involvement of the *loya jirga*. A leader or elder may call the *Kgotla* but does not actively participate in it. Their role is to listen. Everyone in a local tribe or community is invited, but participation is voluntary. Like similar processes, the goal is consensus and forward thinking about what is best for the community. It is more open than some other processes in that anyone may advocate for a decision, and it is the persuasiveness of the arguments presented that decentralizes the authority and power. The event has no set time limit; the *Kgotla* ends by group consensus.

Table 6.1 provides a summary of the ancient practices as well as notes on how they may be adapted for use in a modern corporate business environment.

In a later chapter, I make the case for the inclusion of religious beliefs and local or tribal cultures in a development program, particularly for the international executive or specialist. In many parts of

Table 6.1: Summary of Ancient Practices

Ancient Practice	Adaptation
Vision Quest	The key to a modern vision quest is the idea of a conscious capitalism or shared value creation. A variety of studies show the importance that younger workers place on "mission" and "purpose." Companies can harness the power of collective purpose by acknowledging the importance of social goals. The growth of the benefit corporation movement is a good example.
Council Circle	A corporate and civil society "workout process" that combines traditional problem-solving practices with a long-term reflection process (the Seventh Generation Principle). This can be adapted to a multi-team approach so that teams can represent different generations of stakeholders.
Loya Jirga	The *loya jirga* acknowledges both the importance of community acceptance and the need for value sharing. There are important lessons in negotiating with communities regarding site selection, water rights, and any disruptions of long-term practices and norms.
Kgotla	The *Kgotla* community exchange has similarities to the practice of appreciative inquiry and can be adapted to the corporate environment. The key elements are full participation and a common sense of community that drives the search for a common good.

the world, deep cultural beliefs still guide community activities and create a strong sense of purpose and continuity. These native or cultural traditions have similar value because they have stood the test of time as methods to reach consensus and maintain balance in a larger society.

Current Problem-Solving Practices

Fast forward to today and we find that several companies have developed decentralized decision-making processes to encourage innovation while supporting an overall company vision. The best known of these is General Electric's "Work-Out" process,[7] although there are similar concepts in programs like ninety-day sprints, scrums, and accelerator programs. Variations are also seen in companies that use a collaborative negotiation system like the Mutual Gains Approach, championed by the Consensus Business Institute (CBI) in Cambridge, Massachusetts.[8] CBI was founded by Lawrence Susskind, one the seven founding members of the Program on Negotiation at Harvard Law School. The Mutual Gains Approach uses a four-phase process—preparation, value creation, value distribution, and follow-up—that aligns well with the components of a contemporary workout process described below. The key in each instance is to recognize the needs of an extended set of stakeholders and the opportunity for both economic and social value creation:

1. **Preparation:** A team close to a problem is given responsibility to analyze the issue, refine a problem statement, and consider the positions of all key stakeholder groups.
2. **Ideation:** A formally facilitated program is convened to help work through root causes, opportunities, and potential solutions.
3. **Review:** One or more decision-making executives listen and make recommendations on the options that deserve action.
4. **Decision:** One option is approved for implementation.
5. **Accountability:** The team making the recommendations is accountable for solution implementation.

6. **Communication:** The process and decisions are transparent and communicated to the organization.
7. **Execution:** Resources are dedicated to resolve the problem with regular reporting in short time cycles such as thirty, sixty, and ninety days.

A New Seven-Step Sustainable Model

In order to create our new sustainable-business problem-solving process, we can adapt this model using several common characteristics from sustainable organizations and societies:

Step 1: A team close to a problem is given responsibility to analyze the issue and generate recommendations. It is important that the team possesses three things: a clear objective, clear delegation of authority, and the right people.

Step 2: A program is organized that includes a formal facilitator plus additional resources for design and systems thinking, as appropriate. The program will include an assessment and problem-analysis process that considers three different boundary conditions for the problem:

- **Narrow:** Definition is constrained to impact on direct company resources and assets.
- **Intermediate:** Definition is extended to include all current and anticipated tier 1 business relationships.
- **Broad:** Definition is extended to include all current and anticipated tier 1 and tier 2 business relationships.

The accountabilities of key stakeholders are defined in all three boundary-definition scenarios. A company standard "test for success" reflection mechanism is developed that includes three considerations:

- Outcomes must address economic value creation as well as social and environmental value creation.

- The reflection mechanism should be based on the commitments the company has made in its corporate responsibility statement (CSR) statement, or it can include objectives specifically created for the problem-solving process.
- Ratings are assigned to all recommendations using a five-point sustainability alignment scale (the full model is illustrated in chapter 3):

1. **High Negative:** High economic value but low social value and/ or net negative environmental impact.
2. **Net Negative:** Some positive and negative attributes, but overall net negative for social and environmental considerations.
3. **Neutral:** Economic, social, and environmental values balance out.
4. **Net Positive:** Overall net positive attributes for social and environmental considerations.
5. **High Positive:** No negative attributes. High positive attributes for all three triple-bottom-line considerations.

This is the opportunity to explore how new value is created. Are we saving money? Increasing productivity? Reducing our carbon footprint? Improving worker conditions among suppliers? All recommendations are subject to a forward-impact exercise that asks:

- Will the perceived alignment of the recommendation change over time?
- Are the benefits short-term or do they support long-term value creation?

Step 3: An executive team listens to the presentation and reviews all options with the team:

- Executives are incentivized to create a portfolio of business improvements and innovation that are net positive in nature with strong long-term value creation potential.

- The simplest process is to delegate to the team the responsibility to bring the executives several viable options, from which the executives with take one of three actions: (1) approve one option and discuss next steps; (2) discuss revisions with the team and approve a revised option and next steps; or (3) continue the team activity for another week allowing the team more time to develop one or more options with greater detail. Step 3 is a stage where the executives intervene to facilitate additional resources or outside partnerships, if warranted.
- A representative of the integrated reporting team is present to be sure relevant qualitative descriptions of company action are captured and shared.

Step 4: A decision is made and one option is approved for implementation. The executives approving the decision are now the project sponsors.

Step 5: The team making the recommendation is accountable, so it is important that they feel strong support from the sponsoring executive(s). To facilitate this, senior executives must all be briefed on process guidelines and roles and be prepared to rapidly secure funding and remove barriers where necessary. The organization must also develop clear incentives.

Step 6: The process and decisions are transparent and communicated to the organization.

Step 7: Resources are dedicated to resolve the problem, with regular reporting in short time cycles such as thirty, sixty, and ninety days:
- skilled facilitators must be prepared;
- key staff and team leaders must be trained on the core process;
- specialist resources must be trained and available in systems and design thinking; and
- executives must commit to a review of approved programs and long-term monitoring of the impact of any actions.

An effective and consistent problem-solving process is essential for any company considering market-leading activities. Implementing such a process is also an opportunity to discover new knowledge and build company-specific knowledge about new areas of competitive advantage. The repetition or multiple problem-solving team activities across the organization provides a level of consistency, feedback, and reinforcement that is key to organizational change. The formal programs are also an excellent development opportunity since they provide both a performance value (new business solutions are discovered) and a development value (new skills are learned).

Application of the Sustainable Model

East-West Seed Company (EWS) uses a variation of the workout process in its Innovation Olympics. The company starts by identifying a key challenge such as "connecting farmers to a larger community so they can gain more value from their crops." In 2017, EWS sponsored the event and opened up the program to ten teams of students and entrepreneurs to generate a range of solutions. By structuring the rules of the innovation tournament, guidelines for both economic and social value creation were established, in addition to the social entrepreneur mindset. A panel that included executives from EWS reviewed and judged the presentations, and provided recognition, funding, and ongoing support for the innovations.

Galaxy Entertainment extended the problem-solving idea to its supplier ecosystem. According to Trevor Martin, director of human resources and administration at Galaxy, "You need to be more collaborative and operate with a systems mindset. You can provide inspiration and advice, but you also need to provide tools." Galaxy works with suppliers to problem solve around the limitations of a small business. "The Galaxy vision is designed to be comprehensive, but also to leverage the contributions of the larger community."[9]

LVMH, the global luxury goods company, has used problem-solving groups within its seventy businesses (Maisons) to address challenges tied to its LIFE initiative (LVMH Initiatives for the Environment). The problem-solving groups have created such innovations as the "Natural Clicquot" packaging for its Champagne brand. The boxes are made from grape skin, a by-product of a manufacturing process, and recycled, unbleached paper. This type of action is directly tied to its corporate goal of reducing the impact of its products on the environment.

Reader Reflection

IMAGINE for a moment that you are running a customer conference in a smaller regional city of a developing market. Although your company is based in a wealthy Western nation, you are excited about the high-growth opportunities where local economies have experienced 6 percent GDP growth for almost a decade. The country is considered more difficult to operate in, but the risks seem to be outweighed by the potential rewards. These markets are a key part of your strategic plan and are important for both growth and profitability. You have personally championed the regional market strategy during a recent company leadership retreat.

It is Thursday evening and the event planning has gone well. You do not have a lot of experience in this market but are happy with the preparations and decisions you've made. The event was organized quickly, so you needed to make most of the big decisions yourself. The venue is less than one half the cost you would have encountered in a major city like New York or London. You have invited your organization's best customers and key prospects for three days of product demonstrations and are counting on the program as a key driver of your regional business. You launch the event with your keynote address on Friday morning.

Your cellphone rings. It is one of your staff, who informs you that three important customers have been detained at the airport on unspecified charges. Your customers will be taken into custody until a judge can hear their case the following Monday.

Shortly thereafter, you receive a call from a person who says he is a local attorney who was asked to contact you to help with the situation. You experience some relief. He suggests that the charges could be serious, although he doesn't know all of the details. He offers to help resolve the problem and possibly get the detainees released immediately if you are willing to pay a fee to expedite the process. You plan to meet the attorney right away.

What do you do? Is this "process" just an elaborate request for a bribe? Will any sort of payment be illegal? Do you avoid engagement with the lawyer and risk having your customers sit in jail for three days? Having a local attorney was not on your "to do" list for the conference and it is already late in the evening. Do you solve the problem yourself or engage other stakeholders in the decision process? What if you can't find anyone else to help quickly?

I hope that you never find yourself in this predicament, but I know of several colleagues who have faced similar situations. One of the key models discussed in chapter 2 is the United Nations Global Compact, which specifically asks companies to take an anti-corruption pledge: "Businesses should work against corruption in all its forms, including extortion and bribery." There are specific training programs you can develop on anti-corruption, anti-money laundering, anti-bribery, and related challenges, but it is a bit late when you already have three customers in jail. My general rule in a situation that involves individual safety is to do what it takes to resolve the problem and then work to ensure it doesn't happen again. I also believe that no matter how tight the deadline, it is always better to engage more people in the solution. Longer term, this is about preparation. Talent development organizations can do a better job of preparing global teams by identifying databases and analytics that provide accurate and timely information (covered more in chapter 10). Sources of information on country practices include the World Bank's Ease of Doing Business Index[10] and Transparency International's Corruption Perceptions Index.[11] Information, preparation, and team training are keys to maintaining your sustainability advantage and avoiding such dilemmas.

TAKEAWAY: Consistent Use of Group Problem-Solving and Decision-Making Keeps the Sustainability Agenda on Track

- Day-to-day problem-solving is one of the few practices that offer the repetition needed to accelerate behavior change.
- Business models like a circular economy model will present constant changes in multiple functional areas. Both good and bad practices can propagate rapidly. An enterprise process for working out difficult issues aligned with sustainability helps keep the organization on track.
- Research shows that we are often a poor judge of our own biases but are better at spotting biases in others. Group problem-solving helps dampen individual biases and is beneficial for new activities with uncertain or new conditions.
- Senior management sponsorship and short cycle times for problem-solving activities provide a variety of opportunities for teachable moments, coaching, and communication that can reinforce the spirit of the new business purpose.

In chapter 7, we will see how organizations impact the well-being of their local communities through their commitment to values. As the organization begins to deepen its sustainability experience, more people become involved, and developing talent through shared knowledge is a theme that we begin to explore.

Chapter 7

ANCHORING SUSTAINABILITY INTO THE DNA OF YOUR BUSINESS

"The greatest danger in times of turbulence is not the turbulence—it is to act with yesterday's logic." PETER DRUCKER

Sustainability is now and will continue to be a major driver of innovation. I believe this fervently, and your interest in reading this book suggests you believe this too. While you might be prepared to take my word for it, this view is also the opinion of change agents at global and local companies and thought leaders around the world. Businesses as diverse as Procter & Gamble, Toyota, Kellogg, and Microsoft have committed to making products that are more respectful of the resources consumed, the employees who make and deliver their products and services, and their customers. This practice is partly driven by government mandate, but also by consumer sentiment. According to research firm Nielsen, "66% of global consumers say they're willing to pay more for sustainable brands—up from 55% in 2014. 73% of global millennials are willing to pay extra for sustainable offerings—up from 50% in 2014."[1]

Audrey Choi,[2] the chief executive of Morgan Stanley's Institute for Sustainable Investing; Chris McKnett,[3] managing director and head ESG investing strategist at State Street Global Advisors; Christine Bader,[4] Amazon's former director of social responsibility; and Harish Manwani,[5] Unilever's former chief operating officer, have made similar arguments for sustainable business practices. In fact, more than nine thousand companies and three thousand noncommercial organizations[6] have signed on to the United Nations Global Compact, and thousands of companies now file corporate social responsibility (CSR) reports.

Yet as we look across the landscape of global commerce, we need to ask how many companies are fully committed to sustainability. In 2015 and 2016, we surveyed talent development professionals and asked, "Do you teach sustainability and social responsibility in your leadership development programs?" The results are shown in Table 7.1.

Table 7.1: Talent Development Survey 2015–2016

Do you teach sustainability and social responsibility in your leadership development programs?	2015 (n = 327)	2016 (n = 454)
Yes, in all programs	10.1%	13.6%
Yes, in some programs	21.1%	25.4%
No, but we will next year	31.2%	22.0%
No	37.6%	39.0%

As we examined the data, we concluded that no company had integrated sustainability to a significant degree in training and development across all functions. In 2016, companies that responded in the affirmative to our question typically taught a small number of courses on sustainability, with the following being true:

- Most had done so only in one leadership program or in briefings about corporate social responsibility.
- Of those that said they had plans to do so in 2017 (again, at least one course), most did so only as functional programs instead of an enterprise curriculum.
- A few individual functions, notably human resources, procurement, and supply chain units had done some specialized training, particularly on energy use, water quality, and waste management, or on specific CSR-reporting activities like community volunteer time.

If I compare these results against companies that appear to fully embrace sustainability across the enterprise, a significant difference is evident. I will use Galaxy Entertainment, a Hong Kong–listed company with major operations in Macau, China, as an example.

Galaxy Entertainment: A Deep Commitment to Core Values

In fewer than twelve years, Galaxy Entertainment has become one of the top four casino operators in the world.[7] Dr. Lui Che Woo established Galaxy Entertainment in 2005, and it became the first Hong Kong–listed company to own a gaming license in Macau. In 2017, its full-year revenue exceeded US$62 billion from gaming, hotel, entertainment, restaurant, and retail operations.[8] In an industry known more for excess than sustainability, Galaxy has embraced energy efficiency, anti-corruption and anti-money laundering practices, cultural preservation, and environmental stewardship.

Trevor Martin, the recently retired director of human resources and administration for Galaxy Entertainment whom I interviewed, said, "Large successful companies have an opportunity that is unique because of their size and operating footprint. They can choose to live their values by supporting a large ecosystem of suppliers both locally and globally. Those decisions can have a significant impact on a range of issues such as cultural preservation, community development, and a healthy environment."[9]

Galaxy Entertainment shares a key characteristic with other early adopters of sustainable business practices, which is a deep commitment to core values. I worked with Galaxy prior to its phase two expansion in the Cotai area of Macau. The small Chinese peninsula and former Portuguese colony is already home to four of the world's largest casinos, and hosts many of the largest integrated resorts. Land values are at a premium, and the typical model is to build as large a casino and entertainment complex as space will permit. Instead, Galaxy dedicated part of its land holdings to local businesses that support traditional Macanese food and cultural activities. This is clearly not a strategy based on space optimization or short-term profit, but a decision to take a longer-term view of community well-being. This decision is linked to the vision of company founder Dr. Lui Che Woo, which is the "belief in giving back to the society from which one has benefited."[10]

Galaxy extended its community support by creating a small to medium-size Enterprise (SME) program affecting almost three hundred local businesses, as of the time of writing. The program sponsors entrepreneurs—among them recent startups—who are refreshing Galaxy's supply chain with innovations. Galaxy plays a role in the success of its suppliers by offering training and support programs to help them grow and improve their performance.

My experience from dozens of interviews and company assignments is that a deep support for social value creation is rooted in the values of a founder, key change agent, or executive. Executives of more sustainable businesses often link core values to business purpose, using phrases such as "core values must be part of the company DNA" and "core values must be deeply embedded in the company's culture." It is not a surprise that employees of companies like Tesla (founder Elon Musk), Patagonia (founder Yvon Chouinard), and Grameen Bank (founder Muhammad Yunus) tend to believe in the founder's vision and sense of purpose. Patagonia, founded in 1973, still maintains its mission as "Build the best product, cause no unnecessary harm, use business to inspire, and implement solutions to the environmental crisis."[11] In the case of Galaxy Entertainment, a deep sense of values can also be traced to its founder.

In 2016, Dr. Lui established the LUI Che Woo Prize for World Civilization to improve sustainable development, promote positive life attitudes, and enhance the welfare of humankind. The intent of the prize is to "extol those individuals and organizations who have selflessly dedicated themselves to the nurturing and enrichment of world civilization."[12] In 2015, Galaxy Entertainment also established the Galaxy Entertainment Group (GEG) Foundation to support local charities, civic engagement, and quality of life.

The Sustainable Development Goals are not broadly visible at Galaxy as a management tool, but you can easily see evidence of alignment with SDGs in the environmental KPIs published by the company: the ISO 14001 certification achieved by several properties, the anti-money laundering and combating finance of terrorism activity, and the anti-bribery and anti-corruption programs. Management development assignments often involve participation in one of the many working groups that have oversight of the sustainability agenda, such as the environmental committee and the energy management committee and its sustainable food waste program. In general, this is the model that works in most industries—utilize the SDGs as a senior-level guideline and then translate priority objectives into standards with industry-specific, geographically specific, or functionally specific applications.

East-West Seed Company: A Study in "Seedsmanship"
Another illuminating example of a company that has found a way to embrace sustainability is East-West Seed Company (EWS) in Thailand. By size, industry, market, and customer base, the company is light years away from the highly developed Galaxy Entertainment. But nevertheless, it has had a major impact on the well-being of local communities.

Francis Ferdinand C. Cinco, until recently the head of human resources for EWS, explained the company's sustainability strategy this way: "We didn't talk about sustainability specifically; we talked about helping farmers. We were founded as a seed company dedicated to local conditions, local varieties, and local tastes. That was part of the vision and just something we always did. We make money if our farmers are successful. For us, it's just how we think."[13]

East-West Seed Company, a privately held company founded in 1982, is dedicated to being "the best tropical vegetable seed company in the world."[14] With more than 4500 employees and operations in more than 60 countries, EWS has developed a strong innovation model targeting the 85 percent of the world's farmers who operate small farms. According to EWS, the average small farmer in Asia cultivates 1.1 hectares (about 2.7 acres) and the average small farmer in Africa cultivates 1.9 hectares (about 4.7 acres). In order to meet the demand of a global population expected to exceed 9 billion by 2050, EWS estimates that food production must increase by 70 percent to meet that demand.[15]

I helped set up the East-West Seed Academy in 2012 and conducted interviews with more than thirty employees. In reviewing my notes for this book, I was struck by how often people would offer comments like, "It's better for the farmers" or "We can really make a difference in their lives." If there was ever a company with a sense of social mission at its core, it is East-West Seed. Since I first worked with the company, it has significantly increased the number of employees as well as its market presence, particularly in Asia and Africa. Its internal training academy focuses on "seedsmanship" as well as leadership and professional development. The company believes that this issue of "seedsmanship" is core to its culture and competitive differentiation.

As with many companies that focus on sustainability, EWS embraces several of the SDGs on which it believes it can make a real difference. In particular, it focuses on reducing hunger and improving nutrition, helping women farmers, and eliminating child labor. The company also goes a step beyond by addressing issues consistent with sustainability for which it has equal passion, such as preserving genetic diversity, promoting "orphan" local crops, and sharing knowledge.

Mark Relova, the current group head of Learning and Employee Experience at EWS, says the concept of sustainability "is core to our talent strategy. Corporate citizenship is not a program; it is part of who we are. We always talk to our staff about 'How do we [grow] a social enterprise mindset?'"

According to Mark, attracting talent can be a challenge: "Agriculture is not viewed as the sexy career path in many markets. We compete against big multinationals and tech companies for the best employees. We work really hard to bring the company purpose to life."[16]

Mark's comments about a company's purpose are central to the social rituals and action learning programs used to transmit the company's values and desire to innovate and solve problems. For example, EWS runs a three-day program for its office and operation center employees that involves taking these employees to customer farms. The employees stay overnight, eat and socialize with the farmers, and experience the work schedule and challenges of the small farmer. The goal is to create a personal connection between the employees and the farmers they serve.

EWS envisions itself as the farmers' champion and emphasizes its role in building healthy farming communities. Francis Ferdinand C. Cinco, former head of human resources for EWS, describes the EWS innovation efforts as "an offshoot of internal programs where we encourage people to think big and act bold. These led to some of our work with foundations and our desire to improve knowledge sharing as key to farmer productivity and success."[17] The company created the EWS Foundation in 2012 (based in the Philippines) and also runs an Innovation Olympics for technology farming innovations and a formal knowledge transfer program (EWS-KT) that includes demonstration farms, field visits, and specialized training. The company also sponsors the Simon N. Groot Scholarship Program, named for the company's founder, which is designed to support the next generation of farmers. According to Mark Relova, the "average farmer is fifty-seven years old and we want to encourage talented young people to take up the profession."[18]

Four Types of Knowledge Transfer and Their Impact

So what do we learn from companies that make sustainability core to their business values? Figure 7.1 illustrates the learning challenge and

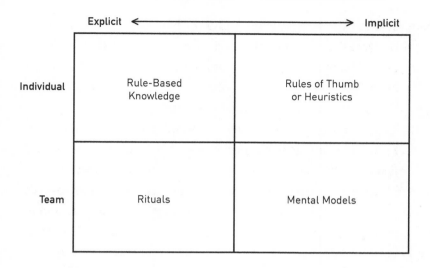

Explicit ←————————————————→ Implicit

	Explicit	Implicit
Individual	Rule-Based Knowledge	Rules of Thumb or Heuristics
Team	Rituals	Mental Models

Figure 7.1: Types of Knowledge Transfer

the four types of knowledge transfer needed to make sustainability part of your company DNA. I'll use the EWS to illustrate how the figure is used.

The upper-left quadrant, "Rule-Based Knowledge," illustrates East-West Academy's Seedsmanship program. Core learning will include the water cycle, crop varietals, soil conditions, and similar subjects. For the EWS target audience of rural farmers, these topics are significant because they form the basis for an initial exchange of value and the development of trust. I call this type of information "knowledge of enduring value." All knowledge in this area shares a common characteristic: this is information we accept as true.

The upper-right quadrant, "Rules of Thumb or Heuristics," is the land of new knowledge discovery. If the upper-left quadrant is information accepted as true, the upper-right quadrant is information we "think" is true. The growth in machine learning and intelligent support systems relies on rule-based algorithms that afford a level of predictive success. When a website suggests a new product for you, it is basing its suggestion on the behavior patterns of people it considers similar to you. This starts with what we call a "rule of thumb" or heuristic. A rule of thumb or heuristic represents the sum of experiences that guide behavior. Rules of thumb are an incredibly important part of the business transformation to sustainability, since they represent new knowledge discovery that can lead to better performance and competitive differentiation.

In the case of East-West Seed, new knowledge discovery and rules of thumb emerge from farmer experience and the observation of patterns. Soil and weather patterns are diverse and complex, so adjustment is needed. As climate change offers new conditions, we need to observe and adapt based on how patterns and probabilities change. Thinking about how we best acquire and share this type of knowledge tells us something about how we want to develop talent and scale new products or practices.

The lower-right quadrant, "Mental Models," is the key area of focus if you want to build sustainability at a company's core. That is the home of "how we think" and "how we make decisions." Heuristics may be food for thought, but mental models are where we do the heavy lifting. Embedding sustainability in your company's DNA is highly meaningful for your employees who have a shared worldview and a common set of decision-making principles they consider valid.

The challenge in many instances is to change an existing mental model that may be decades old. A single course, seminar, or well-written memo will not do the job. New behavior patterns require a lot of experiential learning, feedback, and repetition. Changing mental models on a large scale generally requires modification of incentive and communication practices, as well as leadership behavior.

Several years ago I worked with Mike Osario, then senior vice president for Organizational and Change Management at DFS Group Limited, based in Hong Kong. Mike always emphasized the importance of "organizational health" in sustaining organizational change. Mike's point is that excessive stress and pressure on results are the enemy of purpose.

In my interview with Mike about the importance of sustainability, he explained it this way: "Even with a massive business commitment and a visionary CEO, culture change is about maintaining a healthy balance of business results and social commitments. Without exceptional effort and attention, new changes are always at risk."[19] Mike's comments reinforce the importance of leaders as sustainability advocates.

The figure's lower-left quadrant, "Rituals," is the home of social rituals that almost all companies use to impart a sense of community and culture in their organizations. A social ritual or rite-of-passage event may be used when an employee joins a company or when staff transition to management. East-West Seed effectively uses the overnight farm visits as a way to establish an emotional connection between its business vision and employees. Employees who hear about a farmer who was able to buy a new truck or send a daughter to school because of the higher income generated with the help of EWS's products makes a powerful statement. Such a statement is what I call a "signature event," which is a type of ritual.

Rituals within companies vary depending on the function, business unit, or geographic structure. The key is that people share a common experience. This is the basis for transmitting values and accountability, but also for becoming a "member of the team"; in other words, the basis for a signature event. A signature event has three features:

- First, it is an event that communicates key knowledge, practices, beliefs, and/or core competencies unique to that firm. It is the place where company stories are told.
- Second, it serves to connect each person to the greater community, be that the business, functional group, role, or desired outcome. With sustainability, the boundaries of community expand so the opportunities for creativity and personal connections increase.
- Third, it is a networking event that creates collaborative bonds. It enables information sharing, encourages shared work practices, and often builds key peer relationships.

Signature events serve as critical anchor points for building and maintaining a culture of sustainability and are an essential part of any business transformation. Next, we will discuss the role of talent development within the context of transformation.

Talent Development and Sustainability

In Figure 7.2, I illustrate a four-part model of knowledge. The efficacy of the model is to help companies make decisions about the kinds of tactics and practices they can use to develop talent. Each knowledge type is part of the solution, although the balance will depend on your business size and the maturity of your business ecosystem (topics to be covered in later chapters). The four-quadrant figure can be modified to better serve its purpose by inserting new foci in each quadrant. For example, the earlier term "Rule-Based Knowledge" can be changed to "What I know to be true" and "Rules of Thumb or "Heuristics" to "What I think is true." I often find this helpful in situations where some staff are not native English speakers. "Rituals" become the programs that define "Where I belong" and "Mental Models" describe "How I think."

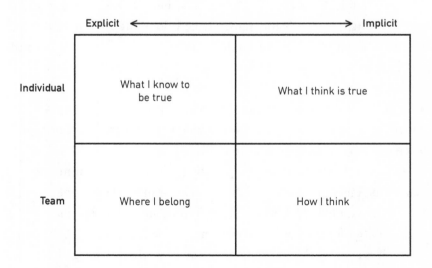

Figure 7.2: Understanding Knowledge Types Version 1

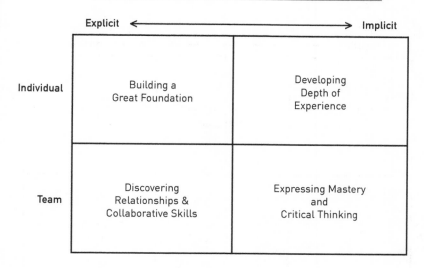

Figure 7.3: Understanding Knowledge Types Version 2

In most consulting assignments, I work with internal teams to help draft iterative solutions. If the model shown in Figure 7.2 doesn't resonate with a team, we co-create new language the team is more comfortable with. For example, see Figure 7.3.

The next step in the process is to consider how we connect the type of knowledge needed to meet our priority sustainability objectives with possible talent development solutions. To achieve this, I expanded the model from a four-solution to a nine-solution matrix by adding a middle row and column (Figure 7.4). The added row acknowledges the differences between group and team activities. The former covers the idea of scaling knowledge to many people, while the latter concerns transferring knowledge to people who share work dependencies. The center column is added because real-world scenarios tend to be less clean and there is always room for blended solutions. As such, the solutions live on a spectrum of choices.

Explicit ←————————————————————————→ Implicit

	Explicit		Implicit
Individual	E-Learning Digital Learning	Apprenticeships Job Rotations	Coaching Appreciative Inquiry
Group	MOOCs	Centers of Excellence	Communities of Practice
Team	Classroom Training Cohort Online Blended Designs	Team Events Signature Events Case Study Teams	Startups Crisis Assignments Action Learning Innovation Labs

Figure 7.4: Turning Knowledge Types into Talent Solutions

Using this framework, transferring foundation knowledge may be done one-on-one with digital learning tools or via a larger group via a MOOC or large cohort program. Individuals may learn rules of thumb from coaching and experience-based job rotations, but they might also learn insights from sharing within a community of practice. Developing a new mental model often occurs from an action learning experience that offers a unique insight into business behavior or from a crisis or startup assignment. The value in these frameworks is that they allow you to think through the nature of the talent development challenge based on specific sustainability definitions and business priorities.

For example, if you choose to focus attention on low-risk activities such as reducing energy use, improving recycling, or reducing water usage, then you are using foundation knowledge and heuristics that can easily be learned from partnerships or consultants. This approach does not yet require a company-wide change in mental models, and the priorities will likely be focused on specific functions and departments. However, if you choose to expand your accountability to include reducing poverty in the communities you serve, you may need an entirely new set of skills for which your organization does not have experience or the appropriate development assignment.

A Sustainability Action Model

The final tool in the DNA toolbox is a five-stage model for determining how rapidly changes are propagating across the business (Table 7.2). As you generate innovations in one area of the business or improve alignment of your products and services, the next step is to undertake broad-based change. The model can be used to rank different sustainability practices. It is based on documentation and direct observation rather than statements. If you see evidence of a consistently applied sustainable practice in only one area of the business, you are at level 2: "evidence of intent and action." If you can observe the same practice in multiple functions or business units over a period of time greater than eighteen months, you are at level 4: "evidence of intent, action, consistency, and repeatability."

Table 7.2: Assessing the Speed of Change

Level	Description	Purpose
1	Can multiple members of your team describe practices consistently?	Evidence of intent
2	Is there documentation of practices in action in one or more functional, geographic, or business units?	Evidence of action as an applied practice
3	Is there evidence of more broad-based practices, consistently applied across the enterprise?	Evidence of action as an organizational practice

4	Is there evidence of broad-based practices, consistently applied over time (>18 months)?	Evidence of consistency and repeatability
5	Are there documented discussions of metrics and use of practice data for innovation and improvement over time? Are there formalized training or social events that mark the practice a standard operating practice (SOP)?	Evidence that the practice is anchored in the business culture

Reader Reflection

IMAGINE that you are the leader of a smartphone company with an expanding international presence. You are not the biggest company in your market space, but you have a loyal and growing customer base. You are popular with everyone's target customers, young millennials, because of your great features but also because of your progressive policies and commitment to social values.

As your company expands into new markets, you have to consider greatly expanding your supply chain for manufacturing but also for logistics and distribution. Up until now, you have had tight control over all suppliers and have required everyone to work under the same code of conduct. However, growth is slowing because of the difficulty of finding new suppliers who meet your stringent standards. Under pressure from shareholders and customers, you created several new joint ventures that provide you faster expansion opportunities, but you have yielded control of your local distribution.

A major media outlet has started publishing stories about working conditions at the workplaces of your joint venture partners. The picture is not flattering and you are not used to the negative coverage. However, these companies are partners and there is no evidence of any wrongdoing by you or your employees. Despite the coverage, sales remain very strong and these new markets now contribute over 20 percent to both your top and bottom line.

How do you respond? Is your partner's problem your problem? How will you respond to anxious loyal customers who buy from you because of your social values? Should you sever ties with the venture partners and risk losing the revenue? Could you have undertaken any steps that might have revealed a potential challenge like this?

The value of anchoring sustainable practice in your business DNA is that you see the risk in business decisions before you make them. A strong mental model of sustainability acts as a business advantage because it makes you aware of the risks in changing boundary responsibilities. In 2011, clothing brand Victoria's Secret was accused of using cotton picked on farms that used child labor.[20] In 2012, we witnessed a garment factory fire in Bangladesh that killed 112 people.[21] In 2013, Samsung was sued over worker conditions in Brazil.[22] Even if you have the best of intentions, these examples illustrate a challenge. How do you ensure that tier 1 and sometimes tier 2 suppliers behave in ways that are consistent with your sustainable business values? The dilemma illustrates the tension that exists between short-term economic considerations and long-term value creation. It also illustrates the challenge of managing complex international supply chains. Businesses have a two-tier challenge. At the first level, companies need core practices and training that allows them to manage accountability for a global supply chain. They must assume responsibility for the actions of suppliers and have practices that allow them to ensure alignment of goals and values. At a second level, when problems occur, company leaders need to respond in appropriate ways. Practicing crisis case scenarios is helpful to refining a company crisis response. The need for strong case development and discussion leadership skills is covered in chapter 10, Strategies for Supporting an Evolving Business.

TAKEAWAY: Three Key Elements Anchor Sustainability in Your Business DNA: Accountability, Clarity, and Common Values

The first lessons on the path to sustainability tell us that, in order for an organization to embrace sustainability as a strategic opportunity, three things need to be done:

- We need to accept accountability for the challenges of sustainability and use those challenges to frame new business opportunities.
- We need clarity on the definition of sustainability so we can translate that into actions for everyone in the organization. The more everyone sees how his or her actions make a difference, the more we participate in a common mission.
- To create a sustainable business that persists over time, we need to embed a set of common values—the DNA of the sustainable business—in a common worldview that will inform our decision-making and our new knowledge discovery.

As many of the Reader Reflections have illustrated up to this point, challenges of all types are a regular occurrence in business transformations. As you explore new boundaries and value propositions, strong organizational values become an important resource. Knowing that key people in your organization "have your back" when a decision is made is a great source of confidence. That confidence will be built on shared experiences and company stories that reinforce company values as the underlying framework for leadership and decision-making.

Your conceptual model of organizational boundaries may need to evolve to include your broader business ecosystem. Your actions and those of your partners will increasingly be seen as interconnected. Start with the premise that it is your responsibility to understand the relationships, capabilities, and organizational health of your partners.

Development activities that generate shared experiences and help embed sustainable values in your business's DNA (and that of your ecosystem) must become a priority. Clarity of purpose must translate into clarity of practice that can be independently applied by people across your organization. The foundation of your new sustainable business practices is the knowledge discovery process we will explore in chapter 8. I will discuss different types of knowledge and how your organization can make the right investments to accelerate the process of sharing new knowledge. The faster you move to create consistency in skill development and decision-making, the faster the process is of anchoring sustainable values in your business's DNA. The key is recognizing the value in learning, not just for economic value creation, but also for creating social good. Learning practices are a competitive advantage and a key driver of sustainable business outcomes.

PART THREE

BUILDING TALENT AND OPERATIONAL EXCELLENCE FOR SUSTAINABILITY

Chapter 8

DISCOVERY, VALUE, AND THE SHARING OF NEW KNOWLEDGE

"The ability to learn faster than your competitors may be the only sustainable competitive advantage." ARIE DE GEUS

Joe Haberman is managing partner for the Global Education Markets Practice at executive search firm Heidrick & Struggles. As an observer of education market trends for almost twenty years, he suggests that senior talent development roles have changed:

The roles today are much more broadly defined. On the corporate side, learning is tied much more into culture change and delivering value though accessibility, social engagement, and knowledge sharing. It's not about training per se, but making the organization more adaptive. In higher education, it's more about outcomes and a tighter orientation between higher education and workforce collaboration. The better corporate environments are all about the value of learning and competitive advantage.[1]

The purpose of any talent strategy is to support your organization's competitive advantage. The key is to connect investments with a key driver (e.g., improved product quality; productivity or service; enhanced social outcomes; improved efficiency). When executed well, greater and more differentiated investments in talent development result in specific competitive strengths that lead to both a successful business over time and a balanced triple bottom line.

A talent development plan for a sustainable business looks at how an organization develops, consumes, shares, and transforms knowledge into business outcomes in the context of broader boundaries and both economic and social goals. The key is to look at the organization as well as the broader market as an experience engine. Ask yourself these questions:

- Where do I see high-value interactions that provide unique insight?
- Can I tap into the performance value of any experience as well as the developmental value?
- How do I convert that experience into sharable knowledge and repeatable action?
- How do I move from successful talent development with an individual or a team to scale?

The first half of this challenge is to understand how a learning environment can be created to enable the discovery of knowledge for a sustainable business, and the other half is to understand the value of that knowledge and where to make the right investments.

As discussed earlier, new sustainable business models will necessitate changes in job boundaries and performance values. New knowledge will be required. Your company may have a well-developed supply chain, but if you've never managed the carbon footprint or labor practices of your suppliers, then you will not have a clear process, training program, or rotational assignment that will be aligned with your purpose as a sustainable organization.

As business writer Everett Rogers first explained in 1962 in his seminal work *Diffusion of Innovations*,[2] we are in the "Persuasion Stage" of sustainability, where early adopters reign. That tends to mean we are still figuring out the right answers and new practices. Changing the way you invest in learning and development will support new competitive advantage.

Creating the Framework for the Learning Organization

Building new organizational capability typically has two main components: (1) a job rotation or development assignment system that is experience- and feedback-based; and (2) a corporate university that serves to share codified content (e.g., foundation knowledge) and provide shared experiences (e.g., social rituals). The corporate university is often the physical presence of talent development in a larger organization, and sometimes the organizational home to the staff responsible for coaching, mentoring, or specialized assignments as well as customer and supplier training.

In most cases, corporate universities were modeled after academic universities. For example, the Royal Bank of Scotland's (RBS) corporate training center was modeled after the Harvard Business School case classroom design. The bank also engaged Harvard Executive Education faculty. If you sat in on an RBS program in the early 2000s, you would be forgiven if you thought you were sitting in Aldrich Hall in Cambridge, Massachusetts. American companies like Corning, Apple, Goldman Sachs, Deloitte, and Coca-Cola all produced award-winning facilities and programs that were major components of their talent development investments. Keystone corporate universities in major markets include Sony University (Japan), Philips Lighting University (Netherlands), Intercontinental Hotels Group Academy (UK), Turkcell Academy (Turkey), ArcelorMittal (India), and East-West Seed Academy (Thailand). All employed variations of the corporate university strategy.

Over the last ten years, corporate universities have evolved in several ways:

1. **Technology:** Corporate universities can be virtual or have a physical campus (or both), and can be the hub for many different forms of formal and informal knowledge sharing and content curation. With mobile devices and cloud computing, content can be created, stored, and shared from almost anywhere to anywhere, and on any device. Information can be provided at a point of interaction; thus, learning can happen in both planned and episodic ways.

2. **Feedback Systems:** Feedback systems are increasingly embedded in both work and learning systems, including sensors, wearable devices, games, intelligent tutoring, and artificial intelligence. As such, it is no longer necessary in some instances to use development assignments, because feedback systems are built into business processes. In other words, the worker (learner) receives immediate performance results from a given project or assignment.

3. **Informal Education Systems:** Video is now the media of choice on almost all social platforms, and business education increasingly includes user-generated content and social media integration. The value of video content is highly dependent on the trust of the video producer (the personal brand), rather than the production standards.

4. **Formal Learning:** Formal learning is generally acknowledged as a classroom model, but this model can include distance learning, flipped learning models (e.g., Khan Academy), and digital online group learning models. Increasingly, formal learning will include algorithm-based just-in-time tutorials and personalized programming. Some education models allow students to learn at their own pace and from their own sources, and the emphasis is placed on rigorous testing. Students receive credit (i.e., certification) by passing a test.

5. **The Gig Economy:** The use of temporary workers or short-term assignments creates non-linear development paths and changes the

accountability for learning new skills. This varies greatly across the globe, but the level of variable work in a business ecosystem is a new issue and has both potential risk and opportunity.

Organizing the Transfer of Knowledge

The starting point for a learning organization is often to create the small community of sustainability advocates who are the leading edge of knowledge discovery. As described in chapter 7, knowledge discovery drives gains in foundation knowledge and helps shape new mental models. Since many knowledge domains are still low maturity, the goal is often to start where you have greater knowledge and less risk.

For some insight, I spoke with Nick Pennell, group operations director for Essentra, an engineering and manufacturing firm that creates extruded plastics, fasteners, packaging, tapes, and displays. Nick is the de facto chief sustainability officer, because he is the senior officer with the most knowledge and passion for sustainability. Nick's previous experience includes working on major sustainability projects with consulting firm Booz & Company. With respect to Essentra's learning strategy, Nick commented, "We have just organized our group's sustainability committee and are now focused on creating value in a structured way. We've created a corporate social responsibility statement and are crafting a new employee value proposition. We haven't created a lot of new training, but rather are focused on creating energy champions, waste champions, and site champions to bring focus to what we are doing and learning."[3]

Using this model, two things become apparent. The first is that knowledge sharing will be a mix of video-based on-demand and synchronous sharing and discussion learning in group settings. However, the majority of knowledge discovery occurs on the job. Second, your job as a learning professional is much more fun. The early stages of organizing the transfer of knowledge involves shopping for publicly available knowledge and an increased emphasis on co-created knowledge with partners, vendors, government agencies, and industry associations. The general organizing principle is shown in Figure 8.1.

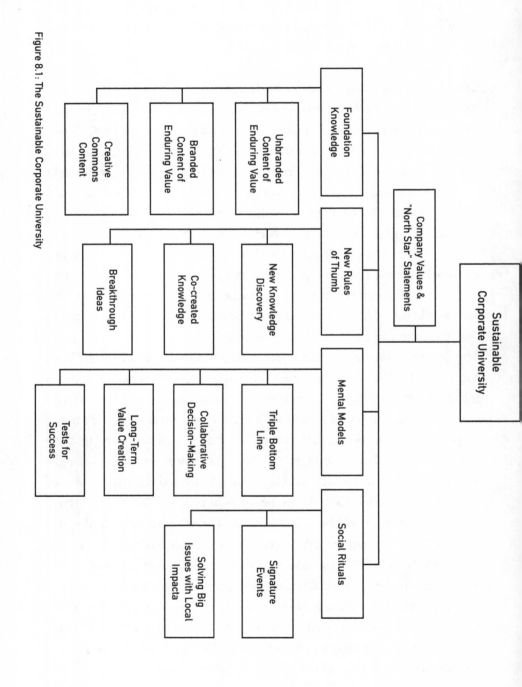

Figure 8.1: The Sustainable Corporate University

Your company's values and North Star statements must be unique to your organization. The example of the W.S. Badger Company illustrates the point. These are really about "who you are" and must express your vision for an economically viable and socially conscious organization. Your North Star statements are longer range, but it is not really necessary to think about a North Star statement in the concept of a three- or five-year plan. These statements are aspirational. As Trevor Martin of Galaxy Entertainment said, "Sustainability is a choice people have to make about the future of the planet." North Star statements influence each of the different knowledge types, but are particularly relevant to mental models.

For example, employees are offered free meals at Galaxy Entertainment facilities in Macau. Most employees filled their plates to overflowing, because the food was free, but often tossed half the food into the trash. Galaxy introduced the "clean plate" initiative to increase resource efficiency. The result was a substantial reduction in food waste. The balance of what is not used is now recycled as animal feed or fertilizer. Making hundreds of small behavior changes is the key to making your North Star statements and company values come to life. Over time, these can become embedded as new mental models. These changes are often best done on the job and generally offer a positive payback.

The Changing Concept of Foundation Knowledge

Foundation knowledge is normally the biggest category of formal training and it is important to provide quality without overinvesting. I break foundation knowledge into three sections. The first two involve branded and unbranded content of enduring value. This is best illustrated by Creative Commons knowledge, a licensing scheme created by Lawrence Lessig in 2001.[4] The Creative Commons allows authors and owners of intellectual property to license their content according to the model shown in Table 8.1.

Table 8.1: Creative Commons Licenses

License	Summary Definition
Attribution License	You can use the content, but you must provide specific attribution for the original author and source.
Share Alike	You can share or use the content but you must apply the same share alike restrictions.
Noncommercial	You can use the content for non-commercial purposes.
No Derivative Works	You cannot remix or create derivative works. The content must be presented as originally designed.

The more the talent development function is involved with new knowledge creation, sustainability experiments, and business prototyping, the more it can take a lead on the release of internally generated or co-created content to ensure that it is appropriately registered for sharing. One new role for a talent development or learning function is the curation and licensing of new knowledge. Given the volume of content creation in many organizations, this can be an important part of social value sharing.

In 2015, I conducted an experiment on my research website, Top5 Learning, where we populated a weekly news magazine with only Creative Commons content. The goal was to see if we could identify high-value but low-cost (free) articles and videos that would be considered useful for the talent development professional. The challenge was to publish quality content but also to judge the degree of difficulty of finding and reviewing the content. To support this initiative, I dedicated a half day of editorial time and one day per week of an analyst's time to collect, collate, and publish what we found. At its peak, the distribution reached seven thousand talent development professionals. The free content was seen at viewing rates equal to 60 percent to 110 percent of our proprietary content, depending on the week.

Since that time, there have been millions of additional content items with a Creative Commons license. Most major search engines like Google, Bing, and Baidu, and video services like YouTube and Vimeo, will let you filter for Creative Commons licenses in your search. There are also specialized search engines that allow you to simultaneously search for content, images, and video from sites like Google, Flickr, YouTube, Pixabay, SoundCloud, and many others.[5]

As a change leader, you will discover that new knowledge discovery will take on many forms in your sustainable organization. The process can involve complex programming algorithms and design concepts, or simple "how to" user-generated video. I have helped many organizations expand the use of user-generated content. In one instance, I worked with a colleague, Mike Pino, to train teams at DFS Academy in Hong Kong to develop new instructional videos using their phones or tablets and the video editing software that comes free on their PCs. We supplemented the training with instructions on how the teams could access low-cost or no-cost images, sound tracks, and videos to supplement their own materials. The results were a series of free videos that could be distributed on DFS's internal Learning Management System (LMS). The East-West Seed Academy uses the same concept with field trips to farms to illustrate solutions and capture real-world video scenarios. Both Creative Commons–licensed content and user-generated content can be useful for low-cost training activities.

Types and Value of Knowledge

While one part of the market is trending towards low-cost content of enduring value, there is still a high demand for our third knowledge section, branded breakthrough content. Branded breakthrough content is generally associated with a world-class research service, author, or university. The uniqueness of breakthrough knowledge creates competitive advantage and thus higher value. Branded content also benefits from superior research, curation, and editing.

The value of breakthrough content starts out high, but this type of content generally has a relatively short shelf life. It is an essential part of competitive advantage but must be put to use rapidly. After a period of time, it is no longer breakthrough and I reclassify it as branded content of enduring value. The cost of this content is lower because more people have access and it is less unique. If the content enters the public domain or is unbranded in nature, the cost may fall dramatically. Commoditized content sells for even less.

The point to remember about breakthrough knowledge and content of enduring value is that they become part an evolving competitive landscape. More is expected from customers and employees, which means the business must always be integrating and scaling this knowledge while seeking new breakthroughs.

I created Figure 8.2 to illustrate the point. Using my consulting files, I identified client purchase decisions for different kinds of courses, e-learning, and digital training content. I set the value of branded breakthrough content at 100 for 2005 and measure everything else as a percentage of that figure. My data model is limited, so this is the case of a learning model that I "believe to be true." Based on my experience, I think the pattern is essentially correct, even if the absolute numbers vary quite a bit. For example, Harvard Business Publishing has been selling its Harvard ManageMentor (HMM) e-learning program for almost two decades. The program is typically sold as an enterprise license, comprising forty-two modules offered in English.

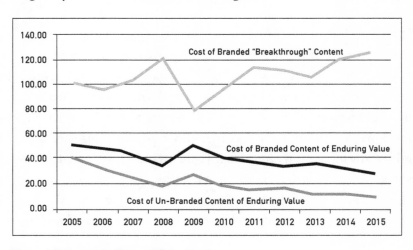

Figure 8.2: Content by Type and Price Matrix

Although the HHM program has added to the total number of modules over time, the cost of an enterprise license has increased with each new version, as has the cost per hour of instructional time. The general trend for vendors selling unbranded content has been the opposite—more modules, more languages, and more total seat time for a declining price per hour of instruction. You would likely be able to buy ten times as many modules of unbranded content in multiple languages for a lower price than a premium-branded product. However, customers regularly pay the higher price to have the more prestigious brand with unique content created by a top business school faculty. Although not all branded content can maintain the top price difference, there remains a substantial premium in the marketplace.

These differences in value pricing extend to a range of learning services and have become more pronounced with the availability of user-generated content, vendor provided-training, and free content. Essentially, branded content has maintained or increased its value, while commodity content has reduced in value.

As we increase our focus on sustainability, I think the investment pattern remains similar, but the focus will change. There will be more emphasis on changing mental models and knowledge discovery. Development experiences will increasingly include partnerships and co-creation experiences. This is where a talent development professional is in a unique position to drive change at scale through knowledge discovery, which results in competitive advantage. Economic viability demands that a business seek competitive differentiation.

Many of these knowledge challenges will persist over time because of low market maturity, which will necessitate added investment in knowledge curation, knowledge shopping, and experience design. Sustainability will mean that some content domains will be openly shared while others will remain subject to market pricing and higher levels of investment. Changing the way you invest in learning and development will support new competitive advantage.

So, What Is the Case for Making Higher Investments?

Strong claims demand strong results, so it is helpful to build a business case for increasing investments. One way to do this is to take a high-level market approach and follow the money. What type of multiples will investors pay for companies with learning content? I identified a number of key business purchases over the past seven years to identify patterns. These are very often private companies, so the data are gleaned from public sources such as press releases and industry reporting. Again, I view this data not as operational research but as a rule of thumb, where observations seem to be playing out. Entertainment content companies like Netflix and China's iQiyi are now developing their own branded content and seeing huge gains in both subscriber growth and stock price. Similarly, investors in corporate learning businesses have been paying higher premiums for businesses with unique content libraries and a strong market brand. The rising valuations for such businesses are illustrated in Figure 8.3. Understanding these trends will allow you to maximize your "knowledge shopping" for competitive differentiation.

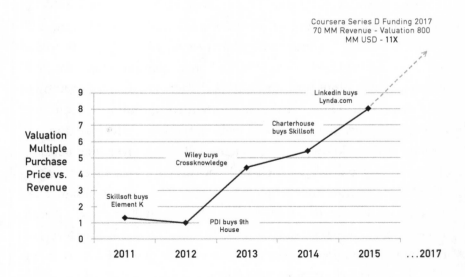

Figure 8.3: Valuation Multiple: Purchase Price vs. Revenue

Another approach is to look at the investment behavior in market-leading companies. When they highlight a strategic priority, where is the evidence that a higher-level investment in learning is part of the solution? Let's take the case of LVMH and the rollout of its LIFE program (LVMH Initiatives for the Environment) in 2012.

LVMH is composed of seventy fashion houses or Maisons that collectively employ more than one hundred and forty thousand people around the globe. LVMH developed a specialized environment department more than twenty-five years ago. Key LVMH programs included an ethnobotany project in Madagascar for Madison Parfums Christian Dior in 1995. LVMH Hennessey became the first spirits company to be ISO 14001 certified (for environmental management) in 1998. It conducted a full carbon footprint analysis at several businesses starting in 2002 and developed a new supplier code of conduct in 2008. LVMH was committed to behaving in an environmentally responsible way, and the 2012 LIFE program was its latest update to the company-wide vision.[6]

When the program was introduced, Group Managing Director Antonio Belloni stated, "The LIFE program is the foundation and backbone that structures all the initiatives deployed by LVMH within the scope of our environmental policy, at all our Maisons, from product design to retailing."[7] The LIFE program sets a series of targets for LVMH Group, and each Maison is expected to contribute to the targets, although each business is given a high degree of autonomy. I spoke with several members of the LVMH team to gauge how such a program is rolled out.

Ian Hardie was head of LVMH House, the in-house executive education program for more than ten years, and he currently serves as global head of learning and development for the Sephora Maison. Ian commented that when the program was rolled out, "It was agreed centrally that it was a priority and led from the center, but with lots of buy-in created. A mix of central-leadership and diplomatic efforts to create the buy-in. Plus, the central team delivered value by providing expertise, contacts, training, etc. that helped the in-Maison staff and lifted them up."[8]

Each LVMH Maison has a separate environment and training staff, as well as a central environmental academy. The academy trains and develops support staff teams in each Maison to help drive performance on key metrics that are shared on a group dashboard that includes an environmental performance index. The LIFE project also has a centralized budget, and each Maison has a budget. The combination of clear leadership commitment and a long-term focus on environmental indicators has created a culture that expects to make continuous progress. Centralized and decentralized budgets and specialized staff, as well as continuous training, specialized academies, and major partnerships with industry groups, represent a substantial commitment to skill and capability development. The LIFE program was updated in 2016 with new targets extended through to 2020.

Sylvie Bénard, environment director at LVMH since 1992, has helped lead LVMH through a range of projects since she attended the first United Nations Earth Summit in Rio de Janeiro in 1992. The LIFE program is the latest iteration of those efforts. Bénard explains, "We try to identify important areas through life cycle analysis, where we can take action and try to find the best tools to measure the issue. Then we look for a project to start with." She notes further, "It is important to never work alone so we are always partnering with a functional manager. My role is to train people and help them understand the impact of their decisions."[9]

The Correlation between Higher Investments in Learning and Company Performance

As part of my consulting practice helping companies make better talent decisions, I created a set of baseline data from information on over twenty thousand publicly traded companies. From that group, we analyzed a subset of companies in ten industry sectors. For each firm, we looked for publicly available company websites and publications such as annual reports. We used key search terms to identify information suggesting a strategic investment in talent development (e.g., terms such as

Corporate University.) We then cross-referenced the companies with third-party sources of information from human resources, business associations, and industry award programs. Companies were considered to have a strategic investment in talent development if they met two of the following four conditions:

1. There was evidence of a strategic investment in talent development as reported in a publicly available company publication (e.g., annual report or press release).
2. An independent third party validated reporting on the company's strategic investment.
3. There was some evidence that the company invested above the industry norm when compared to an industry standard data set.
4. The company received award recognition for being "best in class" for its talent development or corporate university function (e.g., an industry award).

Figure 8.4 compares the relative stock performance of companies graded as having strategic investments in talent development versus those without during specific years. In this instance, we used the Russell 3000 index, which is designed to benchmark the entire US stock market, comprising both large cap and small stocks.

Overall, companies with a strategic investment in learning and development posted consistently higher stock market returns than their competitive peers. The difference was most notable in bull markets, but the growth was seen in both pre-recessionary and post-recessionary activity. As we break the data down by industry sectors, we see a more nuanced story.

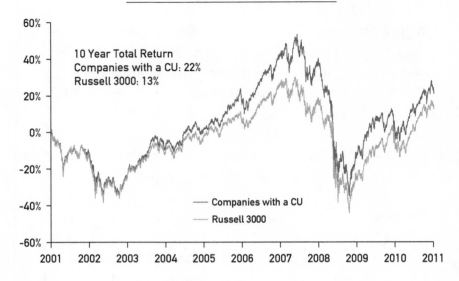

Figure 8.4: Relative Stock Performance of Companies Graded as Having Strategic Investments in Talent Development (Pre- and Post-recession)[10]

Figure 8.5 looks at the stock performance of information technology companies, both with and without a strategic investment in learning. In this instance, the comparison is with the S&P 500 Index. Although the performance variation in some years is small, the overall performance difference over an extended period of time shows a substantial additional return on investment. There are, of course, many factors that influence stock performance, and this analysis is not a direct causal model. Good strategy, a strong balance sheet, excellent products, and many others elements will influence overall business performance. However, I believe it is a reasonable conclusion that a greater focus on strategic learning investments is what creates the adaptive organization that responds faster to market feedback and competitive conditions.

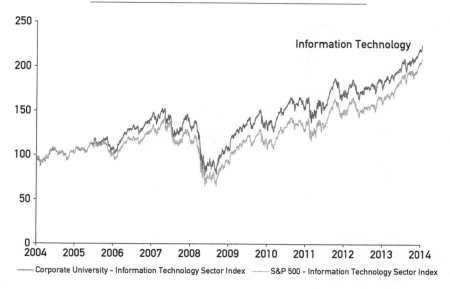

—— Corporate University - Information Technology Sector Index   —— S&P 500 - Information Technology Sector Index

Figure 8.5: Performance of Information Technology Stocks, Both With and Without a Strategic Investment in Learning, vs. S&P 500 Index[11]

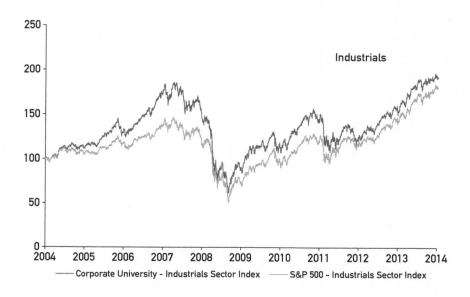

—— Corporate University - Industrials Sector Index   —— S&P 500 - Industrials Sector Index

Figure 8.6: Performance of Industrial Stocks, Both With and Without a Strategic Investment in Learning, vs. S&P 500 Index[12]

Table 8.2: Comparison of Performance across Industries[a]

	SITD	Count	2000	2001	2002	2003	2004	2005	2006	2007	2008	2009	2010
Energy	Y	35	1.3x	1.3x	1.5x	1.0x	1.0x	1.1x	1.3x	1.2x	1.2x	1.4x	1.4x
	N	37											
Consumer Staples	Y	26	1.1x	1.3x	1.2x	1.4x	1.1x	1.2x	1.1x	1.3x	1.3x	1.2x	1.2x
	N	56											
Financials	Y	62	1.3x	1.3x	1.6x	1.6x	1.3x	1.2x	1.3x	1.4x	1.5x	1.4x	1.3x
	N	226											
Utilities	Y	12	1.0x	1.5x	0.7x	1.0x	1.3x	1.3x	1.0x	1.5x	1.4x	1.3x	1.1x
	N	39											
Consumer Discretionary	Y	60	1.0x	0.9x	0.9x	1.0x	1.3x	1.2x	1.2x	1.1x	1.2x	1.1x	1.0x
	N	122											
Information Technology	Y	44	0.8x	0.9x	1.0x	1.1x	1.1x	1.3x	1.5x	1.5x	1.7x	1.6x	1.4x
	N	53											
Industrials	Y	94	1.0x	1.1x	1.2x	1.1x	1.1x	1.1x	1.1x	1.1x	1.4x	1.1x	1.1x
	N	175											
Health Care	Y	40	0.9x	1.0x	1.1x	1.5x	1.5x	1.5x	1.7x	1.6x	1.7x	1.8x	1.7x
	N	18											
Materials	Y	44	0.9x	1.0x	1.1x	1.2x	1.0x	1.0x	1.3x	1.1x	1.2x	1.1x	1.2x
	N	88											
Telecommunication Services	Y	20	1.2x	1.0x	1.0x	1.3x	1.1x	1.0x	1.3x	1.2x	1.3x	1.4x	1.4x
	N	27											

a Corporate University Research Ltd., *Corporate University Database*, Tortola, British Virgin Islands, accessed June 20, 2018, used with permission.

The same pattern can be seen in other sectors like industrials. Figure 8.6 also uses the S&P 500 index for comparison.

Table 8.2 is used to directly compare only the competitive peers from our database using a similar time frame as Figure 8.4 (ten years, pre- and post-recession). It shows that in down-market cycles, in industries dominated by raw materials, pricing, or highly regulated frameworks, the higher investments in talent development did not always pay off (a ratio of less than 1.0). Industries such as materials and industrials had the closest ratios. Other industries, like financials, showed a consistent positive trend, while information technology had the widest swings from negative to positive. In most other instances, particularly in knowledge-intensive industries or industries undergoing substantial disruption, there was a substantial improvement in stock performance (ratio greater than 1.0) correlated with a higher-than-normal strategic investment in talent development (SITD).

At this point, it would be helpful to overlay performance of companies identified as sustainability leaders; unfortunately, that data does not neatly align with our data set (yet). The Dow Jones Sustainability Index is the largest data set for the past five years and offers a variable perspective. The index includes 250 of the 2500 largest global companies in the S&P Global Index. During that time, its average annual return of +9.64 percent trails both the overall Dow Jones Industrial Average (+13.41 percent) and the S&P 500 Index (+12.79 percent).[13] That seems to suggest that companies with a focus on sustainability performed less well than their non-sustainable competitive peers. However, there are reasons to believe that a longer-term focus is the better vantage point from which to draw a comparison. As illustrated in chapter 3, when Unilever introduced its Sustainable Living Plan under CEO Paul Polman, the stock underperformed competitive peers during the early years of the plan, but then outperformed competitive peers in later years.

An eighteen-year retrospective study of companies in 2012 offered the following conclusion: "Over an 18-year period, the high-sustainability companies dramatically outperformed the low-sustainability ones in terms of both stock market and accounting measures."[14] Certain sustainable investment funds, like the ESG Beta Quality Fund from Pax, beat the Lipper Multi-Cap Core Funds index on a five-year basis.[15] Also, the FTSE4Good Ethical Benchmark beat the overall FTSE Share Index with a total return of 48 percent versus 43 percent, also on a five-year basis.

In addition to comparisons of direct economic performance, companies like Morgan Stanley have looked at firms that have risk exposure from what are called environmental or social governance events (ESG). These would include an accounting fraud, disclosure of labor abuses, a mine explosion, an oil spill, or some other such event. The average loss to shareholders was a 64 percent drop in stock price after one year.[16] Overall, there appears to be strong evidence that investing in sustainability both reduces risk and offers potential upside financial returns. Of course, none of these comparisons quantifies the social impact of such performance. We are still trying to find the right ways to describe business contributions to healthier communities with the same conviction and vigor that we present economic comparisons.

Creating Tests for Success

A "test for success" is a guideline for evaluating decision-making. It should be simple and easy to use. An example of a test for success is the YC Scorecard developed at Patagonia (the initials YC stand for Patagonia founder Yvon Chouinard). Each new scorecard is reviewed for issues such as simplicity of design, functional use, and ease of repair. The scorecard frames a series of questions that help evaluate a decision versus your stated sustainability goals. For example:

- Does it cause any unnecessary environmental harm?
- Without sacrificing quality, could it have been made in a less environmentally harmful or more sustainable manner?
- Is the product a responsible choice from birth to death?

A simple example can be seen in the ways that people view text messages and social media content. If you post a message, even if private, consider the impact if it were to be viewed publicly. Would you phrase it the same way?

In chapter 6, on day-to-day problem-solving, we discussed the need for a future-oriented test. A test might include a question like, What would be the long-term impact of this decision on our communities? For a bank, it might be, Are we lending money for business expansion in areas at risk for climate events? For an investment firm, it might be, Will we invest in a carbon extraction industry or textile company without proof of a certified supply chain that prevents child labor?

The tests for success are a way of translating your values into actionable guides.

Where Can I Look for Help?

One typical place to look for outside support are regional and international business schools. Most business schools still treat sustainability as a separate course or program rather than as an integrated concept. New degree and executive education programs now include a focus on sustainability, but such programs remain a small percentage of the overall program enrollment and executive education hours delivered. Many schools have created dedicated research centers that specialize in sustainability, such as the Cambridge Institute for Sustainable Leadership.[17] However, a few pioneers, like the Business School Lausanne under dean Katrin Muff and Sunway University in Malaysia with the support of economist Jeffrey Sachs, are the exceptions. They have made the effort to fully integrate sustainability into the school curriculum.

A second resource is communities of practice and networks where sustainability champions participate in insightful dialog. Professor Alfons Sauquet Rovira of ESADE in Spain is chair of the Academy of Business in Society (ABIS), based in Brussels, and helps organize numerous conferences for businesses and academics to discuss the challenges of a more sustainable world. Professor Bertrand Moingeon at HEC Paris is also responsible for HEC's Africa and Indian Ocean Institute, an area of the world with enormous sustainability challenges. Professor Bobby Parmar of the University of Virginia is developing a program on business ethics that challenges the notion that businesses exist only to satisfy shareholder interests. The key to successful engagement with industry associations and conferences is to have a clear agenda and some level of interactivity so you can interact with peers and resident experts.

Reader Reflection

IMAGINE that you are head of a supply chain department for a manufacturer of computer parts. The components your company builds make you a key supplier to global and domestic brands. You subcontract to hundreds of small suppliers in neighboring countries that provide raw materials, subassemblies, and services. You have been informed that a number of your customers are now participants in global forums on sustainability, and word has trickled down that each of them wants their suppliers to be more focused on a triple bottom line.

You have specifically been asked by one major supplier to report on your subcontractors' operations and to sign assurances that none is in violation of any of the UN Global Compact agreements on human rights and, in addition, that you are in compliance with key agreements from the International Labor Organization (ILO). Since you use dozens of subcontractors, this will be a time-consuming and expensive process. You have checked with your leadership colleagues and no one seems to have the personnel or expertise to meet the requirements. Your CEO is pushing for fast work on this project, because the company fears losing business if it is in noncompliance.

One colleague suggests that you conduct a sample inspection of subcontractors as sufficient due diligence. Another colleague advises that if your subcontractors want to keep your business, they have to sign an agreement that they are in compliance. You are conscious of a contract you lost last year, when your costs increased to the point where your customer moved their business to a competitor. Your biggest fear is that you are operating without good information and do not have anyone who can help. All of the risk seems to be on your shoulders. What will you do?

Anchoring sustainable practices in your business is a multiyear effort that will face the constant and inevitable tension with costs, efficiency, and time. The more complex your organization, the more likely there will be dozens of opportunities for new risk issues and challenges to emerge. You can view this dilemma from one of two perspectives. If you are the large company making demands of your subcontractors, you may see the value in extra documentation. It gives you a clear paper trail. If you are the small contractor, you may see the emergence of new requirements from dozens or hundreds of customers as a cost and time burden. In both instances, clear standards are helpful and illustrate the value of industry associations and multi-company collaborations. The key is to keep the goal in mind and not lose focus. Collaboration and practice sharing can be enormously helpful. It is also useful to keep in mind that there are likely to be many other companies who have faced similar challenges, perhaps in your industry or perhaps in adjacent or different industries. Research skills become an important capability in low-maturity markets, allowing you to find simple solutions to business pain points. Solving these issues faster than the competition also provides a level of competitive advantage and differentiation. In markets where everyone is struggling with common challenges, becoming the sustainability market leader may make you the preferred provider.

TAKEAWAY: Smart Investments in Learning Can Pay Big Dividends

A company attempting to change to a more sustainable business model has four big talent development challenges:

- First, the core foundation knowledge of a business must evolve with changes in boundaries and performance values. Processes need to be redesigned and new knowledge domains added.

- Second, early adopters exist in a space that is more "best practice" than well-defined knowledge domain. A low-maturity strategy means you need to work more with new knowledge (discovery) and variable knowledge (rules of thumb) rather than established expertise. As such, driving efficiency and scale is more difficult.

- Third, changing a business purpose to focus on greater social value creation requires rethinking business rituals and team-building activities. Rituals are key to anchoring new changes over time.

- Fourth, new business models often require changes in mental models. Add-on courses are typically not sufficient to make those changes. One course may work as a catalyst for a few people, but it is not the way to change a corporate culture or long-term business practice. This must be embedded in hundreds of day-to-day activities to anchor the changes in the business culture.

The key to solving these new development challenges is to change your learning investment strategy. Economize where learning is free or low cost, make use of partnerships to burden-share investments, and invest heavily in things that will accelerate change. The relative investment in talent development is much higher if the goal is a transition in mental models, the conversion of variable knowledge into foundation knowledge, and a compressed time scale.

If we define sustainability as both a source of industry disruption and as a knowledge-intensive change, then it seems reasonable to assert that accelerated talent development offers a high probability of generating improved competitive performance.

As I point out in chapter 9, although foundation knowledge in sustainability is in its infancy, short-term or focused projects will allow you to discover possibilities that drive innovation. Developing your talent management strategy is the topic we will turn to next.

Chapter 9

BUILDING YOUR TALENT PLAN

"I am convinced that nothing we do is more important than hiring and developing people. At the end of the day, you bet on people, not on strategies." LAWRENCE BOSSIDY

The United Nations is a unique organization, and in many ways it provided me with a range of talent development experiences. One challenge was to assess and prepare potential leadership candidates for the top jobs in country offices, called the resident coordinator or RC and the resident representative or RR. My role was to help the United Nations Development Programme (UNDP) prepare a slate of three potential leadership candidates. My recommendations would be passed to the agency head and secretary general for discussion with the foreign ministry of that particularly country. Along the way, my partner colleagues and I needed to make sure that (1) the candidate slates had strong gender diversity; (2) member countries and regions were appropriately represented; and (3) candidates were highly qualified and possessed exceptional language skills. We typically rotated candidates on three- to six-year assignments to keep the positions fresh and avoid any issues of corruption or influence. A great deal of pressure was exerted on resident coordinators, as they were constantly moving into new roles and trying to develop high-performing teams at each new location.

I recently interviewed a colleague from my time at the UN, Richard Dictus, now serving as RR for UNDP and RC for the UN in Egypt, to discuss the importance of sustainability and talent development. He commented that "Corporations are major actors in sustainability, although engagement with SMEs is not always as strong in emerging economies. The role of the UN is not to tell corporations what to do, but to create 'moments of realization' and then to facilitate work on very specific issues with measurable outcomes."[1] From a talent development perspective, let us consider how Richard would be prepared for this role. His background provides context.

Richard spent time as deputy director of human resources for UNDP. It is a positive practice for senior leaders to spend time in a staff function, as this helps them gain an appreciation for the challenges and business outcomes associated with key business functions. He also ran various UN funds and programs, including serving as executive director of the UN volunteer program in Bonn, Germany. He received a range of formal training, including the Harvard/MIT public disputes program and completed assignments for the UNDP Pacific Island sector coordinating the interests of many countries. According to Richard, "These assignments give you a focus that is more strongly on equity and pro-poor growth in agriculture and rural development, as well as the needs of the rural poor and most vulnerable segments of society. Connecting with the corporate sector is about understanding the positive aspects of a bottom-line approach as well as other social interests, and then connecting parties together in a collaborative effort."

Richard's learning path included foundation knowledge education for key roles and development assignments that built his knowledge of heuristics. Key UN social rituals helped to create peer networks and organization commitment. His mindset didn't need to change from one absent of social value creation, because most UN employees are mission driven. His rotational assignments gave him direct exposure to environmental challenges in small-island developing states, the challenges of rural poor, the inequalities of many societies, and the challenges of building new teams every few years. As a senior UN leader, he is also charged with making the business case for funding the development work he cares about so deeply. Collectively, the elements of this learning path create a strong sense of the balance needed and the benefits of a strong triple bottom line.

The career challenge for Richard was building an appreciation for business value creation and learning to build bridges between the public and private sectors on sustainability. He observes, "I don't get up every day saying I'm going to focus on goal number one and number two, but everything I do is focused on making positive forward progress on the SDGs. That happens when I create engagement."[2] Although his starting point was on the social side of the value paradigm, Richard's development experience and training path are not unlike the path taken in the commercial sector. The challenge for business professionals is to gain access to social value experiences that balance their development profile.

The typical executive team in any organization is focused on defining the business strategy, making investment decisions, and engaging with customers. The human resource and talent development functions focus on creating a structure that supports the strategy, finding or developing the right talent to execute on the strategy, and developing the culture that aligns and reinforces the right mental models and behaviors. The talent development function for a sustainable organization must reorient itself to support the new business accountabilities (boundaries) and a revised value proposition. Unless the business is a very early adopter of sustainable practices, the typical path to sustainability is as shown in Figure 9.1.

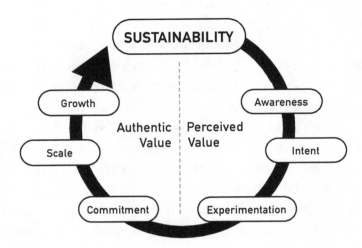

Figure 9.1: Six-Step Model of Sustainability

Creating an appropriate talent plan for the "perceived value" stage involves finding the right people to engage in experiments and demonstration projects. It is the opportunity to ask the questions, What are we trying to learn? and How will that help us in the next phase to build commitment and scale?

The area of perceived value indicates that the company is still exploring how social value creation or new economic value creation, along with positive social outcomes, will affect the business. The perceived value space is where we claim environmental or social benefits that we think are true or that we would like to be true. However, this is also where we can unintentionally get into "greenwashing" by overstating the benefits of our actions. It is important to spend time understanding the new value proposition and whether the value creation is generalized or specific. You may ask yourself questions such as, Are the social changes due only to company actions and are they measurable? Do our actions benefit a specific number of people or the community as a whole? If my claims were subjected to an independent assessment, would the claims for value creation stand up to reasonable scrutiny?

Getting measurement right is the key to making the commitment for change. Authentic value should be measurable in either quantitative or qualitative terms. It is something of an aspirational goal, where we succeed in some areas better than others. It is genuinely difficult to assign value to a natural resource, which is why it deserves deep and genuine investigation. Reducing the value of poverty or inequality to a number is equally challenging, which is why we need to look for improved ways to describe our actions and results. The 169 sub-measures of the SDGs are a good starting point, as are equally relevant measures from leading NGOs and groups that represent specific industries and underserved populations. As Richard Dictus observed, "moments of realization" are often the starting point from which you explore and refine the value proposition. For a company ready to make that transition, the talent planning process must be fully under way so you have a sense of the cost and time it takes to grow the business while maintaining your sense of purpose.

Authenticity and Transparency

Authenticity is a critical element of management behavior in sustainable organizations. It involves communicating from core beliefs. Transparency is about openness and is expected of any business that applies for benefit corporation status or B certification. Transparency in a benefit corporation also requires a third-party benchmark to ensure a level of objective reporting on sustainability goals. Both require reporting on your goals for specific and general social good and publishing your results. Regulatory transparency, truth in labeling, and almost all sustainability certifications require a level of openness, even for private firms.

Authenticity and transparency are not new to leadership development. Bill George, former CEO of Medtronic and author of *Authentic Leadership*[3] and *Discover Your True North*,[4] emphasizes the importance of a mission orientation, self-awareness, and the need to live your values every day. But surveys of public perception suggest that our largest institutions have an authenticity deficit. Recent Gallup polls indicate that only 25 percent of US respondents have either "quite a lot" or "a great deal" of confidence in big business.[5] The 2018 Edelman Trust Barometer, an online survey of over thirty-three thousand respondents in twenty-three global markets, suggests that average trust in major institutions stands at only 48 percent among the global population. However, the same survey indicates that 64 percent of people around the world believe that CEOs "should take the lead on change rather than waiting for government to impose it."[6]

As with many competencies, it is hard to "turn it on" when you want to, so it is necessary to build it into the way you manage, collaborate, and communicate. That suggests you look for these behaviors in hiring, build it into your business practices, and coach it with existing staff. You need to

- hire for talent with a demonstrated history of living their values;
- look for leaders with a long-term history of building strong relationships; and
- hire people who can admit mistakes and learn from failures.

The Importance of Collaboration

Some organizations, like the Nature Conservancy, highlight the importance of a "shared agenda" when talking about business and industry partnerships. I interviewed Dawn Denvir, the new global head of learning for the Nature Conservancy.[7] She emphasized, "We really try to understand everyone's point of view and we're willing to work with anyone who has a commitment to bring together people and nature. We are very much about diversity and inclusion and a shared sustainability agenda." The Nature Conservancy has developed historic partnerships with firms like Dow Chemical by "demonstrating that building nature's value into business strategy could lead to better outcomes for companies and conservation."[8]

Throughout this book, I have used a variety of examples to illustrate the importance of shared decision-making to reduce cognitive bias and how it applies to group problem-solving as a way to internalize sustainable values and best practices. I have also highlighted the importance of knowledge discovery in low-maturity markets and of innovation as a key skill in evolving the sustainable marketplace. However, collaboration and innovation are practices that require active support. By this I mean that leaders must create an environment where the voices from their teams matter more than their own; this specifically means encouraging discussion, approving projects, removing barriers, and encouraging peer-to-peer engagement as opposed to directing behavior.

Creating Value with Multigenerational Talent

For the first time in history, four generations of workers are in the workplace. Baby boomers and generations X, Y, and Z will compose teams and collaborate on projects. Motivations will be diverse and will include success and status, purpose and happiness, discovery and legacy. I freely acknowledge that the older I get, the more attracted I am to projects that offer greater meaning and depth. Any talent development plan needs to use that diversity as a resource.

Talent development for a sustainable organization should value diversity for several reasons. Helping team members understand each other and appreciate new or different perspectives speeds up the process by preventing a regression to old habits.

The value of collaboration in new knowledge creation and the importance of peer-to-peer interactions in development cannot be understated. Passionate employees are a tremendous asset. Their knowledge base should be tapped as a source of strength.

The more seasoned employees are often a source of social and community knowledge that helps provide perspective. In different countries and cultures, age and knowledge, as well as the idea of "giving back," are strong cultural norms that can be used to build the company culture. A diversity of motivations allows the business greater flexibility to design jobs, work conditions, benefits, and compensation. The more personalized the job design, the greater the connection between personal values and the business mission. Consider these points:

- multigenerational talent adds another level of diversity and perspective;
- multigenerational talent can increase the opportunity for knowledge sharing, teaching, and mentoring; and
- multigenerational talent creates greater diversity of motivations that creates more, not less, flexibility in organizational design.

Include Your Ecosystem in Your Talent Plan

One of the simple but consistent takeaways from my interviews is the importance of the business ecosystem to sustainable growth. Ramesh Ramanathan, founder of Jana Small Finance Bank, posed the question, "Does a lack of maturity in a business ecosystem place a limit on balanced growth?" The corollary questions become, If new suppliers and hires have less passion, do you dilute your sense of purpose? and If your business hits a rough patch or has a financial crisis, do the values go out the window?

Over the last several decades, it has been common for many businesses to focus on core capabilities and to outsource other activities to suppliers. Extended supply chains often trade lower costs for reduced oversight of work conditions and practices at supplier companies. In an interview with Nitin Tikle, vice president of strategic sourcing at Mahindra & Mahindra, based in India, he spoke of the importance of building long-term relationships in supplier ecosystems, noting, "We have a complex supply chain, and it is necessary to work with a wide variety of suppliers to truly have an impact on a triple bottom line. In many instances, we work with specific subgroups in areas of water, waste, and chemical recycling on specific solutions."[9]

One specific project was the move away from single-use wood product packaging throughout the company's supply chain. Tikle observed, "We now use reusable collapsible metal cages and other solutions, but we had to innovate on a product-by-product and supplier-by-supplier basis. But when you focus on a project like that, sustainability becomes like the air you breathe—it's everywhere. When you see something wrong, you feel guilty."[10] Some takeaways from Mahindra & Mahindra's story are:

- partners with shared values are more likely to partner on co-creation projects to stay aligned;
- long-term connective relationships create positive dependencies and greater transparency; and
- if you are a larger parent organization, you often have enormous leverage with smaller suppliers. Trading short-term incremental costs to create alignment for longer-term value creation needs to be a business focus.

Become the Employer of Personal Growth

The general goal for any business is to become the employer of choice. I think the better idea is to be recognized as the company that offers the most creative learning environment—the employer of personal growth. The goal in both instances is the same, which is to have prospective hires lining up at your door for the chance to work with you.

Ask yourself who would you love to work for and why. If you are happy and challenged in your company, what it is about your organization that really excites you? Being mission oriented is a great start, but it is often much more than that. Having good pay and benefits also helps, but there are many companies that pay well and offer good benefits but that are not employers of choice. If you are lucky enough to love where you work, you know that your opinion is shaped by your ability to do things you are passionate about. It is the many small things about a workplace that help create and sustain a space where you are always learning something new and are engaged with work that you find challenging and meaningful. Frequently, the companies that attract the most people offer the most exciting and interesting work—work that is connected to a strong mission. That is why listing a company like Apple, Microsoft, or Google on a résumé gives you instant credibility. People assume your experience at such companies means you have special skills.

I have illustrated the connection between your talent selection choice and creating a learning environment in Figure 9.2. The six main development opportunities are at the bottom of the diagram, although each can be further divided based on the scope of the challenge, the time line, and the potential impact. The expectation is that you have a leadership team committed to a collaborative style where they act as discussion leaders, roadblock removers, and investors in education. The three circles on the bottom left capture the types of rotational assignments that are longer term. The daily problem-solving space is shorter term, and the two right-hand categories are more self-directed or action-learning oriented. Although the big categories may not seem substantially different than traditional plans, the emphasis and design of the experience

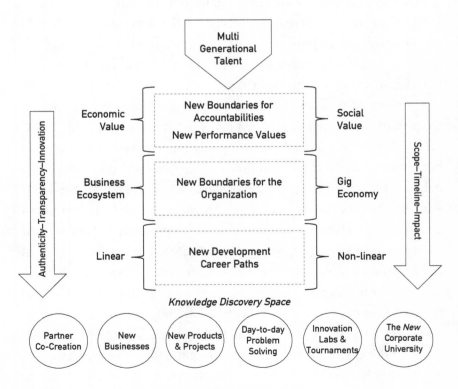

Figure 9.2: Talent Development and the Learning Environment

will be very different due to the boundary changes, the level of new knowledge discovery, and how leaders participate.

Development planning for new sustainable business practices will have fewer "standard" resources such as foundation assignments or job rotations. However, your business will abound with shorter-term experiences that offer a change in perspective. New practice areas may not be well understood, but they can also be unique as knowledge creating or discovery assignments. As such, there are new considerations:

- What projects or functions will best illustrate the new business purpose and have the highest likelihood for success?
  - Early successes are used to build the business case for larger-scale change. Which functional areas, geographic areas, or business units best illustrate the new sustainable business opportunities?
  - What is the performance value of different projects in terms of economic and social gains? Ideally, we want a project that is positive in both social and economic value creation, as opposed to a "net" benefit scenario, where we achieve positive gains with offsets for negative outcomes.
- What is the development value of the project in terms of lessons learned and staff development?
  - Do we have the right people managing these opportunities?
  - What capabilities are needed for success? For transfer and scale? For continued innovation?
  - Can we add staff (assignments) to offer them a unique learning opportunity without sacrificing the new performance value?
- If we do not have the internal capabilities to support new practice areas, where do we look for help?

So how do we take all of this information and start to craft a company-specific talent development plan? We start with nine questions:

1. What is the new sustainable business purpose and strategy?
   a. This is an expansion on the point of focus and asks you to make a decision on your business model (e.g., net benefit, shared value, circular economy). The executive team needs to reflect on new sustainable business concepts and decide how they affect the organization's purpose and competitive differentiation.
   b. Key members of the executive team also need to familiarize themselves with new economic boundary issues like "natural capital," which change the way we look at economic impact and costs.
   c. At this stage, clarity of purpose is essential and we need to decide if we are starting with a demonstration project focused on energy savings, for example, or a broader plan to align all of our products with sustainability standards.
   d. The bolder the action and the faster the scale, the larger the investment and the more complex the changes. Is the primary question one of outside hires vs. internal development or organization structure and job redesign?

2. What are the goals that describe progress on the new sustainable value propositions?
   a. This turns the point of focus into more discreet, measurable outcomes.
   b. Taking bold action requires substantial investment of time and money, so it is important to quantify both the desired economic and social outcomes. Although we are often good at describing economic outcomes in traditional terms, monetizing our impact on the environment, evaluating our products in terms of social impact, or describing our impact on the community is still new territory.
   c. Goals need to be translated for each major type of organizational structure (see question 3), typically business units,

geographic units, functional groups, and hybrid organizations (e.g., shared service or matrixed structures).

d. For most organizations, conducting a balanced dialog on a triple bottom line is a new practice. It may be helpful to have a range of new metrics and business assessments that provide feedback with facilitation by a neutral, but knowledgeable, third party.

e. Communication is key, so there needs to be an open dialog and active communication.

3. What kind of talent will we need to execute on these new goals?

   a. Which job roles will remain static and which ones will evolve?

   b. Are there people in the market that I can hire who have an existing skill set, or do I need to develop skill sets internally?

   c. Focus on hiring for passion and alignment with values.

   d. Ensure sign-off from two or three team members on a new hire for a sustainable team.

4. How do I structure my recruiting and organizational plan?

   a. At the entry level, paying at or above market level is a fundamental part of sustainable business practices. You want to hire and retain the best talent you can afford, and bear in mind that entry-level talent is motivated by safety, mobility, and career interests. I would also add "purpose" to this list.

   b. Develop and communicate career paths. People want to be certain that in joining your organization they will have the opportunity to learn and develop, and either move into new roles or have a variety of projects.

   c. Hire senior-level talent for legacy. Compensation should not be the number-one reason they join. If you need to pay well based on market conditions, move some compensation into deferred programs or longer-term bonuses. Tie compensation to long-term value creation in the triple bottom line.

d. Minimize organizational levels wherever possible to improve communication and transparency. Any organizational change in structure must be evaluated against the potential impact on communication, cohesion, transparency, and consistency of purpose.

e. Are there other companies in the market doing what you need to do? Is there value in hiring such talent as a model? How do we leverage those hires so there are both performance and development outcomes?

5. How will new sustainable business practices change the organizational structure and resource requirements?

a. This question assumes you are an existing organization making a transition and not a startup. Answering this question helps refine the scope and cost of change. You can create a path of change that matches the likelihood of success at each stage with the investment outlay.

b. The basis of good organizational design suggests that "form follows function." For example, if I adopt a circular economy model, how will that change product design? Will I need new job functions to handle end-of-life product returns? Will I need new technology? How will I monitor and report on full life-cycle progress?

c. If you choose to be a B certified company, benchmark with the Dow Jones Sustainability Index, or become ISO 14001 certified, then there are specific requirements for each that will inform certain job and development activities.

d. Hiring and development plans are a direct consequence of how much variance exists between new challenges and current practices. If you make a lot of changes here, then you need to circle back to questions 3 and 4.

6. What is the maturity level of key sustainable business practices and the local business ecosystem?
    a. This provides an assessment of current capability and the basis of a gap assessment.
    b. What is the maturity profile? (Use the five-stage maturity assessment described in chapter 4.)
    c. Are there certain functional areas where you have a clear idea of how to operate with expanded boundaries of accountability?
    d. How do I modify or use development resources for high- and low-maturity areas? What are the economic or social benefits?

7. Where can we run meaningful experiments to gain more information and test key assumptions?
    a. This is an expansion of the point of entry. Persuasion is a key part of change, and good experiments provide the data, stories, and financial arguments for broader-scale actions.
    b. How will changes in a business practice affect how people deliver value, learn new information, and put that to work on behalf of the business? How do I test my assumptions?
    c. What organizations, teams, and roles will offer the most new variable work?

8. What resources do we have to accelerate development?
    a. This amends the assessment of current capability and gap assessment indicated in question 4 and informs a forecast of existing costs and possible time commitments.
    b. What jobs, assignments, or organizations offer unique opportunities for development (development value vs. performance value)?
        i. Begin with considering matching a small number of assignments against the biggest capability needs and gaps.

      ii. The key is to have high-value development jobs and assignments matched with an experienced supervisor with skills as an authentic communicator and key talent developer.

  c. Which positions or people are key generators of critical new knowledge?

  d. What resources can we deploy to capture and codify the new practices that demonstrate incremental or breakthrough innovations?

  e. Which people in the organization have the most positional credibility to drive change? Do they have the skill to be good teachers, coaches, or mentors?

  f. Do I have the right human resource and financial practices to support these changes?

9. How do we scale our new sustainable business practices?

  a. This expands on the plan forecast by adding details and also raises questions about related HR practices, like incentives and retention.

  b. Are our leaders skilled in leading organizational change?

  c. Do we have the resources of an established corporate university or talent development team?

  d. Do we understand how the new challenges affect our best people? Trying to achieve scale in a low-maturity environment puts a greater burden on your high-performers and experts. This suggests a change in expectations for what they do as well as a change in your management, communications, succession planning, and recruiting and recognition systems.

  e. Leaders and individual contributors with specialized knowledge or experience and the capacity to teach are very valuable and likely to be poached by competing firms. How will you support and retain these people?

Using these nine questions as a guide will allow you to design action plans, commit to time lines, and prioritize investments. The development challenges and options listed in Table 9.1 are an illustration of how a company-specific talent development plan may look. Your plan may be substantially larger than the illustration in Table 9.1 (see on pages 176–77), depending on the scale of your business operations, and may require considerable thinking about the relative costs of using external executive education talent (consultants) versus internal resources. Since so many areas involve new knowledge, formally facilitated debriefing sessions and action learning sessions can improve the speed of acquisition and the codifying of new learning. Training executives to serve as discussion leaders is also a strong way to emphasize the importance of the challenges and the organization's commitment to change.

Reader Reflection

IMAGINE you are the head of human resources and also the chief sustainability officer for an agricultural supply business. Your competitive advantage rests on a proprietary technology that uses sensors located on farms to provide business intelligence to farmers, advising them of the optimum time to plant, harvest, and ship products. Your intelligence employs a forecasting model that combines market and international trade data and weather patterns, as well as global warming simulations. You are at heart a high-tech company selling information that can greatly increase the productivity of your client farms.

You are not alone in the company in recognizing that your competitive advantage is tied to the talent and technology you have assembled. Your people are the most productive in the industry and you are rightly proud of the way staff at all levels have embraced your sustainability mission. However, your team has become the envy of others and you are seeing talent being poached by consulting companies and competitors. Several key players have also left to form startups.

More and more staff are speaking at conferences, and many are independently sharing company information or writing about company practices. In addition, the governments of several countries where you have good market share are pressing the company to share more information for free. Government officials argue that such sharing will rapidly decrease hunger levels (SDG 2) and increase sustainable production and consumption (SDG 12). You company is also a member of the UN Global Compact that asks you to "encourage the development and diffusion of environmentally friendly technologies."

Your conflict is this: How can you balance the sustainability agenda with your competitive position? How much information can your company give away without compromising or endangering its business? Should you restrict your staff from publishing or speaking in public? Should you impose non-compete agreements? To complicate matters even further, your business is in a position to raise prices because of your highly productive value proposition. Is this in conflict with your mission and social goals?

Despite the apparent conflicts in this challenge, the issues are driven by success. There are worse problems to have. Maintaining competitive advantage is as difficult as developing it in the first place. What this challenge illustrates well is the issue of balance. As a business grows rapidly, there is a real possibility that we dilute our bench strength, hire the wrong people, overextend our support systems, and lag on training activities. From a talent management perspective, the key is to balance what are highly effective development and training activities with an understanding of your key business drivers. As the last several chapters illustrate, there is value in hiring for passion as well as for legacy. The faster you grow, the more robust and flexible your talent development programs need to be. Your development toolbox can include collaborative green teams that help solve problems and multigenerational programs that provide mentorship while enhancing innovation. The key with a strong competitive position is to prioritize problems and gain perspective on the perceived or authentic value in any solution. The gig economy, complex business ecosystems, and many new challenges will be with us for a long time. The key is to build a strong talent plan that reinforces the leadership behaviors that maintain your sustainable values while the business moves forward.

TAKEAWAY: Build a Company Where Everyone Experiences Personal Growth

- You need a tiered talent plan that emphasizes the different motivations from entry-level to senior-level positions. Multigenerational talent becomes the connective tissue.
- New knowledge discovery is both the challenge and the biggest opportunity. Everyone must be an advocate for learning and every leader must focus on improving the process of innovation, communication, and sharing.
- Your values and purpose become more important that organizational boundaries and structure. Incentives, communication plans, key hires, measurement practices, and key practices all must be aligned with values as the ultimate "test for success."

The focus of this chapter can be summed up by thinking of your organization as an employer of personal growth. When you offer people the opportunity to learn and to learn by doing, and provide meaningful experiments and interesting job assignments to open up the embedding of sustainability, people will come to your door, as the W.S. Badger Company knows.

In chapter 10, I examine the talent development function within the challenge that lies ahead for the sustainable business: how to reframe strategy, evaluate products, generate new social value, and shift resources, while increasing both top- and bottom-line growth.

Table 9.1: Examples of Talent Development Activities for a Sustainable Company

Development Area	Development Challenge	Classification
Understanding of core tenants of sustainable development	Develop a strong understanding of the SDGs and the rationale for each.	Foundation knowledge
Implementing a benefit corporation business model	Learn new practices in social value creation. Translate new vision and purpose into changes at the functional and business unit levels. Change mental models.	Foundation knowledge Mental models Social rituals
Analyzing natural capital financial models	Change mental models. Learn new financial modeling techniques. Build and test model cases for costs and benefits.	Heuristics Mental models Social rituals
Creating financial models for new products and services that provide both economic and social benefit	Assess existing products and services. Learn new financial modeling techniques. Build and test options that match goals.	Foundation knowledge Heuristics
Writing a good benefit corporation report	Produce reports that meet or exceed statutory requirements. Produce narratives that accurately reflect the company story.	Foundation knowledge Heuristics
Communicating social impact	Learn to describe both short-term and long-term social benefits. Communicate progress to key stakeholders.	Foundation knowledge Heuristics
Measuring sustainability and social impact	Learn new techniques for creating new metrics, measurement scorecards, and reporting systems.	Foundation knowledge Heuristics
Negotiating for mutual gain	Adapt negotiation and sales practices to accommodate goals for long-term social and economic value creation.	Foundation knowledge Heuristics Mental models
Business ethics	Establish a strong foundation of business ethics to support new business models.	Heuristics

E-learning, online, or classroom review of key principles related to balancing people, planet, profit, and practices, the United Nations Global Compact, and the Sustainable Development Goals.

E-learning or classroom training on core concepts of clean capitalism, green growth, the importance of B certification as a framework, and the specific variation of the benefit corporation law in your jurisdiction.
Online or classroom case analysis and discussion regarding application of boundary challenges, social value creation, and new heuristics.
Development managers in key functions or business units. Augmented budgets for development activities.
Job rotations and coaching in key development assignments.
Key signature events taught by executives.
New integrated reporting and incentives for high performance.
Innovation events for both products and processes to drive learning and evolve business.

E-learning or classroom review of core concepts of natural capital models.
Partner and meet with NGOs to add complimentary knowledge about natural systems.
Conduct group problem-solving sessions to model systems.
Group debriefing sessions led by senior leaders to debrief options and discuss learning.
Inclusion of natural capital purpose and outcomes in signature events.

Classroom case discussion and innovation labs on the application of new techniques such as smart financing, leasing, and pay-per-use schemes, off-balance sheet operating leases, and performance contracting that improves long-term balance between social and economic value creation.

E-learning on the basics of benefit corporation reporting and statutory requirements.
Team meeting to review samples of goals and desired outcomes and the selection of third-party standards.
Practice sessions to discuss separating "general public benefit" from "specific public benefit." Review of industry best practice reports.
Editorial coaching to create positive story narratives and descriptions of what was learned from failure.

E-learning on the basics of social impact.
Attending conferences and meeting with leading NGOs and social entrepreneurs to learn the challenges and pitfalls of transparency and how to connect values to sustainability and strategy.
Classroom discussions led by outside experts and executives to review the pitfalls of "greenwashing" and the power of strong ethics in communication.
Practice session writing and editing long and short-form communications that connect social outcomes to core beliefs.
Case discussions on the challenges and pitfalls of transparency.
Connecting values to sustainability and strategy.
Working with boundary systems and strategic uncertainty.

E-learning as well as specialty industry conferences on the impact of intangible assets and social outcomes, full life-cycle financial modeling, integrated reporting, and techniques for monetizing social good and assigning financial values to social change.
Classroom training on integrated reporting with case reviews of different techniques such as comparing Gapframe vs. SDSN (Sustainable Development Solutions Network), benchmarking with major indexes, certification models, and gap assessments.
Off-line team assignments to build business test cases with new social and economic variables followed by the application of regression analysis and relational goals.

Classroom reviews of core concepts of principle-based negotiation.
Action learning assignments with technology vendors to implement new integrated reporting requirements.
Team and workflow reviews to align activities and incentives to optimize negotiation preparation, acceptable value creation, and value-sharing practices and the development of sustainable agreements.

E-learning or classroom training on business controls and ethics boundary systems.
Off-line leadership team assignments led by outside facilitator.
Case discussion on ethical dilemmas using multiple stakeholder perspectives.
Specialized training on techniques for dealing with angry stakeholders and crisis management.

Chapter 10

STRATEGIES FOR SUPPORTING AN EVOLVING BUSINESS

"Every single social and global issue of our day is an opportunity in disguise." PETER DRUCKER

I have probably impressed upon you by now that creating a sustainable business model requires a shared commitment within an organization to have social and economic interests simultaneously guide the business. The role of talent development is to help shape the dialog, develop early advocates, capture new knowledge, and anchor the best practices in a new business culture. To use an analogy, you are creating a new building from the ground up, while standing in the framework of the old one.

I learned some of the most important concepts about talent and sustainability from two dissimilar organizations: the United Nations and Galaxy Entertainment. At face value, these organizations don't have much in common, but both operate in talent-constrained environments. When I joined the UN in 2002 as chief learning officer of the United Nations Development Programme (UNDP), all open positions in the Learning

Resources Center were filled prior to my arrival. The reasoning was that a full complement of staff would allow me to hit the ground running. Coming from the private sector, my feeling was the opposite. Leave the positions open until I have the chance to assess our talent requirements. The problem as I saw it was that if you hired first and then created your strategy, it was unlikely that the resources would match.

Working within the UN system was always of matter of working with a highly diverse set of talent and structured work rules. Although the structure initially felt constraining, I understood fairly quickly that most people joined the UN because they wanted to make a difference. I had a team of people from Peru, the Philippines, Kazakhstan, India, Taiwan, Argentina, the US, and another half dozen countries in my New York office alone. In addition, my 156 learning managers represented almost as many countries and cultures. Essentially, I was the outsider joining a community that was purpose driven. The successful talent strategy was about discovering each person's ability, redesigning services to match capabilities, encouraging a shared sense of purpose, and developing partnerships to fill capability gaps. Going in a direction contrary to the system was a losing proposition. Success was about removing barriers and finding new doors to open and unlocking potential.

When I worked with Galaxy Entertainment, one big challenge the company faced was a government requirement that certain job roles be filled by Macanese citizens. The hotel and entertainment companies were growing rapidly, and the island of Macau has a population of only six hundred thousand. Essentially, everyone who wants a job has one. In many instances, if you advertise for a position and someone walks in the door, you hire them. But the goal is not just to hire—that's almost self-defeating when there is always another company wanting to steal your best staff. Rather, the goal is to find the best spot for the person. Job matching and job mobility help ensure you have alignment between a new hire's interest and skills, and so you might lessen turnover from job dissatisfaction.

In Galaxy's situation, one talent development solution was to extend brand building into the community. From a practical perspective, you are helping to reach the next generation of potential employees. By working with the community and giving generously to schools, charities, and local institutions, you build a positive impression of the company and its role as part of the community. Talent development focuses not only on the company as a whole, but also on an interlocking network of communities of interest. Becoming the employer of choice means being more open and transparent, and assuming an active role in social value creation.

In both the UN and Galaxy Entertainment scenarios, social value creation is part of the business model. Unique market conditions provided the opportunity to turn sustainable business practices into a competitive advantage. In many ways, that is the idea behind developing a sustainable talent development organization. So the question to ask yourself is, What are the capabilities I need to make that happen, so that I might capture opportunities and accelerate change whenever and wherever the opportunities exist?

Knowledge Shopping

As you enter the world of sustainable development, there will always be someone who asks about an issue on which you have no expertise. This is the challenge of new knowledge discovery. If a business leader calls and asks if you can help train a team on migrant worker conditions or natural asset pricing, where do you look? One of the most useful tools for a talent development professional is a "heat map," and it is the starting point of building knowledge about any idea.

The heat map concept is a widely used tool for people in the publishing and research professions trying to figure out if an article or book idea is really new and unique. The goal is to outline the core content in a knowledge domain. Let's say, for example, you are the head of talent development in a company and tasked with developing new learning requirements for a sustainable business. The heat map in Figure 10.1 provides a place to start. The categories illustrate common reference points that are easy to

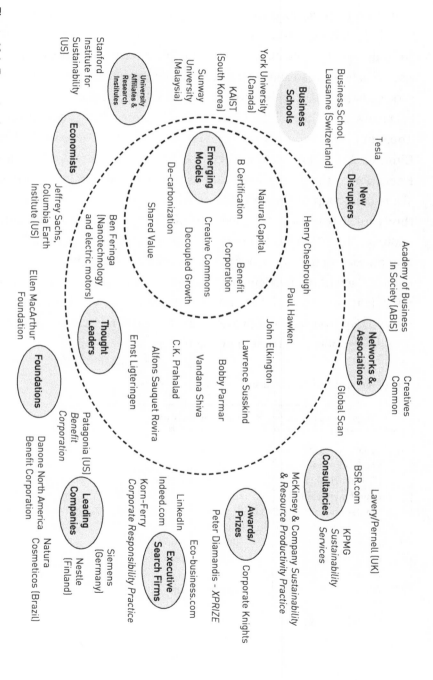

Figure 10.1: Example of a Heat Map

New Disrupters
- Tesla

Business Schools
- Business School Lausanne [Switzerland]
- York University [Canada]
- KAIST [South Korea]
- Sunway University [Malaysia]

University Affiliates & Research Institutes
- Stanford Institute for Sustainability [US]

Economists
- Jeffrey Sachs, Columbia Earth Institute [US]

Emerging Models
- B Certification
- Natural Capital
- Creative Commons
- Benefit Corporation
- De-carbonization
- Decoupled Growth
- Shared Value

Thought Leaders
- Ben Feringa [Nanotechnology and electric motors]
- Henry Chesbrough
- Paul Hawken
- John Elkington
- Lawrence Susskind
- Bobby Parmar
- Vandana Shiva
- C.K. Prahalad
- Alfons Sauquet Rovira
- Ernst Ligteringen

Networks & Associations
- Academy of Business In Society [ABIS]
- Creatives Common
- Global Scan

Foundations
- Ellen MacArthur Foundation

Leading Companies
- Patagonia [US] Benefit Corporation
- Danone North America Benefit Corporation
- Natura Cosméticos [Brazil]
- Siemens [Germany]
- Nestlé [Finland]

Consultancies
- BSR.com
- Lavery/Pernell [UK]
- KPMG Sustainability Services
- McKinsey & Company Sustainability & Resource Productivity Practice
- Korn-Ferry Corporate Responsibility Practice

Awards/Prizes
- Corporate Knights
- Peter Diamandis - XPRIZE

Executive Search Firms
- Indeed.com
- LinkedIn
- Eco-business.com

181

search. You can look at consultancies for applied research and academics for thought leadership. Many recruiters and executive search firms can offer insight on what competitive companies are looking for in new hires and how difficult it is to find such people. Leading companies, award programs, and foundations all offer insights. The combination of alternatives gives you a sense of how broad and deep a new knowledge domain is and how it has evolved over time, and also provides you with target partnerships.

During my tenure at the United Nations, I created a program called Top5, in cooperation with Columbia University and Professor William Eimicke. At the time, he was director of the Picker Center for Executive Education at the Graduate School of International and Public Affairs. We had a group of fifteen students who participated in five teams of three. Each team was assigned one of the five regions of the world addressed by UNDP and were tasked with finding five types of information on each of the five major practice areas in UNDP (hence the Top5 name). Each of the participants was able to be involved part-time, and my staff at the New York Learning Resources Center would set up interviews as appropriate and provide access to UN reports and libraries. The basic model is illustrated in Table 10.1.

Table 10.1: Model for Top5 Students to Follow

UNDP Regions	UNDP Practice Areas	Types of Information
1. Eastern Europe and CIS States (17 countries) 2. Latin America and the Caribbean (33 countries) 3. Arab States (20 countries and territories) 4. Asia & Pacific (9 countries) 5. Africa (46 countries)	1. Democratic governance 2. Crisis prevention and recovery 3. Sustainable energy and the environment 4. HIV/AIDS and other pandemic diseases 5. Gender mainstreaming	1. Practice leaders 2. Organizations (NGOs, charities, etc.) 3. Academic institutions 4. Conferences 5. Publications

The difference between the general heat map (Figure 10.1) and the Top5 model is that the latter forces you to look for specific types of information in specific regions. Our interest in NGOs and charities was specific to the kinds of work the UN did. Although the model missed some smaller areas of interest, it provided an easy-to-use framework and was generally comprehensive. At the end of the exercise, we had a good idea of the key organizations and leaders in each region, what they wrote about, and what they discussed when they met. From this we were able to build our curriculum and research tracking systems to keep tabs on new ideas as they emerged.

In recent years, I adapted the idea to create a company called Top5 Learning, which provides research to support my consulting business. I might be working with an agricultural company like East-West Seed one week and a hotel and casino company like Galaxy Entertainment the next. In almost every assignment, there were areas of knowledge that were new or where the company was seeking new competitive ideas on thought or practice leadership. After some experimentation, we came up with a model that worked well for most companies. We broadened the UN Top5 experiment to include all global regions. We applied the research model to any practice area of interest to a client, but covered five standard sources of information: publications (both long and short form), conferences, leaders (thought and practice), award programs, and investments. The latter two categories were often the most interesting since they provided both a current and a prospective view. The awards tell you something about how peers and industry associations view a set of accomplishments and the trail of venture investments suggest emerging areas of interest or innovation.

New Talent Development Capability	Value Proposition
Knowledge Shopping	• Assess a knowledge domain by identifying key thought and practice leaders, conferences, publications, awards, and investments. • Use the "heat map" to network for ideas and establish the validity of recommendations on development activities, training, or partnerships.

Data Management and Statistical Analysis

The next useful skill set allows you to drill down into the heat map. Data analytics has been a growing field for twenty years, and the ability to understand data relationships, patterns, and principles is an essential skill for contributing to new business models and making differentiated talent investment recommendations. Access to growing pools of data and improved data management tools make it much easier to test and refine new knowledge or make insights. The tendency has been for the HR and talent development functions to have access only to a select pool of HR staffing data, often described in terms that must be translated for other business executives.

Your talent strategy must be based on the same business data that key executives use to make key decisions. Your talent development plan must be worded in specific terms to support decisions that add to competitive differentiation in clear and meaningful ways. Having a seat at the table means positioning the talent development function as a key enabler of the new strategic priority—sustainability. Understanding the language of data analytics and statistical analysis allows you to participate in the conversation as an equal. The business challenge is to reframe strategy, evaluate products, generate new social value, and shift resources, while increasing both top- and bottom-line growth. If you can recommend something that supports those decisions, you will be on the team.

Over the next decade, it is likely that all learning solutions will be blended designs since they enable capture of key learning data that can be processed with machine learning. This has been one of the takeaways from massive open online courses (MOOCs). Although the MOOC design does not drive better learning outcomes in all situations, the online format allows the capture of thousands of more data points. Ever more powerful analytical engines will identify patterns and relationships that previously were too difficult or labor intensive to mine. The use of integrated data systems will connect learning and development interactions with business data and results. Enterprise-level data analytics will transform just-in-time learning by generating insights into when and where an intervention can be connected to changes in social and economic value creation.

New Talent Development Capability	Value Proposition
Data Management and Statistical Analysis	• How can I use statistical analysis to connect business activities to the creation of new social and economic value? • How do I link that value creation to specific people or roles and enhanced capabilities linked to specific priority actions?

Content Editing and Curation

An area of increasing importance is the curation of knowledge. During my time at Harvard Business Publishing (HBSP), I sat on the executive committee that oversaw the different businesses, including Harvard Business Press (books), the Harvard Business Review (magazine, website, and blogs), our higher education business (case studies, exercises, and teaching guides), and our corporate business (conferences, distance learning, and e-learning). Each part of the business had expertise in content design, story-telling, and editing. It was a personal reflection that the talent and business structure of HBSP was more likely the future of a learning organization than the typical structure of a corporate university.

Knowledge creation has increased exponentially over the years, and it is now possible to access great libraries of content anywhere in the world. The missing capabilities are quality editing and curation. A flood of information serves no one. How can one tell what information is reliable and which is not? Are sources of equal value? Is the content copyrighted or not (meaning, is its use freely permitted or permitted for a fee paid to the copyright holder)? A key talent development strategy is to help the organization with both the internal and external knowledge flows, both by helping the organization value different kinds of knowledge and by performing quality editing and curation tasks on different story forms: blogs and notes; longer-form research papers; and digital story-telling such as videos, e-learning, and lessons based on experience.

Effective knowledge curation requires an understanding of both internal and external knowledge and its relative value to the business. Not all knowledge has the same value or offers the same leverage. For example, what is the value of a university partnership conducting research on Gapframe design or integrated reporting? How expensive is it to build data models on natural capital financing? Is the information organized in a way that employees in every function know how it applies to them? How rapidly can the organization take such information and make it available to front-line staff? Does the working knowledge offer the company new competitive advantage? Figure 10.2 offers a simple way to begin organizing content areas by their relative value to the business. Is the knowledge unique to the company? If yes, how much has the company invested? How difficult would it be to replace? Was the knowledge co-created with partners? Is that knowledge documented or is it represented by key staff? Some knowledge is based on a copyright or patent holder and must be licensed (independent research and intellecutal property). Still other knowledge may be in the public domain or considered a commodity available from multiple sources of equal value and quality. In my experience, most talent development functions would not have the skills to answer these questions.

Understanding the value of information allows you to make better judgments about sharing. Sustainable Development Goal 17 asks everyone to "strengthen collaboration on global challenges," and the ninth principle in the UN Global Compact asks everyone to "share environmentally friendly technology." Sharing knowledge is part of social value creation. A challenge for the business is to determine how much knowledge is proprietary and how much to give away. This can have significant revenue, cost, and brand implications. If you want a seat at the executive table, I think there are open chairs for people who can help solve these challenges.

Content or knowledge curation is linked to the Creative Commons, founded by Lawrence Lessig (see chapter 8). It bears repeating that the more the talent development function is involved with new knowledge creation, sustainability experiments, and business prototyping, the more it can take a lead on the release of internally generated or co-created content to ensure that it is appropriately registered for sharing. Given the volume of content creation in many organizations,

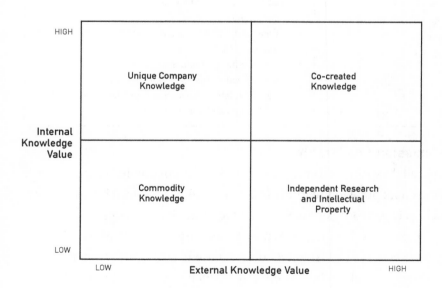

Figure 10.2: What Types of Knowledge Are the Most Valuable to Your Company?

this can be an important contribution both to value capture and social value sharing.

There is also another essential skill area: case development. As a company solves problems associated with sustainability and discovers new opportunities, the early successes and failures are all opportunities for learning. A well-constructed case allows teams to discuss a problem scenario as well as the solutions. Cases offer an opportunity for learning, but they also serve as a social ritual that forms team bonds and helps to change mental models. Role-plays, decision scenarios, text cases, and video cases are all sources of knowledge discovery and can reveal new business practices, ethical dilemmas, and new challenges like social value creation.

New Talent Development Capability	Value Proposition
Content Editing and Curation	• Make use of Creative Commons content to reduce costs. • Share internally generated or co-created content to add new social value creation to the business and community. • Case development (text and video) of key successes and failures. • Improve internal and external knowledge use as the company creates new heuristics and codifies new foundation knowledge meeting sustainability challenges and opportunities.

Discussion Leadership

A parallel capability to content creation is discussion leadership, which is the conceptual foundation of case teaching as practiced by institutions such as Harvard Business School. One of the key challenges for adopting sustainable business practices is the large amount of new knowledge discovery. That suggests that a content-centric or teacher-centric approach is likely to be less effective. Much of the new knowledge will be in the hands of the staff closest to the problem, and group discussions engage them in the learning process. As such, the user-centric or student-centric approach to knowledge sharing benefits from the skill of an excellent discussion leader in much the same way as new knowledge creation benefits from excellent editing and curation skills.

The goal of discussion leadership is to have a skilled discussion leader who asks questions and elicits and extends the peer-to-peer dialog that ensues. The discussion leader can identify key "teachable moments" that may be unique to that group of participants. The best discussion leaders make the process seem effortless. I have taught classes in discussion leadership at several companies and have seen new discussion leaders struggle to keep an exchange going for thirty minutes, while others can take the same material and have a robust dialog lasting ninety minutes or more.

This skill area can be developed in partnership with a university that already possesses experienced practitioners. By co-developing the content and ensuring processes are in place for skill transfer, a full-year investment can provide substantial long-term value.

The case-development process requires three skill sets. First is the actual writing of the case and teaching notes described above in the curation and editing section. Second is the skill with which you brief a team on case preparation and the expectations for case-study teams. This second area is very important but also relatively easy to master. The third part is managing an interactive dialog among fifteen to thirty participants by the discussion leader. This process is one of the most effective ways to teach critical thinking skills.

The best reference material I have seen on this topic is *Education for Judgment: The Artistry of Discussion Leadership*,[1] in which the late Harvard professor Roland Christensen described the case method as the "art of managing uncertainty."[2] This, he argued, is largely because case scenarios often don't have one right answer and may involve multiple learning outcomes. Although the case method has been in service for a long time, it is a skill set that can be adapted and enhanced in service of building a sustainable business organization.

New Talent Development Capability	Value Proposition
Discussion Leadership	• Provide a knowledge transfer environment for the most relevant new business challenges and differentiators. • Provide development of critical thinking skills in new areas critical to the business. • Provide a structured forum for business leaders to interact with key staff on exploring the implications of key business decisions and possible ethical dilemmas.

Experience Design

The final area critical to helping a bold company scale new business processes and talent development is experience design, a craft that has evolved considerably over the years. In-house content design has changed because technology offers new opportunities for realism; however, the core skill remains excellence in story-telling. Self-directed video development, video cases, and teaching scenarios all enhance the learning experience. However, social challenges offer a new set of opportunities. Immersive job development experiences, particularly with real-life problems, can be enlightening. The key skill areas are developing external partnerships and setting the stage for the development experience.

During my tenure at the United Nations Development Program (UNDP), we developed a series of programs with corporate partners (mostly professional services firms) to help solve problems in developing countries. A small team of high-potential managers at a corporate firm would spend four to six weeks in a middle-income country using their consulting skills to solve a local community problem. It provided a development experience that participants universally enjoyed. The goals were always community oriented and the experience was often described as the most important development experiences in the participant's life.

I would describe my own time at the UN in similar terms. Challenging social tasks with a strong emotional component inspire a level of hard work and commitment. I have had the chance to travel from Syria to Togo, Ghana to Nepal, and Armenia to Brazil. The world is full of great opportunities to do good works.

I recall a conversation I had with a world-leading expert in leadership development while I was at the UN. I wanted him to participate in a program we called the Virtual Development Academy, or VDA. We were training sixty to seventy high-potential participants each year from approximately fifty countries. Most of the training was virtual, but we brought everyone together for a two-week intensive experience and I wanted to have a superb faculty. My problem was that I was limited by UN rules regarding how much I could pay. When I pitched the idea by phone, the expert indicated his standard rate was US$20,000 per day but that he would work for a nonprofit like the UN at a discounted rate of $12,000 to $15,000 a day. Unfortunately, my actual limit was closer to $2500 per day. Although I had some flexibility, we were far apart. I told him my limit and he questioned why he should do the job for that amount.

In most instances this may have been the end of the conversation, but good experience design means the learning experience must have a value proposition that is positive for all stakeholders. Although I had little cash to work with, I did have unique access to a lot of other things. I suggested he would be working with an audience he would never otherwise meet while doing great work for the world. I would start the program at an 11th-century library in Syria in the ancient Fertile Crescent. We would all travel to a desert oasis, where he would teach his cases in the restored amphitheater of Assyrian kings. At night we would debrief in a big tent under a starlit sky and enjoy local food. I threw in that he would stand in the same place as ancient philosophers like Aristotle. Although I had no idea if Aristotle had ever been there, it seemed like a good close to my argument. He agreed to participate.

New Talent Development Capability	Value Proposition
Experience Design	• Improve internal content development in video cases, e-learning, and self-directed staff videos. • Link experience design to your new mission orientation. • Build capability in story-telling that reinforces the emotional connection from strong social value creation.

Developing External Partnerships

Developing external partnerships is a great opportunity for talent development in non-traditional areas like social value creation. In many instances, there are opportunities if you apply a little creativity and assess your resources. Rethinking your business boundaries will also provide a new set of options and challenges. Many executives and employees may have existing relationships with nonprofits. It is also true that many nonprofits are often cash poor. Your ability to add resources, convene meetings, or underwrite travel can open doors to many opportunities that will have disproportionate development value.

While at UNDP I found opportunities to use a partnership model to increase social value creation while reducing costs. UNDP had a practice area focused on democratic governance that helped promote free national elections. We identified an opportunity to partner with the Dutch Development Agency that focused on local elections in sub-Saharan countries. We combined training resources to improve the services available to both organizations while enhancing the alignment between our outcomes at the national and local level.

Corporations also have the opportunity to self-fund social value initiatives when they see strong alignment with the company purpose. One of my former clients in Thailand whom we have discussed, East-West Seed Company (EWS), developed a nonprofit subsidiary, the SEVIA Foundation, which uses EWS staff and external resources to teach farmers sustainable practices and what they call "seedsmanship." EWS sells hybrid seeds to farmers in developing markets like India, Thailand, and the Philippines, but sets social goals to help build local capability, improve local seed stock, and enhance farmers' lives. The training from SEVIA is offered for free. The business targeted new areas for growth in sub-Saharan Africa and paved the way with SEVIA activities in Tanzania, Benin, and Nigeria. Having better-educated and more productive farmers offers opportunities for East-West Seed while helping to sustain and improve local communities.

One opportunity for any sustainable business is to find an NGO, charity, or local community group aligned with your business purpose and strategic priorities. Such organizations offer real and beneficial opportunities for co-created value.

New Talent Development Capability	Value Proposition
Develop External Partnerships	• Assess internal connections and networks for partnership opportunities. • Find potential partners with depth of expertise in areas where you have little. • Build relationships with external partners that offer unique development opportunities in social value creation.

Reader Reflection

IMAGINE you are the leader of a subsidiary of a business that has a strong manufacturing presence in equatorial countries. You are one of several manufacturing sites that make up a global supply chain. Your part of the business has been growing, thanks to competitive local labor costs, investments in local infrastructure, and strong productivity growth. As a geographic subsidiary, you have your own support staff for human resources, training, and sustainability, and a reasonable amount of autonomy to make decisions. However, you are expected to coordinate with the heads of functional departments and with corporate HQ.

Your business operates with a triple bottom line that has been enshrined in your profit-and-loss statement. Because your plant is located in a developing country with a history of inequality, you have been tasked with taking a leadership position on SDGs 5 (Gender Equality) and 10 (Reduced Inequalities). Objectively, your metrics say you are making progress. You have hired more women into management positions, increased salaries across the board, improved equal treatment of staff, and greatly expanded training opportunities. But there are other serious issues you are very concerned about. Rising temperatures have made many dietary staples and fresh water more expensive. Women have traditionally shouldered the burden of home care and child rearing, which makes it more difficult for female staff to work overtime, leading to increased absenteeism. Unbearable heat means that incomes are being consumed by the costs of food, electricity, health care, and elder care. People in the poorest communities are suffering the most.

You are committed to the idea of sustainability, but heat is not on your list of SDGs. However, it seems to be the new face of inequality. But how do you solve the problem? The more communities and families suffer, the more difficult it is for you to increase the number of women in your workforce and the greater the impact on productivity. If you increase wages further, you may lose business to cheaper providers. What is your level of commitment to solving the inequality problems? Where do you draw the line?

Just when you thought you had a clear framework for seventeen Sustainable Development Goals, a new one emerges. Will higher temperatures create a new wave of inequality? It is distinctly possible. As the first section of the book illustrates, the term "sustainability" has evolved quite a bit over the last one hundred-plus years. It is reasonable to expect that it will continue to change. Therein lies the value in new strategies that support an evolving business. Each of the talent development capabilities illustrated in this chapter is designed to improve the quality of your information, enhance your market awareness, reduce your risk, or fill an emerging knowledge gap. Collectively these capabilities provide you with the ability to see emerging trends and have more time for internal dialog and solution development. A heat map, as illustrated in Figure 10.1, can help you develop a new curriculum model, but it can also provide you with clarity on the overall market. Some questions can help with perspective. Ask yourself,

- Does anyone else around me see this emerging SDG or am I the first?
- Is there a small group of early adopters that I can partner with?
- If I do several heat maps over time, will I see a change in perceptions or an increased awareness of the problem?

Used well, these capabilities will enhance your organizational agility and improve your response time.

TAKEAWAY: Opportunity Lies in the Intersection of New Knowledge Creation, Sustainability Experiments, and Business Prototyping

Business transitions to sustainable practices require investment in unique skill development. Part of the effort will focus on new knowledge discovery and the development of new internal knowledge. The talent development function will need to evolve to provide appropriate support. Four key areas for growth include

- data management and statistical analysis;
- content editing and curation;
- discussion leadership; and
- experience design.

You are probably wondering where these investments can pay off. This is the focus of the next chapter.

Chapter 11

KEY AREAS FOR TRAINING AND GROWTH

"Education is our passport to the future, for tomorrow belongs to the people who prepare for it today."
MALCOLM X

In our discussion of talent planning and development, growing and retaining talent includes hiring, onboarding, and training, as well as offering an environment that optimizes talent potential. The process covers incentives to culture and key business practices. In relation to sustainability, it also includes new areas of accountability and new performance values. While this process undoubtedly sounds familiar to you, I wish to emphasize that even with the best investments in talent, sustaining a mission-based business over time is hard: the business grows, the sustainability movement evolves, and customer preferences change. In addition, bold changes in business models can often drive a company into uncertain territory, and companies can lose their way. We've seen executives at high-growth companies like Satyam Computer, Tyco, Computer Associates, and Enron convicted of fraud, misuse of company funds, or worse.[1]

In the case of sustainability, there is a temptation to engage in "green-washing," which is the practice of painting a company's actions as much greener or sustainable than they really are. Checks and balances are a necessary part of good governance, and good governance is a product of shared accountability, business controls, and strong ethics. In this chapter, I will discuss values in relation to the new sustainability curriculum.

Changing the Way You Do Product Design

Product design is one of the most important considerations for sustainability. A complex product with unusual materials may make it hard to service, repair, or recycle. Certain choices may increase the use of limited resources, extend a supply chain, or challenge end-of-life disposal. As noted earlier, Patagonia founder Yvon Chouinard created a series of design standards that have been codified into the Patagonia YC Scorecard.[2] The scorecard is used to review and score new product options on issues such as simplicity of design, functional use, and ease of repair. This is a test for success. The scorecard is based on a ten-point scale and scored by several design team members. The average scores from the team serve as a way to examine how the products measure up in their "functional, social, and environmental performance."[3] Criteria include the following:

- Does it cause any unnecessary environmental harm? Without sacrificing quality, could it have been made in a less environmentally harmful or more sustainable manner?
- Is the product a responsible choice from birth to death?[4]

The product scorecard can then be matched with customer-facing measures such as satisfaction, quality, and fit. From a development perspective, this drives several considerations:

- Does your company have a test for success like the YC scorecard that guides decisions?

- Are incentives aligned to reward successful use of your test for success?
- Are business practices simple, easy to apply, and effective?

In this instance, the talent development question in product development is, how do you drive consistent team behavior with an evolving core process? The use of practical scorecards and guides lessens demand for pre-training or classroom training. The emphasis shifts to the process itself and the facilitation of real-world decision-making or product-development scenarios by team leaders. New staff are trained on the job by seasoned staff and during actual product development activities. Scaling successful processes is more about leadership behavior, the consistency and clarity of your practices, and the vibrancy of your integrated reporting. The more such frameworks are used, the more people think about the choices they make and are motivated to collectively seek improvements.

Changing the Way You Do Sourcing

Sourcing or supply chain management is one of the key target areas for improvement in a sustainable business. This also includes a separate procurement function in many organizations. The simplest and most direct impact of sourcing is a company's carbon footprint. The global supply chain favors manufacturing in low-wage jurisdictions, which may mean long-range shipping of manufactured goods. As such, sustainable supply chain management offers a huge opportunity to ameliorate carbon emissions from transportation, as well as to improve the choice of materials, manufacturing processes that produce emissions, labor practices, wages, worker safety, and local community well-being and development. The range of possible impact also offers enormous opportunities to improve sustainable outcomes while also driving business efficiency and reducing costs.

As many companies have discovered, supply chain choices can have a significant impact on brand identity and corporate risks. In 2012, *The*

New York Times reported on problems in Apple's supply chain, noting,

Two years ago, 137 workers at an Apple supplier in eastern China were injured after they were ordered to use a poisonous chemical to clean iPhone screens. Within seven months last year, two explosions at iPad factories, including in Chengdu, killed four people and injured 77.[5]

The report was a significant challenge for a company known for quality and innovation. Global footwear and apparel company Nike had experienced problems as far back as the 1990s, with reports of abusive and coercive labor practices in suppliers. Although both companies have bounced back from opposition campaigns, they were forced to recognize that a strong consumer brand means leading the industry in sustainability practices.

Global food company Kraft Heinz has gone so far as to make what it called a modern-day anti-slavery statement:

The Kraft Heinz Foods Company and its direct and indirect subsidiaries (collectively "Kraft Heinz") is committed to Growing a Better World by enhancing the quality of people's lives through sustainability, health and wellness, and social responsibility. Kraft Heinz places a high value on an ethical and transparent supply chain, and supports initiatives aimed to eradicate slavery and human trafficking. Kraft Heinz demands all business partners demonstrate a clear commitment to protecting the rights of workers worldwide, and does not tolerate the use of forced labor—including human trafficking and slavery.[6]

One of the key phrases in this statement is "direct and indirect subsidiaries." This opens up the idea that if you work with or for the Kraft Heinz Company you are responsible for both tier 1 suppliers and tier 2 suppliers (suppliers of your suppliers).

What has changed since the original Nike and Apple problems is the adoption by 194 countries around the world of the UN Sustainable Development Goals. Most large companies, like Nike and Apple, are also participants in the United Nations Global Compact. There are now clearer definitions and measures, as well as more independent groups that seek to monitor and report on problems. Ten years ago, it may have been sufficient to look at worker safety in your primary suppliers and ask them to sign a statement. Now you might be responsible for reports on wage purchasing power parity, toxic chemical exposures, and waste stream reporting, as well as tier 2 supplier usage of migrant workers, the presence of labor fees paid to recruiters to get a job, and a host of other possibilities. Each change in boundary accountability raises the bar on knowledge and skill requirements.

Finance and Integrated Reporting

The finance and reporting areas are ground zero in any attempt to remake a company to focus on more sustainable business practices. Expanding boundary definitions in a business, such as "natural asset pricing," can have profound implications for business costs and product decisions. Dow Chemical Company (US) works with the Natural Capital Coalition[7] on ways to value both the costs and benefits of sustainable and non-sustainable resources. The company uses the Ecosystem Services Identification & Inventory (ESII) Tool (downloadable as an app). The goal is to input data from the use of a natural ecosystem (like wetlands and estuaries) and then examine the trade-offs from business activities. For example, in making a decision about the use of water in production processes, the company can value the cost of land and installing water filtration resources under its control with the natural recharge rates of the water source and any costs for maintaining the water volume and quality. The company can also consider the same business and natural costs for any company discharge.

The ESII software uses information about physical and biological processes to help create outputs that can be integrated with more typical financial analytics. If you are in engineering, operations, or the supply chain function, there is a clear need to partner with the finance department on the development of scenarios to be used in decision-making. As the typical keeper of company scorecards and reporting dashboards, the finance department will need to upskill in new areas to form a better understanding of natural asset valuations, monetizing of both direct and indirect effects, and improved integration of business reporting. In Dow's case, the company established a Valuing Nature goal that has two parts:

- *By 2020, all capital, real estate, new business development, and new product-development projects at Dow will be screened using Nature's Future Value assessments, a tool [it] developed with The Nature Conservancy to measure the value of ecosystem services.*
- *By 2025, Dow will deliver US$1 billion in value through projects that are both good for business and better for nature.*[8]

A major contributor to the development of a natural capital protocol has been sportswear company Puma, which has been experimenting with an EPL (environmental profit and loss) accounting system since 2010. The challenge has been to capture data on all of the inputs and outputs needed to produce one kilogram (2.2 pounds) of raw material in a supply chain that may include dozens of different types of material such as leather, cotton, or wool sourced from different regions. A further complication is the need to consider the impact over a multiyear time frame and trying to interpret that data within an annual report. Over time, natural capital data models will contain tens of thousands of data points and reinforce the need for enhanced data management and statistical modeling skills.

Integrated reporting will be an increasingly important area, since the company will need to understand costs and benefits from decisions across the company. If the business uses a new practice called "net benefit," then one function (likely finance) will need to consider the total impact of all decisions, both negative and positive, to gather an overall company score. If the company uses Global Reporting Initiative (GRI) reporting standards,[9] then there will be numerous reporting requirements across the business that need to be organized and synthesized for general disclosures, management practices, and topic-specific reporting on economic, social, and environmental goals. If your company chooses to register as a B Corp and undergoes a B Impact Assessment, then there may be additional public reporting as well as independent assessment and auditing requirements.

Two leaders in the area of integrated reporting are Harvard Business School (HBS) professors Robert Eccles and George Serafeim. They have created an executive education program at HBS called Aligning Sustainability with Corporate Performance. Dr. Eccles in particular has argued for the integration of what had been separate reporting cycles for traditional financial reports and often nonfinancial CSR reports.[10] This approach tries to capture both the traditional value metrics used in standard corporate reports and what are often called "externalities," which is the value captured by our communities and the environment.

The significance of integrated reporting on investment decisions is substantial, since intangible assets measure a larger percentage of a company's shareholder value. Qualitative performance indicators, as well as qualitative statements about short- and long-term goals that include the influence of externalities, become a key part of both reporting and company dialog. Done well, integrated reporting influences decision-making and becomes a form of management control as well as governance for the sustainable organization.

The preceding three content areas—product design, sourcing, and integrated reporting—generally make a lot of sense to people when I give presentations. They can relate to the practices, see the business value, and feel "at home" discussing the expansion of boundaries in each area. The next domain is less comfortable. Although "ethics" is not an unknown topic, the practice of operationalizing ethics in day-to-day business is less clear and worthy of management time. As a business begins to discuss broader issues of social value, ethics form the foundation of effective management controls and organizational decision-making.

Business Ethics

Business ethics have a strong connection to the business values that underlie sustainability. In turn, values and sustainability goals address endemic issues such as those underlying poverty and inequality. These issues can also include worker health, safety, and education; factors like the illegal movement of money; and fraudulent business practices. Galaxy Entertainment in Macau has made ethical compliance a core part of its training by providing new-hire training, annual workshops, and specialized programs on money laundering, bribery, terrorism, and corruption. Galaxy has also developed the Know Your Customer (KYC) program and conducts various risk assessments to reinforce its management practices.

A greater focus on social outcomes can immerse your business in diverse subjects, from local drug addiction, as happened at W.S Badger Company;[11] to money laundering, as happened at Galaxy Entertainment;[12] to migrant worker issues, as happened at Patagonia.[13] Ad hoc discussions of new business scenarios are a strong part of developing organizational competence and a shared mental model. This is where leaders add great value by serving as discussion leaders, asking open-ended questions, and eliciting peer-to-peer dialog. Such discussions often enhance shared knowledge but also create a call to action.

Professor Bidhan "Bobby" Parmar at the University of Virginia has done considerable research on the purpose of business, and observes, "When companies exist only to maximize profits for shareholders we get disasters, like the BP oil spill [or] . . . engineers cheating on emission tests at Volkswagen." He emphasizes that the real debate is not if we should care about profits, but *how*.[14] New sustainable business models put additional stakeholder groups on par with shareholders. It is no longer the case that everything must be done to maximize shareholder value. A balance in value creation (e.g., profits, jobs, and healthy communities) requires strong boundary systems that allow the company to make progress but also deal with the inevitable tensions and mistakes.

Ethical standards in a sustainable business need to have flexibility, since both the challenges and expectations are evolving. The example of Unilever helps illustrate the challenge. The company is routinely cited for its commitment to sustainability. It is rightly credited with making substantial reductions in water, energy, and greenhouse gas emissions, and for increasing the percentage of sustainably sourced agricultural products to more than 50 percent. However, leaders at Unilever had to deal with long-standing problems from the company's Hindustan Unilever Limited subsidiary, which was closed in 2001 due to mercury pollution. Although the actions that led to the mercury pollution preceded many who are currently in the front office, how the company applies new ethical and sustainability standards is a major test. Maintaining strong values requires leaders to address failures by balancing multiple stakeholder perspectives.

The development path for a larger business making a bold transition to a sustainable business model requires basic training for all managers on ethical standards. These are often codified in statements to guide everyday behavior. Beyond that, selected employees need to have skills in stakeholder analysis, dealing with contrary stakeholders, and negotiating practices for delivering on shared value creation.

If business ethics is a challenging subject of conversation, the next area for focus will need a special introduction. As I have discovered from many presentations, starting a conversation on religion or national identity often sets off warning bells in a leadership group. However, despite my reservations, I feel that this is a critical conversation.

An increasing number of businesses, both large corporations and SMEs, now rely on cross-border or international customers. Technology has reduced the barriers to selling outside a home market, and consequently talent development must accommodate the changing realities of globalization as well as the way sustainable business practices are recognized by different countries and their impact in those countries. Two areas often missing from international talent development are the topics of nationalism, or national identity, and religion.

In countries like the Philippines and Indonesia, public distrust in government and rising inequality have led to the election of populist presidents Rodrigo Duterte and Joko Widodo. Both are nontraditional candidates and political outsiders. A referendum in the UK led to the Brexit vote and a retreat from the European Union, while rising nationalism has been a key part of elections in India and China. The United States and many European countries have seen a rise in anti-immigration sentiment, and once-secular democracies like Turkey, India, and Pakistan have seen a rise in conflicts between religious philosophy and national law. In regional provinces of northern India, for example, unelected councils, called *khap panchayats*, may often be involved in local disputes.

In a company with a complex global supply chain, there is an increased need to understand how religion and national identity affect local attitudes, decision-making, and dispute resolution.

Understanding the Importance of Religion and National Identity

During my time working for the United Nations Development Program, I visited a number of countries, from Thailand to Togo to Armenia, where people have very strong connections with national identity or religion. The senior business leaders or government officials were often trained in the best local or international schools, and many were highly articulate and multilingual. However, when I was invited to people's homes for dinner, it was easy to see the diversity of generations and extended families with very different backgrounds. The deep-seated beliefs of families and friends, as well as perceptions fed by local and international media, play a role in how communities perceive a business or the need for social change. If you now find yourself responsible for issues like poverty and inequality, you will need at least a broad understanding of national identity and religion.

Over 75 percent of the people on planet Earth espouse a belief in or connection with one of the five major religions: Christianity, Islam, Judaism, Hinduism, and Buddhism.[15] Another 1.1 billion consider themselves agnostic/atheistic or align themselves with a folk religion. That represents 90 percent of us. The guiding principles of each of these major faiths or philosophies are highly aligned with helping people, preserving nature, and doing good. These belief systems are also the foundation for traits such as trust, commitment, loyalty, and respect that form the basis for strong ethical systems. However, nothing in my suggestion is intended to convert someone from their chosen faith. I view a better understanding of faith and philosophy as a tool to improve collaboration and increase shared value creation and positive sustainable change. International talent development should, therefore, include a greater understanding of both national identity and religion.

A wonderful story about the impact of religion and local culture comes from Southeast Asia. Rosewood has been a highly sought-after resource in almost all tropical regions of the world. The wood is extremely strong and produces a light fragrant odor many years after being cut. It is used in furniture, musical instruments, and as a building material. For many years, the forests of Thailand, Cambodia, and Laos were generally not overcut, until other global sources became overharvested. According to a BBC documentary *The Silent Forest*,[16] during a nine-year period most of the larger rosewood trees in Thailand, Cambodia, and Laos were felled to support Chinese demand for *hongmu* (rosewood) furniture. According to the BBC, "The value of that rosewood is greater than all of the illegally harvested elephant ivory, rhino horn, and tiger parts in the world." Rosewood furniture is seen as conveying status, an increasingly important value proposition for a rising middle class. A poor local farmer can make three months of a typical wage for only a week's worth of harvesting rosewood. It is a strong incentive.

This example creates an intersection of resource depletion and poverty with high economic demand, hardly an isolated issue in many parts of the world. The impact of religion can be seen in the adornment of large rosewood trees with yellow cloths. In many villages, adorning rosewood trees in this way reduced the illegal harvests. In Buddhist culture as well as traditional native practices, the yellow ribbons signify that the tree has a spirit. You can easily see this practice even in large cities like Bangkok, where parking lots, walls, and buildings are often built to accommodate a large tree perceived as special. That cultural tradition is passed on to current generations: twelve-year-old boys in Thailand, Myanmar, Laos, and Cambodia often spend four to six weeks on retreat with Buddhist monks, wearing the yellow robes and learning the applied practice of Buddhist life.

Religion is increasingly a flashpoint for cultural misunderstandings. These are often areas where the economic value creation model of a business can come into conflict with local social challenges like poverty, education, safe cities, and immigration. An understanding of faith and religion offers the international leader a better way to interact with local communities and build bridges with shared value creation. It offers lessons on missteps to avoid and stakeholder concerns that require attention, and opportunities for working productively with communities.

Reader Reflection

IMAGINE you are a small business loan supervisor with a large community bank. While your career is in its early stages, you have already been promoted once. You have a good relationship with your boss and know that a new, higher-paying job with more responsibility may open up shortly. You are rightly proud of your accomplishments and feel that you can do well if you commit to working hard. You have a real passion for sustainability, but are envious of friends who work in businesses where their contribution seems to have a more direct impact.

Among your friends and acquaintances is one who works for a pharmaceutical company that trains nursing students to meet the needs of inner-city communities and another who works for a small manufacturing company with a goal of zero carbon emissions. As you process paperwork and review loan applications, you don't always see the social benefit from your activities. You see the trend among banking and investment companies that are evaluating how their lending supports positive social outcomes. For example,

- a bank that has made loans to a consortium of small businesses to improve the local business ecosystem;
- another bank that is focusing part of its portfolio on coastal communities that are threatened by global warming; and
- other lenders that have made specific provisions for supporting sustainable energy and infrastructure projects.

You'd like to be involved in something similar, but your bank does not seem as progressive.

You have shared your interest and concerns with colleagues, and many seem to feel as you do. You have also started volunteering in local community activities and feel good about both what you do and the results of your volunteer work.

Is it time for a change? Should you bring your concerns to your boss or someone else in the organization? Should you start a grassroots movement within the bank? Who do you approach and how do you get started? Does it make more sense to leave your job for a more progressive business?

If you are a business leader or a talent deployment professional, this reader reflection is a warning sign. There is ample evidence that millennial--generation workers are highly attracted to mission- and purpose-based organizations. There is also every reason to believe that this tendency will not only continue but accelerate with each successive generation of workers. The sustainability advantage is not just about finding new opportunities with customers, but also about attracting the best and brightest employees. Are you the employer of choice? Do you offer the most personal growth opportunities with sustainable change? Every industry will face a challenge of clearly articulating their position on sustainability.

How does your company contribute to social good while remaining financially viable? How can you connect each employee's work with the overall goals? Your ability to create positive employee engagement on this issue will separate your business from your industry peers.

TAKEAWAY: There Is No Future without Change, So Embrace It in Every Area of Your Business

Take into consideration these aspects of developing your learning curriculum that we have covered so far:

- First, establish the new business model and boundaries as your source of reference.
- Second, identify the content of enduring value that needs to be updated, not replaced.
- Third, incorporate new breakthrough activities like new product development that have been changed and expanded with redefined boundaries.
- Fourth, look at the business models in functional and geographic areas that create the need for specialized training in areas like recycling and reuse, energy efficiency, money laundering, or supplier management.
- Fifth, expand training and development to reinforce your business values with ethics training or by providing international leaders with training on religion and national and regional cultures.

In this chapter, we discussed how making a bold transition to a sustainable business model requires basic training for all managers on ethical standards. Selected employees need to have skills in stakeholder analysis, dealing with angry stakeholders, and negotiating practices for delivering on shared value creation. Product design and the supply chain also come into the picture, and while complex supply chains offer challenges to align with the sustainability initiatives of the company purchasing those products and services, there are ways to move the supply chain forward.

In chapter 12, we will take the temperature of the organization and the leaders driving change. The discussion comes in the form of five direct questions that result in an honest appraisal of where things stand.

CAN YOU DELIVER PASSION, PURPOSE, AND HIGH PERFORMANCE?

"A year from now, you will wish you had started today."
KAREN LAMB

I f you think of yourself as a sustainability champion, it suggests you
have passion for creating a better world or that you see sustainability as an opportunity for innovation. Perhaps you see value in both
perspectives.

Consider the sustainability champions we have read about in this
book. Ramesh Ramanathan of Jana Small Finance Bank shows the
importance of the investor-promoter as the "lighthouse" of sustainable
values. Bernard Arnault, CEO of LVMH, has driven the sustainability
agenda for over twenty-five years. Vice President and Chief Sustainability Officer Rebecca Hamilton of W.S. Badger Company demon-
strates how the second generation of a founding family can continue
the tradition. Nick Pennell has started the process as Essentra's group
operating director; Greg Lavery of Rype Office has driven change as an

entrepreneur; and Trevor Martin of Galaxy Entertainment supports the sustainability agenda as head of human resources. Change leaders can emerge from many different places in an organization.

To help you convert your passion into transformation at any level or degree in your organization, I have divided this chapter into five sections based on questions that are important for any sustainability champion to consider. My suggestions are relevant whether you are a lone sustainability champion or a talent development professional charged with developing a community of such champions. For each question, I offer resource ideas or a set of suggested steps to get you started.

The five questions you need to ask yourself are:

1. Am I personally prepared to act as a sustainability champion?
2. To what degree is my organization committed to change, and what capabilities do we have to carry out change?
3. How fast can we scale a business transformation?
4. How can I and my organization connect to a vibrant sustainability community for support and ideas?
5. Where can I find additional resources on sustainability?

Am I Personally Prepared to Act as a Sustainability Champion?

The first task is to continue your sustainability education. You may have some or a lot of knowledge about sustainability, but the importance of continuing education cannot be understated. As described earlier, the typical process is to become familiar with strategic models, such as the United Nations Sustainable Development Goals (SDGs) and the UN Global Compact, and then the business, geographic, and functional or industry-specific models that are relevant to your role or project. Your objective is to be sufficiently familiar with the goals and concepts in order to educate others and improve both the accuracy and depth of any dialog in team meetings.

One of the first places to start is the United Nations websites dedicated to the SDGs and the UN Global Compact:

- https://www.un.org/sustainabledevelopment/sustainable-development-goals
- https://www.unglobalcompact.org

These will provide you detail on the individual goal commitments and measures.

You will also find plenty of information at other UN agencies associated with specific goals, such as the UN Environment Programme, the UN website for the Climate Change Report, and intergovernmental websites such as the World Bank:

- https://www.unenvironment.org/explore-topics/sustainable-development-goals
- http://www.un.org/en/sections/issues-depth/climate-change
- https://www.worldbank.org/en/programs/sdgs-2030-agenda

Websites of foundations and industry associations can provide you with project descriptions associated with specific goals or sub-measures. Here are links to the UN Foundation and the World Economic Forum:

- http://www.unfoundation.org/what-we-do/issues/sustainable-development-goals/
- https://www.weforum.org/agenda/archive/sustainable-development/

Consider using a heat map to help organize the direction your education needs to take. If, for example, you are focused on environmental issues, you can start with an overview of the SDGs and enter specific SDGs like Life Below Water (Goal 14), Climate Action (Goal 13), or Clean Water and Sanitation (Goal 6). On many UN reports, you will see both internal and external experts that you can list by name on your heat map and later search. From there, you can review content on websites like the UN Environment Programme or regional and industry websites like the Marine Stewardship Council, Friend of the Sea, the Clean Water Foundation (Canada), or Ecomark (India). (I have listed the URLs for each of these sites in the Appendix.) These resources may be used as points of reference in your heat map to build a series of general and specific sustainability references.

Remember, reporting on general and specific public good is a requirement of benefit corporations and a good model for all CSR reports. By searching each site, you will find thought leaders, publications, partners, or collaborators. The heat map serves as your initial networking diagram that provides a starting point for phone calls, emails, and web searches to connect with people in your new sustainability community. Doing this methodically and well pays big dividends in new ideas and lessons learned.

> After familiarizing yourself with the general and specific concepts, it may be useful to do some self-reflection. I started the book by researching my own family history, and it was helpful to remind myself how much I have participated in activities now considered problems. Self-reflection can lead to insights, learning, and performance improvements. As a caution, let me say that if you do not embrace sustainability fully, the inconsistencies will be apparent to people resistant to change and the path to success will be harder.

How Committed Am I?

I believe that we all get four votes for sustainability: (1) as a citizen who selects politicians; (2) as a consumer who makes personal choices of what to buy; (3) as a businessperson who helps shape the behavior of those around them; and, (4) as an investor who can choose what kinds of companies he or she will support. So Table 12.1 presents a simple nine-question quiz that can provide insights into where you stand as a change leader for sustainability. The quiz is not a knowledge test, but an indicator of your general commitment.

Table 12.1: Personal Sustainability Assessment

How Aligned Is Your Personal Behavior with Sustainability Principles?		
My Votes	Is it more or less true that . . .	Ranking
Citizen	I consider a politician's record on sustainability issues when voting.	1 2 3 4 5 6 7 8 9 10
Citizen	I make efforts to improve or serve my local community.	1 2 3 4 5 6 7 8 9 10
Consumer	I consider sustainability issues when deciding where to live and how to commute.	1 2 3 4 5 6 7 8 9 10
Consumer	I recycle or repurpose wherever possible.	1 2 3 4 5 6 7 8 9 10
Consumer	I avoid single-use products that are not biodegradable.	1 2 3 4 5 6 7 8 9 10
Consumer	I try to buy products with labels that certify fair trade and good working conditions.	1 2 3 4 5 6 7 8 9 10
Business	I work at a company with clear sustainability standards.	1 2 3 4 5 6 7 8 9 10
Business	I make my voice known within my company to encourage sustainable business practices.	1 2 3 4 5 6 7 8 9 10
Investor	I consider a company's record on sustainability when I buy stocks or invest for my retirement.	1 2 3 4 5 6 7 8 9 10
	Your Alignment Score	

If you scored above 60, then you are making an effort to embrace sustainability in your life and you generally have a strong commitment. However, if you scored low in one area, it's an opportunity to consider why. What inconsistencies in behavior led you to rate yourself less than an 8, 9, or 10? If you have moderate scores for a number of questions, ask yourself why your behavior is variable.

If you scored less than 60, your commitment probably lags in two or more of your voting choices. This is the same challenge that everyone in your business organization will face. As a sustainability champion, you have to be prepared to leverage existing commitments to sustainability while highlighting gaps between statements and actions. Your personal actions and behavior will matter. If you scored less than 30, you need to take a step back and organize a personal action plan. You are not yet ready to serve as a sustainability champion.

To What Degree Is My Organization Committed to Change, and What Capabilities Do We Have to Carry Out Change?

The next step is to do a simple assessment of your organization's readiness. Each of the categories in Table 12.2 is a capability required for a successful business transformation. This assessment does not measure the emotional commitment of the organization—just the strength of capabilities. It provides you with a rough idea of where you need to invest energy as a sustainability champion. Who do you need to get on board and how fast can the organization move from a demonstration project to broad-based change?

Table 12.2: Organizational Capabilities Assessment

Is Your Company Ready for Sustainable Change?		
Category	Is it more or less true that ...	Ranking
Business Model	Your leaders have a clear business model that produces both economic and social gain.	1 2 3 4 5 6 7 8 9 10
Leadership	Your leaders can promote a business vision for sustainability and champion changes in the business culture.	1 2 3 4 5 6 7 8 9 10
Job Design	Job descriptions and accountabilities have been modified to accommodate broader social goals and responsibilities.	1 2 3 4 5 6 7 8 9 10
Key Hires	You have clearly articulated your sustainability vision in recruiting and retention.	1 2 3 4 5 6 7 8 9 10
Integrated Reporting	Your organization has clear metrics and measures visible to everyone in the organization for both economic and social value creation.	1 2 3 4 5 6 7 8 9 10
Operating Processes	Process improvement activities are tested for alignment with sustainability goals and modified to reduce conflicts.	1 2 3 4 5 6 7 8 9 10
Training & Development	Your organization provides training on key issues like energy efficiency, healthy communities, and sustainable production.	1 2 3 4 5 6 7 8 9 10
Measurement Systems	You have clear metrics and reporting dashboards visible to everyone in the organization for both economic and social value creation.	1 2 3 4 5 6 7 8 9 10
Communication	Your leaders share success stories and encourage team innovation in support of the new sustainable business model.	1 2 3 4 5 6 7 8 9 10
Incentives	People are acknowledged, rewarded, and promoted for delivering social value, as well as economic value.	1 2 3 4 5 6 7 8 9 10
Your Organization's Readiness Score		

If you rate your organizational readiness with a score above 75, then you have substantial organizational resources and it is likely you will have a strong community of sustainability champions. Share the assessment with others to see if they agree with your score. It's an efficient way to create a discussion about the organization's commitment and possible priority areas for investment.

If you scored your organization's capabilities at less than 75, you have gaps in one or more key areas. It is commonplace for organizations to lack full integration across functions, but this also highlights strengths to build on. The change to a sustainable business model is not yet anchored in your culture and you need to place greater emphasis on expanding your community of advocates. A score of less than 50 means you have a lot of work to do. It is likely that you need to focus on demonstration projects to communicate what can be done and how sustainability benefits both the business and community.

Another way to assess readiness is to form a small team to assess the alignment of your products and services. (This idea was covered in chapter 3 and is an easy way to start a senior-level discussion.) You may find you have products that are fully aligned with the SDGs, while others clearly have a negative impact on the environment or people. When you look at products and services, you can also make direct connections to business revenue and negative social impact. Decisions on how fast or slow to transition away from products with a negative environmental or social impact are an equally valid test of executive commitment.

My final tool for judging commitment (Table 12.3) looks more specifically at what is typically called the triple constraint in project management: time, cost, and scope. I offer this model because project management concepts are deeply embedded in many organizations and using common language makes a dialog easier.

Table 12.3: Triple Constraint Assessment

Sustainability Commitment Index		
Category	Is it more or less true that ...	Ranking
Time	Your leadership team spends time aligning the business to the new sustainability plan.	1 2 3 4 5 6 7 8 9 10
Time	Managers across the organization are active in enabling change and removing roadblocks.	1 2 3 4 5 6 7 8 9 10
Time	Daily meetings and routine actions clearly reflect an ongoing focus on sustainability.	1 2 3 4 5 6 7 8 9 10
Cost	Budgets have been modified to reflect changing resource demands.	1 2 3 4 5 6 7 8 9 10
Cost	Budgets are allocated for social value creation.	1 2 3 4 5 6 7 8 9 10
Cost	Longer-term investment plans in new products and services are tied to the sustainability agenda.	1 2 3 4 5 6 7 8 9 10
Scope	New practices have been introduced to align product and service design with new social and economic value-creation principles.	1 2 3 4 5 6 7 8 9 10
Scope	All business functions are working on changes to incorporate new sustainability goals and operating practices.	1 2 3 4 5 6 7 8 9 10
Scope	You actively work with partners and vendors in your ecosystem on the basis of mutual gain and long-term value creation. You require partners to have a commitment to sustainability.	1 2 3 4 5 6 7 8 9 10
Your Organization's Commitment Score		

The scoring concept here is similar to the other assessments. If you score your organization's commitment greater than 60, then your organization is making the effort to embrace sustainable business practices but needs to stay focused on priority areas to maintain its progress.

A score of less than 60 indicates that commitment is more variable and not everyone is embracing sustainability as a priority. Actions speak louder than words. A score of less than 40 suggests that your organization is not fully committed to sustainability and you need to work harder with key influencers who can help drive change. Equally valuable in this assessment is the balance of your scores between time, cost, and scope. It reflects how resources are deployed and offers a simple gap assessment between words and actions.

How Fast Can We Scale a Business Transformation?

If you rated highly on the assessments, you likely have both commitment and capability. Acknowledging that there will be gaps, nevertheless you have substantial resources and an organization that is eager to do something special. The steps outlined below offer a model to follow to make sure each sustainability champion is engaged in the business transformation. The process starts by working with the executive team on the choice of business model and any experiments that are used to build a more substantive business case for change. At each stage will be challenges to overcome and goals to achieve. Addressing these challenges means considering where the opportunities are to add new value and ascertaining what capabilities will help drive success.

Step 1: Validating the Sustainability Business Model

At the top of the chapter, I wrote that if you think of yourself as a sustainability champion, it suggests you have passion for creating a better world or that you see sustainability as an opportunity for innovation. With respect to the latter, the goal of a sustainable business model is to create competitive differentiation and new value creation. However, introducing fundamental changes to the business may also create fear and uncertainty. This is where a small pool of sustainability champions can really make a difference.

Challenges to Overcome	Key Talent Development Activities
Fear of change, lack of knowledge, and uncertainty.	Help design the demonstration projects that test assumptions about new business models (covered in chapter 2). Frame key questions to be answered by the demonstration project so you can model the structural, staffing, and business process changes that will allow the business to scale. Broadly communicate success stories to reduce uncertainty by establishing a path for success. If appropriate, use the opportunity to hire and develop new advocates to support any future demonstration projects.

Step 2: Experiment, Test, and Refine Ideas

A demonstration project that gains insight into the potential future of the business is the place to develop high-value business knowledge. This is where a strong understanding of business analytics allows a sustainability advocate to analyze how changes in business practices create new outcomes, both economic and social. You will also be able to refine how changes in accountability for new social outcomes will change job design, performance scope, and costs.

Challenges to Overcome	Key Talent Development Activities
Expanding boundaries and defining new performance values.	Design the demonstration project in ways that will allow you to collect and analyze data. Conduct regression analysis on key actions to demonstrate relationships between actions and new economic and social outcomes. Use that data to make recommendations about investments needed to replicate and scale the demonstration project results.

Step 3: Capture New Knowledge

Replicating early successes and scaling new business processes involves creating a repeatable path of key activities. That is essentially what we call a skill.

Challenges to Overcome	Key Talent Development Activities
Old mental models, a lack of key support capabilities and skills, and the fact that it is often too early for broad internal expertise to be developed.	Identifying lessons learned and codifying the lessons into practices that can be shared. Build case studies of both successes and failures to encourage innovation.

Step 4: Consolidate Key Practices

This is the stage where you convert the early lessons learned into scalable training and development programs to replicate sustainable practices across the business. This is also the opportunity to start building social rituals among the sustainability advocates to strengthen their sense of community.

Challenges to Overcome	Key Talent Development Activities
Change resistance and old problem-solving practices that will tend to regress towards outdated operating practices.	Changing mental models. Developing an instructional model based on the type of knowledge and how it will be applied in different parts of the organization. Building social rituals for the established sustainability champions.

Step 5: Build Operational Excellence

The goal is to turn words and mission statements into action by aligning business functions and scaling best practices. We are now beyond demonstration projects and we need to make sustainability the rule rather than the exception. Achieving new economic and social value creation, driven by a new business vision, should now be the primary focus.

Challenges to Overcome	Key Talent Development Activities
Lack of consistent leadership behavior and new hire transitions.	Move from social rituals for the change team to everyday organizational practices. Recruiting, onboarding, major role transitions, and organizational recognition programs should now be designed as signature events to drive intent, scale, and consistency.

Step 6: Create New Opportunities

The goal of step six is to move out of the shadow of transformation. The organization must be routinely acting according to its principles and looking for new ways to create social and economic value as part of its business growth strategy.

Challenges to Overcome	Key Talent Development Activities
Underinvestment, staff and leadership transitions, and maintaining ecosystem alignment.	Expanding the pool of internal experts and partners, and building out the organization's sustainable ecosystem. Building a talent development function fully aligned with the principles of sustainability.

TAKEAWAY: Change Depends on You Becoming a Sustainability Champion—on Your Readiness and Willingness to Act

In this chapter we discussed the importance of self-assessment and readiness. The various questions, references, and assessments provide opportunities for self-reflection but also serve as starting points for dialogue with colleagues in your organization.

I have asked you to consider a series of dilemmas in this book. Each presents a potential conflict for you to resolve, but essentially there are no "right" answers—rather, only options to choose from. They illustrate some of the challenges to be faced by the change agent within an organization:

- Are there conflicts between SDGs and competitive position?
- Will you face reputational risks or environmental impacts that are unforeseen?
- How deep and strong do your values go?
- Are you less responsible for environmental or social impact that occurs at a distance?

The challenge for the change agent is not to anticipate all possible problems, but to prepare your organization to be adaptable and equipped to recognize the available options within the context of a strong set of business values. Building a strong team and supporting ecosystem offers the best opportunity to be both economically viable and socially strong.

You will note we have addressed only three of the five questions posed at the beginning of this chapter. The remaining two questions ask you to identify a supportive community and find additional resources. Chapter 13 and the appendix are designed as a digest of resources to explore. Within those listings are numerous assessment and advocacy resources as well as potential partner organizations. I encourage you to start the process of building your community by exploring organizations of interest and reaching out to potential experts and partners. Successful collaborations build communities and the right starting point is your personal journey of exploration.

Chapter 13

RESOURCES FOR SUSTAINABILITY CHAMPIONS

"How wonderful it is that nobody needs to wait a single moment before starting to improve the world." ANNE FRANK

There are many ways that you and your organization can connect to a vibrant sustainability community for support and ideas.

One of the best resources for any sustainability champion is a vibrant community of like-minded individuals. Fortunately, there are growing communities of interest around the world. A certified B Corporation typically has a community page that highlights local B Lab organizations and offers helpful links for educators. There are also wonderful industry groups like the Brussels-based Academy of Business in Society (ABIS), the Geneva-based World Business Council for Sustainable Development, and the US-based GreenBiz. It is generally fairly easy to find a sustainability institute linked to a major university like the Cambridge Institute for Sustainability Leadership or the ESADE

Institute for Social Innovation in Spain. With a little bit of effort, you can generally find conferences, peer-to-peer networking, and education resources in almost every country or region of the world.

In the appendix, you will find over 300 resources to get you started on issues from carbon credits to zero waste. I have tried to reference many of the organizations cited in this book as well as a variety of other helpful sites, although my list barely scratches the surface. The deeper you look into any industry, regional area, or goal category, you will find hundreds more. The resources are generally organized according to the Sustainable Development Goals (SDGs), although many relate to several categories. For example, if you are interested in Peace, Justice and Strong Institutions (Goal 16), you will find overlap with Goal 10: Reduced Inequalities as well as Goal 8: Decent Work and Economic Growth.

In the same way, I have categorized the Ecosystem Services Identification & Inventory (ESII) Tool for calculating physical and biological process under Goal 12: Responsible Production and Consumption, and it clearly has application for Goal 15: Life on Land; Goal 14: Life below Water; and Goal 6: Clean Water and Sanitation.

The remainder of this chapter restates the SDGs and provides some examples of resources as an illustration.

Sustainable Development Goals and Examples of Resources

SDG 1: No Poverty

End poverty in all its forms everywhere

Sustainable Development Goals No Poverty and Zero Hunger are closely related. Oxfam International operates in ninety countries and is focused on the eradication of poverty and the enhancement of human rights. Oxfam was founded in 1995 and named after the Oxford Committee for Famine Relief. The Oxfam International Confederation operates as an umbrella organization for twenty member organizations. Organizations such as Heifer International are crossover organizations that focus on the family farm to reduce poverty, hunger, and inequality. So although I list them here, they apply equally well in other categories.

SDG 2: Zero Hunger

End hunger, achieve food security and improved nutrition, and promote sustainable agriculture

The Global Hunger Index provides comprehensive data on global hunger by region and country. The International Food Policy Research Institute (IFPRI) compiles the data. The index also provides insights on child mortality and related indices. The World Food Programme (WFP) also publishes reports on hunger and food insecurity. The WFP *Food Reports* are developed collectively by twelve institutions from the Food Security Information Network.

SDG 3: Good Health and Well-Being

Ensure healthy lives and promote well-being for all at all ages

The Good Health and Well-Being goal covers a range of topics from reducing infant mortality, the spread of communicable diseases, substance abuse, and traffic injuries, to increasing access to health care. I do not list many links for this goal, primarily because there are too many to list. Every country has numerous resources that are easy to find, and this is an excellent category for making a connection to your local community. A major global player worth mentioning is Doctors Without Borders/Médecins Sans Frontières, which has operated around the world since 1971 and provides critical medical services in conflict and crisis areas. Its efforts were recognized with a Nobel Prize in 1999.

SDG 4: Quality Education

Ensure inclusive and equitable quality education and promote lifelong learning opportunities for all

The focus of this book is corporate education, which is only nominally covered under SDG 4. The focus of this goal is greater access to education for all, including quality primary education and more structured vocational and higher education programs. The key references link access to quality education to reductions in poverty and inequality and upward mobility. However, access to lifelong learning is mentioned as a sub-measure and I strongly recommend Khan Academy to both children and adults as an excellent source of education information and micro learning. Khan Academy is also an excellent example of a virtual learning center that provides problem-based "how to" education.

SDG 5: Gender Equality

Achieve gender equality and empower all women and girls

EDGE describes itself as the global business certification standard for gender equality. EDGE Certification stands for Economic Dividends for Gender Equality Certification. EDGE lists more than two hundred certified businesses in fifty countries. The certification concept addresses key areas such as equal pay, training and promotional opportunities, work practices, and company culture. White Ribbon is an organization committed to ending violence against women and girls and is signified by men and boys who wear white ribbons signifying a "pledge to never commit, condone or remain silent about violence against women and girls."

SDG 6: Clean Water and Sanitation

Ensure availability and sustainable management of water and sanitation for all

The Natural Capital Coalition is a member organization that tries to solve the problem of placing value on natural assets like clean water, as well as the wetlands, estuaries, and aquifers that sustain the asset over time. The organization offers excellent resources that include a database, case studies, member events, news, and analysis. It does particularly interesting work in making the connection between business finance, economic models, and reporting and the issue of natural capital values. There are many other water and sanitation resources available on a regional basis, such as the Clean Water Foundation in Canada and WaterAid in the United Kingdom.

SDG 7: Affordable and Clean Energy

Ensure access to affordable, reliable, sustainable, and modern energy for all

This goal offers resources from an extensive diversity of public and private organizations, including a number of consulting firms. The energy sector has been a robust area for innovation and investment, and you will find global organizations like the International Renewable Energy Agency, which works with member countries, as well as member organizations like WindMade that specifically promotes the use of renewable wind power. To be eligible for a WindMade membership, a company must get at least 20 percent of its energy needs from wind energy. To receive the WindMade certification label, an organization must be able to verify usage above 25 percent.

SDG 8: Decent Work and Economic Growth

Promote sustained, inclusive and sustainable economic growth,
full and productive employment, and decent work for all

Organizations like End Slavery Now address the need to end forced labor, human trafficking, and child labor. Although initially started as an independent nonprofit organization, it now operates under the auspices of the National Underground Railroad Freedom Center in the United States. The goal also includes a broad range of sub-measures such as worker rights, migrant working conditions, fair pay, and consistent economic development. The International Labour Organization (ILO), based in Turin, Italy, addresses many of these issues. Decent Work and Economic Growth also involves access to banking, finance, and insurance systems. If you wish to network in these areas, the Microfinance Association is a good place to start.

SDG 9: Industry, Innovation, and Infrastructure

Build resilient infrastructure, promote inclusive and sustainable
industrialization, and foster innovation

The Corporate Sustainability Index (ISE) is an investment index based on the B3 Exchange in Brazil (formerly BM&F Bovespa). Sustainable Development Goal 9 is all about "inclusion and sustainable industrialization," and the sustainability index offers a way to compare companies that perform in a more socially responsible manner. The index started in 2005 in partnership with the International Finance Corporation (IFC). The ISE and related indexes like the Dow Jones Sustainability Index (US), the STOXX Index (Eurozone), and the Jantzi Social Index (Canada) all offer investors a means to examine a company's commitment to sustainability.

SDG 10: Reduced Inequalities

Reduce inequality within and among countries

The purpose of this goal is to look at inequality from national and regional perspectives. How do you improve the voice of people in developing countries and improve equal access to markets and institutions? This goal also addresses the movement of people for work and issues like foreign direct investment. The World Economic Forum, the World Trade Organization, and regional economic commissions like the Asia-Pacific Economic Cooperation (APEC) all have resources worth looking at. The latter is particularly good if you are in the hospitality industry and want to drill down on topics like tourism.

SDG 11: Sustainable Cities and Communities

Make cities and human settlements inclusive, safe, resilient, and sustainable

The Urban China Initiative publishes the Urban Sustainability Index Report, which reports on more than twenty sustainability metrics for 185 cities in China. The report is relevant because it covers one of the largest population markets in the world, but also because of the diversity of sustainability measures. A variety of other associations and standards-based organizations provide guidelines on sustainable building practices, such as LEED certification (US) and the Pearl Building Rating

System (PBRS) in Abu Dhabi. A number of academic institutions also feature special research programs, such as the Massachusetts Institute of Technology (MIT) Senseable City Lab.

SDG 12: Responsible Consumption and Production

Ensure sustainable consumption and production patterns

The bluesign® system guides the input providers in the textile manufacturing process with a template for how to interact in a sustainable supply chain. It also provides consumers with a standard that says textiles were manufactured using sustainable practices. The Global Impact Sourcing Coalition is a member organization that strives to create a more inclusive supply chain. The coalition members include Facebook, Microsoft, Bloomberg, and Tech Mahindra. Each member takes a pledge to hire disadvantaged (impact) workers with the overall goal of hiring one hundred thousand impact workers by 2020.

SDG 13: Climate Action

Take urgent action to combat climate change and its impacts

I have listed a variety of links to sites that provide information on carbon footprint calculators. These can be useful resources when looking at your personal carbon impact. There are also wonderful organizations like the Earth Institute at Columbia University, which brings together scholars from around the world to conduct basic research on earth science and then share that information with governments and industry. The major reporting source for climate change is the Intergovernmental Panel on Climate Change (IPCC) at the UN. The first major report was published in 1990.

SDG 14: Life Below Water

Conserve and sustainably use the oceans, seas, and marine resources for sustainable development

The Ocean Conservancy is an advocacy organization that seeks to preserve our oceans and the communities that depend on it for survival. It helps organize an annual international coastal cleanup that attracts thousands of volunteers from around the world. The group also sponsors research, advocates for legislative change to protect the marine environment, and works with companies on specific campaigns, such as reducing ocean plastic pollution.

SDG 15: Life on Land

Protect, restore, and promote sustainable use of terrestrial ecosystems, sustainably manage forests, combat desertification, and halt and reverse land degradation and halt biodiversity loss

Organizations like the World Resources Institute are not neatly categorized under one SDG since they provide information on "climate, energy, food, forests, water, and cities and transport." They do a variety of projects on land with climate change and deforestation, but they also have helpful information about Life below Water and Sustainable Cities. Other organizations, like the European Commission (agriculture and rural development, organic farming) and the USDA National Organic Program promote sustainable agriculture practices.

SDG 16: Peace, Justice, and Strong Institutions

Promote peaceful and inclusive societies for sustainable development, provide access to justice for all, and build effective, accountable and inclusive institutions at all levels

Like many of the SDGs, there is a lot of territory to cover here. Several large intergovernmental agencies, like the United Nations Development Programme (UNDP), the World Bank, and the Organisation for Economic Co-operation and Development (OECD), work on anti-corruption, anti-bribery, and anti-money laundering initiatives. These are critically important for any organization with a large international presence and cross-border cash flows. These are also very big issues for any country without strong civil society institutions. There are also a variety of regional initiatives that work specifically on equal justice, such as the Equal Justice Initiative in the United States and the International Legal Assistance Consortium.

SDG 17: Partnerships for the Goals

Strengthen the means of implementation and revitalize the global partnership for sustainable development

The subcategories under these goals largely speak to cooperation between governments, the enhancement of trade with the least-developed countries, and the sharing of environmentally friendly technologies. The most important resources are the UN Global Compact website and the United Nations Sustainable Development Knowledge Platform. I have also included some business associations like Academy of Business in Society (ABIS), because many of the member companies are global in nature and have complex and extended supply chains. Support for less-developed economies and international trade can be highly influenced through effective and supportive supply chain policies that provide long-term relationships and the economic and educational support to increase awareness of sustainable practices.

Closing Thoughts on Being a Sustainability Champion

The challenges of sustainability can seem daunting. A list of seventeen goals and 169 measures can feel overwhelming. But therein lies the opportunity for change and the chance to be a leader in the biggest business transformation the world has ever seen. As I mentioned in an earlier chapter, I think that everyone gets four votes. I encourage you to use yours wisely. Make personal changes, get involved as a citizen and voter, and help drive change at work. Start where you can, learn more about what excites you, and strive to make a difference.

If you still have a sense of caution, reflect on each of the four votes I suggested you have and consider how powerful your voice can be. Your role as a global citizen has never been more powerful. Government officials in the UK created whole new industries by raising landfill taxes to encourage recycling, reuse, and remanufacturing. Chinese government policy has helped catalyze its auto sector to produce over 50 percent of the world's electric vehicles in 2017.[1] Major cities including Mumbai, New Delhi, New York, and Seattle have banned various types of single-use plastics.[2] Well-conceived government policy can create both jobs and positive social change.

Your vote as a consumer has always been a powerful voice. Companies increasingly recognize that consumers want choice. Organic and natural products are increasingly popular. Major fashion houses are now more focused on how their products are created. Textile companies are under greater scrutiny for worker conditions. Major media companies have made eliminating slavery and child labor a regular feature. All of this is the result of consumer demand and greater public awareness.

Your role as an investor is equally about choice. As mentioned in chapter 8, a number of studies and sustainability fund five-year averages show that investing in business with a strong mission orientation can produce competitive or higher than average returns. It turns out that investing in sustainability and long-term value creation makes good sense.

Your role as change agent in your company can be equally important and fulfilling. Each of the 17 SDGs and 300-plus resources listed in the appendix are a golden opportunity for learning, and all change starts by learning something new. As Albert Einstein once said, "The problems of today can't be solved with the same thinking that created them." You are on the front lines of a business revolution that is about more than money or another cool product. You are creating the kind of sustainability advantage that will affect you, your community, and succeeding generations. That is something worth doing. As an anonymous sage once observed, "Live life like a camera. Capture the good, develop the negative, and if things don't work out, take another shot."

If you want a future with a healthier planet, vibrant communities, and exciting work to be done, then you need to help make it happen. That is the role of the sustainability champion. Welcome aboard!

AFTERWORD

My great-grandfather Matthew McAteer died long before I was born. Yet he created a legacy for me that endures. He would have lived in Northern Ireland at a time of great transition. His forefathers would have spoken Gaelic, but he lived in a generation where the call of jobs from the United States and England made the English language a necessity. The name McAteer, spoken *Mac an tSaoir* in Gaelic, means son of a craftsman.[1] For Matthew and several generations of McAteers, the factories, railroads, and construction sites of the United States were a place where the sons of craftsmen could earn upward mobility and the opportunity of a better life. His generation and those that followed deserve credit for unlocking opportunities and creating the innovations that define our life today.

During Matthew's life, the basic science of global warming was established, and during his son's generation the world experienced a new era of innovation and industrial development unlike any seen before. My father and mother experienced both the advantages of that industrial era and the problems unleashed by new social and economic challenges. They grew up in the Great Depression and survived World War 2. Insightful leaders of the time oversaw the creation of the United Nations and many of the intergovernmental bodies that try to manage the challenges of sustainable development. With each generation we made progress, yet we have left much to be done. Although the UN held its first Conference on the Law of the Sea (UNCLOS)[2] the year I was born, almost two thirds of the ocean remains nominally regulated with no overall enforcement mechanism for violations.[3] The post–World War 2 era saw the benefits of decolonization, but it also saw an increase in deforestation and ocean dumping, and a weakening of the earth's ozone layer.

My great-grandfather's personal story and that of the family members that followed are not unlike those lived by many families of immigrants today. They seek a good job, safety and security, and the opportunity to do better. Each generation—Matthew's and the four that followed—inherited a world of greater economic prosperity and knowledge. Although new discoveries offered insights into the mysteries of life on earth, they also began to shine a light on global warming and many of the ills that plague the human race. From mistakes and accidents to discoveries and reflections, we have created an understanding of what we have done wrong and how we can do better. What changed over time is the world itself: a much larger population, a greater demand for resources, and a pattern of behavior that is unnecessarily wasteful and damaging. The legacy of a better world for future generations is in danger.

The record of the last 150 years has been my time line for a journey into the causes of unsustainable business practices. By now, it should be clear that we have problems and that we need to think differently about the path forward. Although the task is large, history tells us there are always people willing and able to step forward and lead the way.

So, why do I have so much faith that great leaders can add so much new value? Jack Zenger and Joe Folkman published a study in 2015[4] that looked at the comparative performance of leaders at a major commercial bank as evaluated by participants using 360-degree feedback instruments. The participant evaluations (subordinates, peers, managers, or colleagues) placed leaders into one of three categories: top 10 percent, bottom 10 percent, or middle 80 percent. The study showed that people rated as poor leaders (bottom 10 percent) created $1.2 million in losses; those rated as good leaders (the middle 80 percent) created $2.4 million in gains; and those rated as great leaders (top 10 percent) created gains of $4.5 million.

A study published by McKinsey in 2008 examined the impact of organizational excellence on nine leadership criteria such as the "leadership team" and "work environment and values" and "direction," and concluded: "On average, the companies ranked most highly according to these organizational criteria tend to have operating margins twice as high as those of the lowest-ranked."[5]

Another McKinsey study that examined the value of women leadership in firms concluded, "We demonstrated that companies with more women in their management teams score more highly, on average, on their organizational performance criteria than companies with no women in senior positions."[6]

In a 2012 study, *The Leadership Premium*,[7] global consulting firm Deloitte opined, "The gap between the value of a company with good leadership and that of a company with weaker leadership could be more than 35.5 percent. On average, we discovered a premium of 15.7 percent for particularly effective leadership—and a discount of 19.8 percent for its opposite."

Bain consultants Michael Mankins and Eric Garton conducted research that indicates that certain companies, like Apple, Netflix, and Google "are 40% more productive than the average company."[8] The same study says that "an engaged employee is 44% more productive than a satisfied worker, but an employee who feels inspired at work is nearly 125% more productive than a satisfied one."[9]

It seems safe to say that inspired leadership can have a substantial impact on performance. Imagine for a moment that we are able to apply that same level of inspiration and great talent to the challenges of sustainability. How much faster could we solve problems? How much more attractive would the pursuit of social value creation and sustainability-oriented innovation be if we were to attract the best and brightest to the cause? It seems like a goal worth pursuing!

I am a strong advocate of learning and innovation. I believe they are two sides of the same coin and equally necessary for successful change. Yet discovery without the ability to put ideas into action is not enough. We also need strong leadership at all levels of an organization. For my great-grandparents, using their life savings to transit the Atlantic Ocean on the hope of a better tomorrow, the future was full of risk. They were traveling without a playbook and with little money, into a world they barely knew, with only their wits, intelligence, and motivation for a better life. The true lesson of such efforts is that we need to have faith in our ability to do better and embrace challenge. Such challenges inspire us to achieve more. My great-grandparents knew that accepting the status quo was acknowledging a life of hardship without hope. They chose to act! As we look at the practices that sustain life on our planet today, we can make the same observation. Going in the same direction should not be acceptable, but each of us has a choice to make.

Mahatma Gandhi is widely acclaimed as a man of his time and a man for all times. He once observed, "You must be the change you want to see in the world." We must act with such conviction and have faith in our abilities to embrace the serious challenges that face us. We must choose to deliver to future generations not a world in crisis, but a world committed to something better. Good intentions, shared commitment, and responsible practices are the starting point. Going forward, we must all commit to raising the bar for our own expectations and those of our colleagues. *Ask good questions, relentlessly pursue better ideas, and serve as champion of a common commitment to sustainable behavior.* To that end, I hope this book serves to speed you on your journey.

ACKNOWLEDGMENTS

Why sustainability? This book is, quite simply, the result of my desire to move the sustainability agenda forward in some meaningful way, rather than complaining about politicians or business leaders. Although I've worked with many companies on their talent development plans or corporate universities, sustainability was rarely an integral part of the strategy.

As I explored the challenge with colleagues and clients, I began to examine my own behavior and my level of commitment. The outcome of this examination was a multiyear plan with three main objectives. The first was to expand my research on the challenges of business transformation and sustainability so I could offer clients a better way forward. Would solutions that work well for a large company work equally well in a small one? The second was to invest in a sustainable business that created products that people use every day. The business would allow me to put my ideas into practice and broaden my network, especially with smaller businesses and entrepreneurs. The result of that investment is KPPM Global, a health and beauty products company that continues today. The third objective was to write a book that captured my thoughts and offered options and solutions to those who champion sustainability. How do you transform an organization to operate in a more consistently sustainable manner?

Along the way, I have received encouragement from friends and colleagues including Hal Movius, David Goehring, Debra Hunter, Alfons Sauquet Rovira, Thomas Stewart, and Bertrand Moingeon. I also garnered many insights talking with my daughter Claire as we traveled together across Asia on our annual trips. Our visits to the rural regions of Thailand, Nepal, and Cambodia offered both time for exploration as well as opportunities to reflect on how cultures and sustainability challenges have evolved over time.

I also owe thanks to colleagues at the United Nations like Malcolm Goodale and Juancho Montecillo and to the many former clients who gave freely of their time to listen and discuss ideas. Special thanks go to the team at KPPM Global for engaging with me on the importance of sustainability and for their patience as we tested different ideas and business practices. In particular, Sawai NaNakorn, Thaweesak Suksrinual, Panita Boonthawong, and Rugpong and Saruda Purivittayatera all deserve special acknowledgment.

Putting my thoughts into words was made easier with the helpful encouragement of the team at LifeTree Media and my editor Don Loney. Don has an easygoing style and I thoroughly enjoyed our discussions and brainstorming during the book's creative process. I typically made an early morning video call from Bangkok while Don participated the previous evening from Toronto. The twelve-hour time difference worked well as Don offered ideas that I could put into practice that day and I often read his e-mail critique the next morning over coffee.

The overall writing process was made easier by the strong encouragement of my fiancée Krittiyanee. Her perspectives as an entrepreneur and small business founder offered both a reality check as well as ongoing support. Her business activities in Thailand, Myanmar, Vietnam, and Laos also offered insight on the challenges of building sustainable businesses in different countries and markets.

A final word of thanks goes to my extended family in the United States, Europe, Australia, and Thailand, and to my many friends around the world. It's hard to be precise about where ideas germinate or how they evolve. Many comments and ideas made their way into my research journal—some only a reference to track down later or a partial idea to be completed another day. Everyone's participation is appreciated. In the end, I hope I've done justice to such an important topic and paved the way for an improved focus on sustainability.

APPENDIX:
LIST OF RESOURCES

Resource	SDG Goal	SDG Goal	Website URL
ABNT Ecolabel (Brazil)	12	Responsible Consumption and Production	http://www.abnt.org.br
Academy of Business in Society (Brussels)	17	Partnerships for the Goals	https://www.abis-global.org
Action Against Hunger	2	Zero Hunger	https://www.actionagainsthunger.org
Action for Conservation	4	Quality Education	https://www.actionforconservation.org
Active Transportation Alliance	11	Sustainable Cities and Communities	https://activetrans.org
AFIDEP	3	Good Health and Well Being	https://www.afidep.org
African Impact	5	Gender Equality	https://www.africanimpact.com/girl-empowerment-programs-in-africa/
African Pangolin Working Group	15	Life on Land	https://africanpangolin.org
Agriculture Biologique Certifications (France)	15	Life on Land	https://certifications.controlunion.com/en/certification-programs/certification-programs/ab-agriculture-biologique-france
AIAB (Italy)	15	Life on Land	https://aiab.it
All We Can Save	13	Climate Action	https://www.allwecansave.earth
Amref (Health Africa)	3	Good Health and Well Being	https://amref.org
Animal Welfare Approved (AWA)	15	Life on Land	https://agreenerworld.org/certifications/animal-welfare-approved/

Resource	SDG Goal	SDG Goal	Website URL
ASEAN Sustainability CSR Reporting	17	Partnerships for the Goals	http://asean-csr-network.org/c/component/tags/tag/14-sustainability-reporting
Asia Pacific Economic Cooperation	10	Reduced Inequalities	https://www.apec.org
Asia Sustainability Reporting - CSR Matters	17	Partnerships for the Goals	https://csrmatters.com
Association for Talent Development - ATD	4	Quality Education	TD.org
Au Fil des Seounes (France)	11	Sustainable Cities and Communities	https://aufildesseounes.jimdofree.com/
Audubon International Certified Sustainable Communities	11	Sustainable Cities and Communities	https://www.auduboninternational.org/sustainable-communities-program
B Certification	12	Responsible Consumption and Production	https://www.bcorporation.net
B Impact Assessment	12	Responsible Consumption and Production	https://app.bimpactassessment.net/login
BCA Green Mark (Singapore)	11	Sustainable Cities and Communities	https://www.bca.gov.sg/greenmark/green_mark_buildings.html
BEAM Hong Kong	11	Sustainable Cities and Communities	https://www.beamsociety.org.hk/en_index.php
Benefit Corporation, The	12	Responsible Consumption and Production	http://benefitcorp.net
Bicycle Kitchen	11	Sustainable Cities and Communities	https://bicyclekitchen.org
Bill and Melinda Gates Foundation	3	Good Health and Well Being	https://www.gatesfoundation.org
Black Lives Matter	10	Reduced Inequalities	https://blacklivesmatter.com
Blue Sphere Foundation	14	Life Below Water	https://www.bluespherefoundation.org
Bluesign	12	Responsible Consumption and Production	https://www.bluesign.com
BM&F Bovespa Corporate Sustainability Index (ISE)	9	Industry Innovation and Infrastructure	http://www.b3.com.br/en_us/market-data-and-indices/indices/sustainability-indices/corporate-sustainability-index-ise.htm

Resource	SDG Goal	SDG Goal	Website URL
BMP Certified Cotton (Australia)	12	Responsible Consumption and Production	https://www.cottonaustralia.com.au/mybmp
Bonobo Project	15	Life on Land	http://www.bonoboproject.org
Borgen Project	1	No Poverty	https://borgenproject.org
Break Poverty Foundation	1	No Poverty	https://breakpoverty.com/en/the-foundation/
Calgary Wildlife Rehabilitation Society (Canada)	15	Life on Land	https://calgarywildlife.org
California Endowment	10	Reduced Inequalities	https://www.calendow.org
Canadian Society for International Health	3	Good Health and Well Being	https://www.csih.org/en
Carbon Disclosure Project (CDP), The	7	Affordable and Clean Energy	https://www.cdp.net/en
Carbon Footprint	13	Climate Action	https://www.carbonfootprint.com
Carbon Footprint Calculator	13	Climate Action	http://www.carbonify.com/carbon-calculator.htm
Carbon Footprint Calculators - Business	13	Climate Action	https://www.carbonfootprint.com/businesscarboncalculator.html
Carbon Footprint Calculators - Personal	13	Climate Action	http://calculator.carbonfootprint.com
Carbon Footprint Calculators - Personal	13	Climate Action	https://www.nature.org/greenliving/carboncalculator/index.htm
Carbon Neutral Certification	13	Climate Action	https://www.carbonneutral.com/certification
Carbon Reduction Institute (Australia)	13	Climate Action	https://noco2.com.au
Carbon Reduction Label	13	Climate Action	http://www.ecolabelindex.com/ecolabel/carbon-reduction-label
Cement Industry Sustainability Manufacturing Program (PCA)	9	Industry Innovation and Infrastructure	https://www.cement.org/structures/manufacturing/cement-industry-sustainability-manufacturing-program
Center for Ecoliteracy	12	Responsible Consumption and Production	https://www.ecoliteracy.org
Center for Regenerative Agriculture	15	Life on Land	https://www.ojaicra.org

Appendix

Resource	SDG Goal	SDG Goal	Website URL
Center For Remanufacturing and Reuse (CRR)	9	Industry Innovation and Infrastructure	http://www.remanufacturing.org.uk
Center for the Advancement of the Steady State Economy (Herman Daly)	17	Partnerships for the Goals	http://www.steadystate.org/herman-daly/
Center for Watershed Protection	6	Clean Water and Sanitation	https://www.cwp.org
Central Asia Institute	5	Gender Equality	https://centralasiainstitute.org/improving-girls-education-in-developing-countries/
CERES	15	Life on Land	https://www.ceres.org
Certified Gluten Free	15	Life on Land	https://gfco.org
Certified Wildlife Friendly	15	Life on Land	http://wildlifefriendly.org
Child Labor Coalition	8	Decent Work and Economic Growth	http://stopchildlabor.org
Children's Institute	3	Good Health and Well Being	https://www.childrensinstitute.org
Clean Development Initiative	13	Climate Action	https://cdm.unfccc.int/about/index.html
Clean Development Mechanisms (CER Credits)	13	Climate Action	https://cdm.unfccc.int/about/index.html
Clean Water Foundation (Canada)	6	Clean Water and Sanitation	http://cleanwaterfoundation.org
Clean Water Services	6	Clean Water and Sanitation	https://www.cleanwaterservices.org
Climate Council of Australia	13	Climate Action	https://www.climatecouncil.org.au
Climate Justice Alliance	16	Peace, Justice and Strong Institutions	https://climatejusticealliance.org
CO2 levels in Atmosphere	13	Climate Action	https://www.co2.earth
Coastal Conservation and Education Foundation (Philippines)	14	Life Below Water	https://www.coast.ph
Columbia Mountains Institute of Applied Ecology (Canada)	4	Quality Education	https://cmiae.org

Appendix

Resource	SDG Goal	SDG Goal	Website URL
Commissioners	16	Peace, Justice and Strong Institutions	http://businesscommission.org/commissioners
Concern Worldwide	1	No Poverty	https://www.concernusa.org
Conservation Alliance	8	Decent Work and Economic Growth	http://www.conservationalliance.com
Conservation International	13	Climate Action	https://www.conservation.org/Pages/default.aspx
Corporate Knights – The Magazine for Clean Capitalism	12	Responsible Consumption and Production	http://www.corporateknights.com
Corporate Knights Global 100	12	Responsible Consumption and Production	http://www.corporateknights.com/magazines/2018-global-100-issue/2018-global-100-results-15166618/
Crees Foundation (Peru)	11	Sustainable Cities and Communities	https://www.crees-foundation.org
Crocevia Center International (Italy)	11	Sustainable Cities and Communities	https://www.croceviaterra.it/
Croeni Foundation	1	No Poverty	https://www.croeni.org/initiatives/poverty-prevention/
Cuso International	1	No Poverty	https://cusointernational.org
David R. Atkinson Center for a Sustainable Future (Cornell University)	11	Sustainable Cities and Communities	https://www.atkinson.cornell.edu
Deploy US	17	Partnerships for the Goals	https://www.deployus.org
DGNB (Germany)	11	Sustainable Cities and Communities	https://www.dgnb.de/en/
Dignitas International	3	Good Health and Well Being	https://dignitasinternational.org
Doctors Without Borders	3	Good Health and Wellbeing	http://www.doctorswithoutborders.org
Dow Jones Sustainability Index	9	Industry Innovation and Infrastructure	https://www.spglobal.com/esg/csa/indices/
Earth Institute – Columbia University	13	Climate Action	http://earth.columbia.edu
Earth Isand Institute	13	Climate Action	https://www.earthisland.org
Eco Albania (Albania)	13	Climate Action	http://www.ecoalbania.org/en/home19/
Eco Benin (Benin Africa)	13	Climate Action	https://www.ecobenin.org

Resource	SDG Goal	SDG Goal	Website URL
Eco Justice Canada Society	16	Peace, Justice and Strong Institutions	https://ecojustice.ca
EDGE Certification for Gender Equality	5	Gender Equality	http://edge-cert.org
Educate Girls Foundation (Skoll)	4	Quality Education	https://skoll.org/organization/educate-girls-foundation/
Educate Girls Globally	4	Quality Education	https://www.educategirls.org
Educating Girls Matters	4	Quality Education	http://www.educatinggirlsmatters.org/howtohelp.html
Elders, The	16	Peace, Justice and Strong Institutions	https://www.theelders.org
Electric Utility Industry Sustainable Supply Chain Alliance	9	Industry Innovation and Infrastructure	https://www.euissca.org
End Human Trafficking Now	8	Decent Work and Economic Growth	https://endhtnow.org
End Poverty Now	1	No Poverty	https://www.endpovertynowinc.org
End Slavery Now	8	Decent Work and Economic Growth	https://www.endslaverynow.org
Energy Storage Association	7	Affordable and Clean Energy	https://pastureproject.org/about-us/regenerative-grazing-benefits/
Engineers Without Borders (EWB)	1	No Poverty	https://www.ewb-usa.org
Ennvironmental Law Institute	16	Peace, Justice and Strong Institutions	https://www.eli.org
Environmental Law Alliance Worldwide	16	Peace, Justice and Strong Institutions	https://www.elaw.org
Environmetal Law and Policy Center	16	Peace, Justice and Strong Institutions	http://elpc.org
Equal Justice Initiative	16	Peace, Justice and Strong Institutions	https://eji.org
Equality Now	5	Gender Equality	https://www.equalitynow.org
ESII Ecosystem Services Identification and Inventory Tool	15	Life on Land	http://www.esiitool.com/why-esii
Espors d'enfants (Children's Hope Association - France)	4	Quality Education	https://espoirsdenfants.org/

Resource	SDG Goal	SDG Goal	Website URL
Europen – the European Organization for Packaging and the Environment	12	Responsible Consumption and Production	http://www.europen-packaging.eu
Fair Factories Clearinghouse	8	Decent Work and Economic Growth	https://www.fairfactories.org
Fair for Life	8	Decent Work and Economic Growth	http://www.fairforlife.org
Fair Labor Practices and Community Benefits	8	Decent Work and Economic Growth	https://www.scsglobalservices.com
FairTrade Certification	8	Decent Work and Economic Growth	https://www.fairtradecertified.org
Fairtrade Federation	8	Decent Work and Economic Growth	http://www.fairtradefederation.org
Fairtrade International	8	Decent Work and Economic Growth	https://www.fairtrade.net
Family Farm Defenders	12	Responsible Consumption and Production	https://familyfarmers.org
Feed The Children	2	Zero Hunger	https://www.feedthechildren.org
Feed The Hungry (LeSEA Global)	2	Zero Hunger	https://www.feedthehungry.org
FLOCert	8	Decent Work and Economic Growth	https://www.flocert.net
Food and Water Watch	6	Clean Water and Sanitation	https://www.foodandwaterwatch.org
Food For The Hungry	2	Zero Hunger	https://www.fh.org
Food For The Poor	2	Zero Hunger	https://www.foodforthepoor.org
Food Loss and Waste Accounting and Reporting Standard	12	Responsible Consumption and Production	http://flwprotocol.org
Food Security Information Network	2	Zero Hunger	https://www.fsinplatform.org
Forest Ecology Network	15	Life on Land	http://www.forestecologynetwork.org
Fossil Fuel Dependency by Country	13	Climate Action	https://www.worldatlas.com/articles/countries-the-most-dependent-on-fossil-fuels.html

Appendix

Resource	SDG Goal	SDG Goal	Website URL
Foundation for Education and Development (Thailand)	8	Decent Work and Economic Growth	http://ghre.org/en/home/
Foundation for National Parks and Wildlife (Australia)	15	Life on Land	https://www.fnpw.org.au
Freedom from hunger	2	Zero Hunger	https://www.freedomfromhunger.org
Friends of the Oxtongue	11	Sustainable Cities and Communities	https://friendsoftheoxtongue.com
Friends of the Sea	14	Life Below Water	http://www.friendofthesea.org
Gender and Development Network	5	Gender Equality	http://gadnetwork.org
Girls' Secondary Education in Developing Countries (MacArthur Foundation)	4	Quality Education	https://www.macfound.org/programs/girlseducation/
Global Citizen	10	Reduced Inequalities	https://www.globalcitizen.org/en/
Global Health Innovation Fund (Merck)	3	Good Health and Well Being	http://www.merckghifund.com
Global Healthy Workplaces Certificate	4	Quality Education	https://www.globalhealthyworkplace.org
Global Impact Sourcing Coalition	12	Responsible Consumption and Production	https://gisc.bsr.org
Global Poverty Project	1	No Poverty	https://www.globalcitizen.org/en/content/topics/global-poverty-project_1/
Global Reporting Initiative (GRI)	12	Responsible Consumption and Production	https://www.globalreporting.org
Go Compare	7	Affordable and Clean Energy	http://www.gocompare.com/gas-and-electricity/what-powers-the-world/
Goodweave	12	Responsible Consumption and Production	https://goodweave.org
GPE (Global Partnership for Education)	4	Quality Education	https://www.globalpartnership.org/what-we-do/gender-equality
Gravity Water	6	Clean Water and Sanitation	https://www.gravitywater.org

Resource	SDG Goal	SDG Goal	Website URL
Green Blue – Sustainable Packaging Coalition	12	Responsible Consumption and Production	http://greenblue.org/work/ sustainable-packaging-coalition/
Green For All (Dream Corps)	11	Sustainable Cities and Communities	https://www.thedreamcorps.org/ our-programs/green-for-all/
Green Gas	7	Affordable and Clean Energy	https://greengasmovement.org
Green Seal	9	Industry Innovation and Infrastructure	http://www.greenseal.org
GreenBiz	9	Industry Innovation and Infrastructure	https://www.greenbiz.com
Greenpeace	13	Climate Action	https://www.greenpeace.org/ international/
Hachijojima Mizukaiyama Green and Water Conservation Society (Japan)	6	Clean Water and Sanitation	http://mizumiyama.blog14.fc2.com/
Health Europa	3	Good Health and Well Being	https://www.healtheuropa.eu
Health Forward Foundation	3	Good Health and Well Being	https://healthforward.org/grantees- and-applicants/what-we-fund/ foundation-defined-grants/ healthy-communities/
Health Systems Global (HSG)	3	Good Health and Well Being	https://healthsystemsglobal.org
Healthy Communities Foundation	3	Good Health and Well Being	https://hcfdn.org
Heifer International	1	No Poverty	https://www.heifer.org
Hong Kong Eco-label	12	Responsible Consumption and Production	http://www.hkfep.com
Human Rights Campaign	5	Gender Equality	https://www.hrc.org
Human Rights Campaign Equality Index	16	Peace, Justice and Strong Institutions	https://www.hrc.org/campaigns/ corporate-equality-index
Humanitarian Innovation Fund	6	Clean Water and Sanitation	https://www.elrha.org/programme/hif/
HUMY (Formerly Projects Plus Actions - France)	15	Life on Land	https://www.humy.org/

Appendix

Resource	SDG Goal	SDG Goal	Website URL
Hunger Project	2	Zero Hunger	http://www.thp.org
Inequality.org (A project of the Institute for Policy Studies)	10	Reduced Inequalities	https://inequality.org
Instituto Peabiru (Brazil)	13	Climate Action	https://peabiru.org.br/quem-somos/
Integrated Reporting	9	Industry Innovation and Infrastructure	https://integratedreporting.org
International Food Policy Research Institute	2	Zero Hunger	https://www.ifpri.org
International Labor Organization (ILO)	10	Reduced Inequalities	https://www.ilo.org/global/lang--en/index.htm
International Legal Assistance Consortium	16	Peace, Justice and Strong Institutions	http://www.ilacnet.org
International Peace Institute	16	Peace, Justice and Strong Institutions	https://www.ipinst.org
International Programme on Fair Recruitment (FAIR) at ILO	8	Decent Work and Economic Growth	https://www.ilo.org/global/topics/labour-migration/projects/WCMS_405819/lang--en/index.htm
International Renewable Energy Agency	7	Affordable and Clean Energy	http://www.irena.org
International Solid Waste Association	15	Life on Land	https://www.iswa.org
International Youth Foundation's Global Youth Well-being Index	4	Quality Education	https://www.youthindex.org
IPA (Innovations for Poverty Action)	1	No Poverty	https://www.poverty-action.org
ISO 14000 Series Environmental Management	9	Industry Innovation and Infrastructure	https://www.iso.org/iso-14001-environmental-management.html
Jantzi Social Index	9	Industry Innovation and Infrastructure	https://www.sustainalytics.com/jantzi-social-index/
Japan Environmental Action Network	14	Life Below Water	http://www.jean.jp/en/
Japan Tropical Forest Action Network	13	Climate Action	http://www.jatan.org/eng/index-e.html
Judicial Watch	16	Peace, Justice and Strong Institutions	https://www.judicialwatch.org

Appendix

Resource	SDG Goal	SDG Goal	Website URL
Kahea - The Hawaiian Environmental Alliance	11	Sustainable Cities and Communities	http://www.kahea.org
Kaua'I Bee Team	15	Life on Land	https://kauaibeeteam.org
Khan Academy	4	Quality Education	https://www.khanacademy.org
Korea Green Foundation (Korea)	13	Climate Action	http://www.greenfund.org/en/
Kresge Foundation	10	Reduced Inequalities	https://kresge.org
Latin American Confederation of Water and Sanitation Community Organizations (CLOCSAS)	6	Clean Water and Sanitation	http://www.clocsas.org
Le Partenariat (International solidarity organization - France)	17	Partnerships for the Goals	https://www.lepartenariat.org
LEED	11	Sustainable Cities and Communities	http://leed.usgbc.org/leed.html
LEED for Sustainable Cities Certification	11	Sustainable Cities and Communities	https://new.usgbc.org/leed-for-cities
Living Streets Alliance	11	Sustainable Cities and Communities	https://livingstreetsalliance.org
Low Carbon Economy Certified (Australia)	11	Sustainable Cities and Communities	http://lowcarboneconomy.com.au
Malala Fund	4	Quality Education	https://malala.org/girls-education
Marine Stewardship Council	14	Life Below Water	https://www.msc.org
Massachusetts Institute of Technology (MIT) Senseable Cities Lab	11	Sustainable Cities and Communities	http://senseable.mit.edu
Maui Tomorrow Foundation	11	Sustainable Cities and Communities	https://maui-tomorrow.org
Medical Teams International	3	Good Health and Well Being	https://www.medicalteams.org
Mentors International to End Poverty	1	No Poverty	https://mentorsinternational.org
Microfinance Association	8	Decent Work and Economic Growth	http://www.microfinanceassociation.org
Migrant Workers Dignity Association (Canada)	8	Decent Work and Economic Growth	https://dignidadmigrante.ca

Resource	SDG Goal	SDG Goal	Website URL
National Academy of Sciences	13	Climate Action	http://www.pnas.org
National Green Tribunal (India)	17	Partnerships for the Goals	https://greentribunal.gov.in
National Oceanic and Atmospheric Administration (US)	13	Climate Action	http://www.noaa.gov
National Resources Defense Council	13	Climate Action	https://www.nrdc.org
National Sustainable Agriculture Coalition	12	Responsible Consumption and Production	https://sustainableagriculture.net
National Sustainable Agriculture Coalition	12	Responsible Consumption and Production	https://sustainableagriculture.net
National Underground Railroad Freedom Center	8	Decent Work and Economic Growth	http://www.freedomcenter.org
Natural Capital Coalition	6	Clean Water and Sanitation	https://naturalcapitalcoalition.org
Nature Collective	11	Sustainable Cities and Communities	https://thenaturecollective.org
Nature Conservancy, The	15	Life on Land	https://www.nature.org
Neighbors Against Poverty	1	No Poverty	http://www.neighborsagainstpoverty.org
Network for Business Sustainability	9	Industry Innovation and Infrastructure	https://nbs.net
Network for Good (End Poverty in Africa)	1	No Poverty	https://www.networkforgood.org/topics/international/africa/
New York Times Climate Section	4	Quality Education	https://www.nytimes.com/section/climate
No Kid Hungry	2	Zero Hunger	https://www.nokidhungry.org
Numi Foundation	11	Sustainable Cities and Communities	https://numifoundation.org
Ocean Care	14	Life Below Water	https://www.oceancare.org/en/startpage/
Ocean Conservancy, The	14	Life Below Water	https://oceanconservancy.org
Ocean River Institute	14	Life Below Water	https://www.oceanriver.org

Resource	SDG Goal	SDG Goal	Website URL
Ocean Wise	14	Life Below Water	https://ocean.org
Oceanic Global	14	Life Below Water	https://oceanic.global
Ocearch	14	Life Below Water	https://www.ocearch.org
One Percent for the Planet	13	Climate Action	https://www.onepercentfortheplanet.org
Open Society Foundations	10	Reduced Inequalities	https://www.opensocietyfoundations.org
Overseas Development Seas	1	No Poverty	https://www.odi.org
Oxfam International	1	No Poverty	https://www.oxfam.org//
Oyster Recovery Project	14	Life Below Water	https://oysterrecovery.org
Pasture Project - Regenerative Grazing	12	Responsible Consumption and Production	https://pastureproject.org/about-us/regenerative-grazing-benefits/
Pearl Rating System (Abu Dhabi)	11	Sustainable Cities and Communities	https://www.upc.gov.ae/en/estidama/pearl-rating-system/pearl-building-rating-system
Pembina Institute (Canada)	7	Affordable and Clean Energy	https://www.pembina.org
Pesticide Action Network (Germany)	12	Responsible Consumption and Production	https://pan-germany.org
Piedmont Environmental Alliance	13	Climate Action	https://www.peanc.org
Planet-Water	6	Clean Water and Sanitation	http://www.planet-water.org
Plastic Free Seas (Hong Kong)	14	Life Below Water	https://www.plasticfreeseas.org
Plastic Polution Coalition	12	Responsible Consumption and Production	https://www.plasticpollutioncoalition.org
PlasticCo Project (Ecuador)	12	Responsible Consumption and Production	https://www.plasticoproject.com
Progressio	1	No Poverty	https://www.progressio.org.uk
Quality Assurance Standard (for Carbon Offsets)	7	Affordable and Clean Energy	https://qascarbonneutral.com/carbon-offset-standards/

Resource	SDG Goal	SDG Goal	Website URL
Racial Equity Here	16	Peace, Justice and Strong Institutions	https://racialequityhere.org
Rainforest Action Alliance	13	Climate Action	https://www.ran.org
Rainforest Alliance Certified	15	Life on Land	https://www.rainforest-alliance.org/find-certified
Relief Web	3	Good Health and Well Being	https://reliefweb.int
Responsible Purchasing Network	12	Responsible Consumption and Production	http://www.responsiblepurchasing.org
Rock The Earth	13	Climate Action	https://rocktheearth.org
Rompientes Foundation (Chile)	11	Sustainable Cities and Communities	http://rompientes.org/
Save the Blue Heart of Europe	13	Climate Action	https://www.balkanrivers.net/en
School Communities Recycling All Paper (Australia)	11	Sustainable Cities and Communities	https://www.scrapltd.com.au
Shared Value Initiative (Michael Porter)	9	Industry Innovation and Infrastructure	https://www.sharedvalue.org
Sierra Club	15	Life on Land	https://www.sierraclub.org
SIMBIO - Sistemi Innovativi di Mantenimento della Biodiversità (Italy)	12	Responsible Consumption and Production	https://simbio.life/en/home/
Singaporean Green label Scheme	12	Responsible Consumption and Production	https://www.sgls.sec.org.sg
Slow Food	12	Responsible Consumption and Production	https://www.slowfood.com
Socical and Environmental Entrepreneurs	12	Responsible Consumption and Production	https://saveourplanet.org
Society for Human Resource Management - SHRM	4	Quality Education	SHRM.org
Something Good In The World	4	Quality Education	http://somethinggoodintheworld.org

Appendix

Resource	SDG Goal	SDG Goal	Website URL
Sonke Justice Center	5	Gender Equality	http://genderjustice.org.za
SR3 (Sealife Response, Rehabilitation and Research)	14	Life Below Water	https://www.sealifer3.org
Stanford University Social Innovation Review	9	Industry Innovation and Infrastructure	https://ssir.org
STAR Communities	11	Sustainable Cities and Communities	http://www.starcommunities.org
State of the Planet Blog – Columbia University	13	Climate Action	http://blogs.ei.columbia.edu
STOXX Global ESG Leaders Index	9	Industry Innovation and Infrastructure	https://www.stoxx.com/ index-details?symbol=SXWESGP
Sustainability at Harvard	9	Industry Innovation and Infrastructure	https://green.harvard.edu
Sustainability Disclosure Database	9	Industry Innovation and Infrastructure	http://database.globalreporting.org/ SDG-12-6/about-sustainablility-reporting
Sustainable Apparel Coalition	8	Decent Work and Economic Growth	https://apparelcoalition.org
Sustainable Development Goals	17	Partnerships for the Goals	https://sustainabledevelopment.un.org/ sdgs
Sustainable Manufacturing Toolkit (OECD)	12	Responsible Consumption and Production	https://www.oecd.org/innovation/green/ toolkit/#d.en.192438
Sustainable Packaging Coalition	12	Responsible Consumption and Production	https://sustainablepackaging.org
SXI Switzerland Sustainability 25	9	Industry Innovation and Infrastructure	https://www.six-swiss-exchange. com/indices/data_centre/shares/ sxi_ssust_en.html
TeachMideast	5	Gender Equality	https://teachmideast.org/articles/ introduction-women-gender-roles- middle-east/
Transform To Net Zero	13	Climate Action	https://transformtonetzero.org
UCI Urban Sustainability Index (China)	11	Sustainable Cities and Communities	http://www.urbanchinainitiative.org/en/
UN Food and Agriculture Organization (FAO)	2	Zero Hunger	http://www.fao.org/home/en/

Resource	SDG Goal	SDG Goal	Website URL
UN Global Compact	17	Partnerships for the Goals	https://www.unglobalcompact.org
UN Global Compact 100 Index	17	Partnerships for the Goals	https://www.unglobalcompact.org/take-action/action/global-compact-100
UN Intergovernmental Panel on Climate Change (IPCC)	13	Climate Action	http://www.ipcc.ch
UN Women	5	Gender Equality	https://www.unwomen.org/en
United Nations Girls Education Initiative	4	Quality Education	http://www.ungei.org/news/247_2165.html
United Nations Sustainable Development Knowledge Platform	17	Partnerships for the Goals	https://sustainabledevelopment.un.org
University of California Davis Agriculture Sustainability Institute	12	Responsible Consumption and Production	https://asi.ucdavis.edu
University of California Sustainable Power and Energy Center	7	Affordable and Clean Energy	https://spec.ucsd.edu
Urban Institute	3	Good Health and Well Being	https://www.urban.org
USDA Organic	15	Life on Land	https://www.usda.gov/topics/organic
Utopia Scientific	4	Quality Education	http://www.utopiascientific.org
Verified Carbon Standard program	7	Affordable and Clean Energy	http://verra.org/project/vcs-program/
Wanicare Foundation (Netherlands)	15	Life on Land	http://www.wanicare.com
Waste and Resources Action Programme (WRAP)	12	Responsible Consumption and Production	http://www.wrap.org.uk
Waste Free Oceans	14	Life Below Water	https://www.wastefreeoceans.org
Water Aid (UK)	6	Clean Water and Sanitation	https://www.wateraid.org/uk/
Water Innovation Engine (Global Innovation Fund)	6	Clean Water and Sanitation	https://www.globalinnovation.fund/the-water-innovation-engine/
Water Journalists Africa	6	Clean Water and Sanitation	https://waterjournalistsafrica.com/openwaterdiplomacylab/
Water.org	6	Clean Water and Sanitation	https://water.org/our-impact/water-crisis/

Resource	SDG Goal	SDG Goal	Website URL
Watershed Research Cooperative (Oregon State University)	6	Clean Water and Sanitation	http://watershedsresearch.org
Western Watersheds Project	6	Clean Water and Sanitation	https://www.westernwatersheds.org
White Ribbon	5	Gender Equality	https://www.whiteribbon.ca
Wild Seed Project	15	Life on Land	https://wildseedproject.net
William T. Grant Foundation	10	Reduced Inequalities	http://wtgrantfoundation.org/focus-areas/reducing-inequality
Women's Human Rights Institute	5	Gender Equality	http://learnwhr.org
World Business Council for Sustainable Development	9	Industry Innovation and Infrastructure	https://www.wbcsd.org
World Economic Forum	10	Reduced Inequalities	https://www.weforum.org
World Fish Center	14	Life Below Water	https://www.worldfishcenter.org
World Food Program	2	Zero Hunger	https://www.wfp.org
World Population Clock	9	Industry Innovation and Infrastructure	http://www.worldometers.info/world-population/
World Population History	9	Industry Innovation and Infrastructure	http://worldpopulationhistory.org
World Resources Institute	15	Life on Land	https://www.wri.org
World Trade Organization	10	Reduced Inequalities	https://www.wto.org
World Vision Partnership to End Poverty	1	No Poverty	https://www.worldvision.org.uk/who-we-are/world-vision-partnership/
World Wildlife Fund	15	Life on Land	https://www.worldwildlife.org
Zambian Carnivore Programme (Zambia)	15	Life on Land	https://www.zambiacarnivores.org
Zero Waste Business Council Certification program	12	Responsible Consumption and Production	https://true.gbci.org
Zero Waste Europe	11	Sustainable Cities and Communities	https://zerowasteeurope.eu

NOTES

Chapter 1: A Journey of Self-Discovery

1. "UK Inflation Calculator," Ed Parry, UK Personal Finance Guides, accessed June 12, 2018, https://www.moneysorter.co.uk/calculator_inflation2.html#calculator.

2. Jim Morrison, "Air Pollution Goes Back Way Further than You Think," *Smithsonian*, January 11, 2016, https://www.smithsonianmag.com/science-nature/air-pollution-goes-back-way-further-you-think-180957716.

3. Viviana A. Zelizer, *Pricing the Priceless Child: The Changing Social Value of Children* (Princeton, NJ: Princeton University Press, 1994), 6.

4. Johannes Friedrich and Thomas Damassa, "The History of Carbon Dioxide Emissions," World Resources Institute, May 21, 2014, https://www.wri.org/blog/2014/05/history-carbon-dioxide-emissions.

5. Max Roser, "Economic Growth," Our World in Data, accessed August 10, 2018, https://ourworldindata.org/economic-growth.

6. "Summary Findings," United States Department of Agriculture Economic Research Service, October 16, 2017, https://www.ers.usda.gov/data-products/international-agricultural-productivity/summary-findings.

7. "Threats: Soil Erosion and Degradation," World Wildlife Fund, accessed August 10, 2018, https://www.worldwildlife.org/threats/soil-erosion-and-degradation.

8. Tom Hatton, "Air Pollution in Victorian-Era Britain: Its Effects on Health Now Revealed," *The Conversation*, November 15, 2017, http://theconversation.com/air-pollution-in-victorian-era-britain-its-effects-on-health-now-revealed-87208.

9. Jim Morrison, "Air Pollution Goes Back Way Further Than You Think," *Smithsonian*, January 11, 2016, https://www.smithsonianmag.com/science-nature/air-pollution-goes-back-way-further-you-think-180957716.

10. Svante Arrhenius, "On the Influence of Carbonic Acid in the Air upon the Temperature of the Earth," *The London, Edinburgh and Dublin Philosophical Magazine and Journal of Science* 41, no. 5 (1896): 237–76.

11. Svante Arrhenius, *Worlds in the Making: The Evolution of the Universe* (London: Harper and Brothers Publishers, 1908), 63.

12. Johannes Friedrich and Thomas Damassa, "The History of Carbon Dioxide Emissions," World Resources Institute, May 21, 2014, https://www.wri.org/blog/2014/05/history-carbon-dioxide-emissions.

Notes

13. "World Population by Year," World Population Statistics, accessed September 5, 2018, http://www.worldpopulationstatistics.com/population-rankings/world-population-by-year.

14. Waldedmar Kaempffert, "Warmer Climate on the Earth May Be Due to More Carbon Dioxide in the Air," *The New York Times*, October 28, 1956.

15. *British Clean Air Act of 1956*, chapter 52, United Kingdom National Archives, http://www.legislation.gov.uk/ukpga/Eliz2/4-5/52/enacted.

16. "The Keeling Curve," Scripps Institution of Oceanography, accessed August 10, 2018, https://scripps.ucsd.edu/programs/keelingcurve.

17. "The Rich History of the City of Paterson, New Jersey," Paterson History, accessed July 18, 2018, http://www.patersonhistory.com.

18. "How Do You Begin to Clean up a Century of Pollution on New Jersey's Passaic River?" National Ocean and Atmospheric Administration (NOAA) Office of Response and Restoration, May 31, 2016, https://response.restoration.noaa.gov/about/media/how-do-you-begin-clean-century-pollution-new-jerseys-passaic-river.html.

19. Rachel Carson, *Silent Spring* (New York: Houghton Mifflin, 1962).

20. "E-waste Rises 8% by Weight in 2 Years, as Incomes Rise, Prices Fall," International Solid Waste Association (ISWA), December 13, 2017, https://www.iswa.org/home/news/news-detail/article/e-waste-rises-8-by-weight-in-2-years-as-incomes-rise-prices-fall/109.

21. C.P. Baldé, V. Forti, V. Gray, R. Kuehr, and P. Stegmann, *The Global E-waste Monitor—2017* (Bonn/Geneva/Vienna: United Nations University (UNU), International Telecommunication Union (ITU) & International Solid Waste Association (ISWA), 2017), 5.

22. "The Tail of the Fish," The Atlantic Cod Fishery, accessed August 14, 2018, http://www.atlanticcodfishery.com/history-of-the-fishery.html.

23. "Newfoundland's Cod Fishery," *CBC*, May 9, 2004, http://www.cbc.ca/news2/background/fishing/cod.html.

24. World Wildlife Fund, *A Roadmap for a Living Planet* (Gland, Switzerland: WWF International, 2008), 7, accessed October 19, 2018, http://d2ouvy59p0dg6k.cloudfront.net/downloads/roadmap_sign_off_fin.pdf.

25. Elizabeth Warren, interview by Charlie Rose, "'This Fight Is Our Fight': Charlie Rose" (video), *Bloomberg*, April 20, 2017, https://www.bloomberg.com/news/videos/2017-04-20/-this-fight-is-our-fight-charlie-rose-video.

26. Jacqueline Williams, "Australia Debates: Does Warming Planet Really Need More Coal?," *The New York Times*, October 14, 2017, https://www.nytimes.com/2017/10/14/world/australia/australia-adani-carmichael-coal-mine.html.

27. Ibid.

28. "Jack Ma Sees Decades of Pain as Internet Upends Old Economy," *Bloomberg*, April 24, 2017, https://www.bloomberg.com/news/articles/2017-04-23/jack-ma-sees-decades-of-pain-as-internet-upends-older-economy.

29. Andrew Freedman, "The Last Time CO_2 Was This High, Humans Didn't Exist," *Climate Central*, May 3, 2013, http://www.climatecentral.org/news/the-last-time-co2-was-this-high-humans-didnt-exist-15938.

30. "Scientific Consensus: Earth's Climate Is Warming," NASA: Global Climate Change: Vital Signs for the Planet, accessed July 30, 2018, https://climate.nasa.gov/scientific-consensus.

31. United Nations Department of Economic and Social Affairs, Population Division, *World Population Prospects 2015—Data Booklet* (New York, 2015), 3–5, https://esa.un.org/unpd/wpp/Publications/Files/WPP2015_DataBooklet.pdf.

32. "Daily CO$_2$," CO$_2$ Earth, accessed May 14, 2018, https://www.co2.earth/daily-co2.

33. Elizabeth Kolbert, *The Sixth Extinction: An Unnatural History* (New York: Henry Holt & Company, 2014).

34. Willy Blackmore, "Refilling Silver Lake Reservoir Is Inexcusably Wasteful. Better to Live with an Empty Pit," *Los Angeles Times*, April 30, 2017, http://www.latimes.com/opinion/livable-city/la-oe-blackmore-silver-lake-reservoir-20170430-story.html.

35. United Nations Food and Agriculture Organization (FAO), *General Situation of World Fish Stocks*, accessed September 5, 2018, http://www.fao.org/newsroom/common/ecg/1000505/en/stocks.pdf.

36. United Nations Food and Agricultural Organization (FAO), *State of the World's Forests 2012* (Rome: FAO, 2012), page 9, Figure 2, http://www.fao.org/3/a-i3010e.pdf.

37. World Bank, *Atlas of Sustainable Development Goals 2018: From World Development Indicators* (Washington, D.C: World Bank, 2018), https://openknowledge.worldbank.org/handle/10986/29788.

38. World Economic Forum, *The New Plastics Economy: Rethinking the Future of Plastics* (Geneva: World Economic Forum, 2016), http://www3.weforum.org/docs/WEF_The_New_Plastics_Economy.pdf.

39. Zeena Saifi, Victoria Brown, and Tom Page, "Start-up Devours Pollution with New Plastic Recycling Method," *CNN*, March 9, 2018, https://edition.cnn.com/2018/03/09/world/miranda-wang-tomorrows-hero/index.html.

40. Dhaval Kulkarni, "Maharashtra Plastic Ban: DNA Captures the Acceptance, Criticism, and Scepticism It Has Drawn," DNA, March 31, 2018, http://www.dnaindia.com/mumbai/report-maharashtra-big-ban-theory-2599527.

41. Intergovernmental Panel on Climate Change, *Climate Change 2007: Impacts, Adaptation and Vulnerability* (New York: Cambridge University Press, 2007), https://www.ipcc.ch/publications_and_data/ar4/wg2/en/ch8s8-4-2-4.html.

42. Karen Williams, "Pogo the Possum and the First Earth Day," Retroist, April 22, 2016, https://www.retroist.com/2016/04/22/pogo-the-possum-and-the-first-earth-day.

Chapter 2: Connecting Sustainability to Your Life Experience

1. Mark Malloch Brown, "Statement by Mark Malloch Brown, Administrator United Nations Development Programme, at the World Summit on Sustainable Development," Johannesburg, South Africa, August 30, 2002, https://sustainabledevelopment.un.org/index.php?page=view&type=255&nr=19701.

2. "Sustainability Metrics and Indices," Wikipedia, last modified August 30, 2018, https://en.wikipedia.org/wiki/Sustainability_metrics_and_indices.

3. United Nations World Commission on Environment and Development, *Our Common Future* (Oxford: Oxford University Press, 1987), 27.

4. Wade Hoxtell, Domenica Preysing, and Julia Steets, *Coming of Age: UN-Private Sector Collaboration Since 2000* (New York: United Nations Global Compact, 2010), https://business.un.org/en/assets/f30f513d-d6e2-4ece-a8e0-7e39552decbd.pdf.

5. "Sustainable Development Goals," United Nations Development Programme, accessed June 20, 2018, http://www.undp.org/content/undp/en/home/sustainable-development-goals.html.

6. "Transforming Our World: The 2030 Agenda for Sustainable Development," United Nations Sustainable Development Goals Knowledge Platform, October 21, 2015, http://sustainabledevelopment.un.org/post2015/transformingourworld.

7. "Dow Jones Sustainability Indices," RobecoSAM, accessed December 2, 2018, http://www.sustainability-indices.com.

8. Corporate Knights, http://www.corporateknights.com.

9. "AEPC Launches Indian Apparel Industry Sustainability (AISA) Programme to Promote Sustainable Practices in the Apparel Industry," Apparel Export Promotion Council, July 13, 2017, http://www.aepcindia.com/news/aepc-launches-indian-apparel-indus-try-sustain-ability-aisa-programme-promote-sustainable.

10. e.g., Sustainable Packaging Coalition, Charlottesville, Virginia, https://sustainablepackaging.org.

11. e.g., Events Industry Council, Washington, D.C., http://www.eventscouncil.org.

12. Cement Sustainability Initiative, https://www.wbcsdcement.org.

13. Cement Sustainability Initiative, *Cement Industry Energy and CO_2 Performance—Getting the Numbers Right (GNR)*, accessed September 3, 2018, http://www.wbcsdcement.org/pdf/GNR%20dox.pdf.

Chapter 3: Sustainability and Emerging Business Models

1. "About Unilever," Unilever, accessed July 20, 2018, https://www.unilever.com/about/who-we-are/about-Unilever.

2. Patrick Cescau (group chief executive, Unilever), "Unilever's Growth Strategy," presentation at Unilever investor seminar, London, March 13, 2007, https://www.unilever.com/Images/2007-investor-seminar-unilevers-growth-strategy-speech-patrick-cescau-ceo_tcm244-422224_en.pdf.

3. Jack Neff, "In Surprise Move, Unilever Names Polman CEO," *AdAge*, September 4, 2008, http://adage.com/article/news/surprise-move-unilever-names-polman-ceo/130735.

4. "Unilever Unveils Plan to Decouple Business Growth from Environmental Impact," Unilever Press Release, November 15, 2010, accessed October 18, 2018, https://www.unilever.com/news/press-releases/2010/10-11-15-Unilever-unveils-plan-to-decouple-business-growth-from-environmental-impact.html.

5. Jo Confino, "CEO Survey Is Gloomy Reading for the Corporate Sustainability Movement," *The Guardian*, September 20, 2013, https://www.theguardian.com/sustainable-business/ceo-survey-corporate-sustainability-movement.

6. "The Unilever Sustainable Living Plan," SDG Gateway, accessed October 18, 2018, https:// gateway.sdgcharter.nl/user/391/our-impact.

7. Unilever, *2016 Full Year Results: Competitive and Profitable Growth in Challenging Markets*, January 26, 2017, accessed July 24, 2018, https://www.unilever.com/Images/ ir-q4-2016-full-announcement_tcm244-497533_en.pdf.

8. "Unilever's Sustainable Living Brands Continue to Drive Higher Rates of Growth," Unilever, May 18, 2017, https://www.unilever.com/news/press-releases/2017/unilevers-sustainable-living-brands-continue-to-drive-higher-rates-of-growth.html.

9. "Unilever PLC Common Stock Historical Prices," NASDAQ, accessed July 15, 2018, https://www.nasdaq.com/symbol/ul/historical?tf=1y.

10. "About Unilever," Unilever, accessed June 21, 2018, https://www.unilever.com/about/ who-we-are/about-Unilever.

11. C.K. Prahalad and Stuart L. Hart, "The Fortune at the Bottom of the Pyramid," *Strategy + Business* no. 26, January 10, 2002, https://www.strategy-business.com/ article/11518?gko=9a4ba.

12. Sheila Bonini, Stephan Görner, and Alissa Jones, "How Companies Manage Sustainability: McKinsey Global Survey Results," McKinsey & Company, March 2010, https:// www.mckinsey.com/business-functions/sustainability-and-resource-productivity/ our-insights/how-companies-manage-sustainability-mckinsey-global-survey-results.

13. Michael Porter and Mark Kramer, "Creating Shared Value," *Harvard Business Review*, 2011, https://hbr.org/2011/01/the-big-idea-creating-shared-value.

14. Michael Porter, "The Case for Letting Business Solve Social Problems," TEDXGlobal 2013 video, June 2013, https://www.ted.com/talks/michael_porter_ why_business_can_be_good_at_solving_social_problems/up-next.

15. John Mackey and Rajendra Sisodia, *Conscious Capitalism: Liberating the Heroic Spirit of Business* (Cambridge: Harvard Business Review Press, 2012).

16. "With Planet 21, AccorHotels Aims to Provide a Positive Hospitality Experience," Accor Hotels, accessed June 23, 2018, https://mercure.accorhotels.com/gb/mercure-hotel/ sustainable-development.shtml.

17. William Stanley Jevons, *The Coal Question* (originally published London: Macmillan and Company, 1866, now available from The Library of Economics and Liberty, Carmel, Indiana), chapter 7, http://www.econlib.org/library/YPDBooks/Jevons/jvnCQ7.html.

18. United Nations Environmental Programme (UNEP) International Resource Panel, *Decoupling Natural Resource Use and Environmental Impacts from Economic Growth* (Nairobi, Kenya: UNEP, 2011), 8, http://wedocs.unep.org/bitstream/han-dle/20.500.11822/9816/-Decoupling%3a%20natural%20resource%20use%20 and%20environmental%20impacts%20from%20economic%20growth%20 -2011Decoupling_1.pdf?sequence=3&isAllowed=y.

19. Patrick Hull (global learning director, Unilever), during presentation at ABIS conference, Brussels, Belgium, November 15, 2017.

20. Ellen MacArthur Foundation, *Towards the Circular Economy Volume 3: Accelerating the Scale-up across the Global Supply Chains*, January 24, 2014, https://www.

ellenmacarthurfoundation.org/publicationstowards-the-circular-economy-vol-3-accelerating-the-scale-up-across-global-supply-chains.

21. "Platform for Accelerating the Circular Economy," World Economic Forum, accessed August 1, 2018, https://www.weforum.org/projects/circular-economy.

22. Beth Kowitt, "This Dairy Company Says Its Business Model Is the Future of Corporate America," *Fortune*, April 25, 2017, http://fortune.com/2017/04/25/danone-white-wave-benefit-corporation.

23. Ellen Berrey, "How Many Benefit Corporations Are There?" SSRN, May 5, 2015, http://ssrn.com/abstract=2602781.

24. "Italy Became a 'Lamp Shining a Light' for Other Countries to Pursue Better Business Benefit Corporation Structure Has Moved Beyond the U.S.," Nativa, October 13, 2017, https://nativalab.com/en/italy-became-a-lamp-shining-a-light-for-other-countries-to-pursue-better-business-benefit-corporation-structure-has-moved-beyond-the-u-s.

25. "About B Corps," Certified B Corporation, accessed September 20, 2018, https://www.bcorporation.net/what-are-b-corps/the-b-corp-declaration.

26. See Certified B Corporation website: https://bcorporation.net.

27. CK Staff, "The A-List of B Corps," *Corporate Knights*, April 16, 2015, http://www.corporateknights.com/channels/social-enterprise/list-b-corps-14291706.

28. "Fair Labor Association (FLA)," Patagonia, accessed September 1, 2018, https://www.patagonia.com/fair-labor-association.html.

29. "Fair Factories Clearinghouse (FCC)," Patagonia, accessed September 1, 2018, https://www.patagonia.com/fair-factories-clearinghouse.html.

30. "The Conservation Alliance," Patagonia, accessed September 1, 2018, https://www.patagonia.com/conservation-alliance.html.

31. "Sustainable Apparel Coalition," Patagonia, accessed September 1, 2018, https://www.patagonia.com/sustainable-apparel-coalition.html.

32. Anya Khalamayzer, "7 Companies Advancing the Circular Economy by Selling Products as a Service," GreenBiz, February 15, 2018, https://www.greenbiz.com/article/7-companies-offering-circular-economy-service.

33. "PyeongChang Olympics Organizers to Raise Funds to Offset Carbon Emissions," *Yonhap News*, December 28, 2017, http://english.yonhapnews.co.kr/news/2017/12/28/0200000000AEN20171228006900315.html.

34. Ibid.

Chapter 4: Smaller Companies Need a Different Solution

1. Organisation for Economic Co-operation and Development (OECD), *Meeting of the OECD Council at Ministerial Level* (Paris, June 7–8, 2017), 6–10, https://www.oecd.org/mcm/documents/C-MIN-2017-8-EN.pdf.

2. Thomas Stewart (executive director, National Center for the Middle Market) in discussion with the author, November 25, 2017 and August 2, 2018.

3. Ibid.

4. United States Small Business Association, Office of Advocacy, *Frequently Asked Questions*, September 2012, page 1, https://www.sba.gov/sites/default/files/FAQ_Sept_2012.pdf.

5. "What Is an SME?" European Commission, accessed September 10, 2018, http://ec.europa. eu/growth/smes/business-friendly-environment/sme-definition_en.

6. Paul Vandenberg, Pornpinun Chantapacdepong, and Naoyuki Yoshino, eds., *SMEs in Developing Asia: New Approaches to Overcoming Market Failures* (Tokyo: Asia Development Bank Institute, 2016), 2–9, https://www.adb.org/sites/default/files/publication/214476/ adbi-smes-developing-asia.pdf.

7. United Nations Social and Economic Commission for Asia and the Pacific, *SMEs in Asia and the Pacific*, 2009, 3–5, https://www.unescap.org/sites/default/files/7%20-%201.%20 SMEs%20IN%20ASIA%20AND%20THE%20PACIFIC.pdf.

8. EaPGREEN—Partnership for Environment and Growth, *Environmental Policy Toolkit for Greening SMEs in EU Eastern Partnership Countries* (Paris: OECD, 2015), 18, https:// www.oecd.org/environment/outreach/Greening-SMEs-policy-manual-eng.pdf.

9. United States Small Business Association, Office of Advocacy, *Small Business Profile*, 1, https://www.sba.gov/sites/default/files/advocacy/United_States.pdf.

10. "Small and Medium Enterprises (SMEs) Finance," World Bank, accessed September 15, 2018, http://www.worldbank.org/en/topic/smefinance.

11. "Jobs and Development," World Bank, updated September 18, 2018, http://www.world-bank.org/en/topic/jobsanddevelopment/overview.

12. W.S. Badger Company, *2016 Annual Impact Report*, 13, https://www.badgerbalm.com/pdf/ Badger-2016-Annual-Impact-Report.pdf.

13. "Local Area Unemployment Statistics: Unemployment Rates for States, Seasonally Adjusted," United States Department of Labor, Bureau of Labor Statistics, accessed July 25, 2018, https://www.bls.gov/web/laus/laumstrk.htm.

14. Rebecca Hamilton (vice president, Research and Development and chief sustainability officer, W.S. Badger Company) in discussion with the author, July 3, 2018.

15. Ibid.

16. W.S. Badger Company, *2017 Annual Impact Report*, 5, https://www.badgerbalm.com/pdf/ Badger-Annual-Impact-Report-2017-B-Corp.pdf.

17. New Hampshire Department of Health and Human Services, Office of Health Equity, *NH Refugee Resettlement—Country of Origin FY 2009–2017*, January 31, 2018, https:// www.dhhs.nh.gov/omh/refugee/documents/ref-pop-chart.pdf.

18. Gautam Bhushan (executive vice president and zonal head, Jana Small Finance Bank) in discussion with the author, June 12, 2018.

19. Supriti, Ramesh Ramanathan, and Sharon M. Barnhardt, *Urban Poverty Alleviation in India: Landmark Government Initiatives for the Urban Poor since Independence* (Bengaluru, India: Ramanathan Foundation, 2002).

20. Ramesh Ramanathan (chair, Jana Small Finance Bank) in discussion with the author, June 19, 2018.

21. HM Revenue & Customs, *Landfill Tax: Increase in Rates* (policy paper), March 16, 2016, https://www.gov.uk/government/publications/landfill-tax-increase-in-rates/ landfill-tax-increase-in-rates.

22. Greg Lavery (director, Lavery/Pennell) in discussion with the author, June 5, 2018.

23. Tanni Deb and Chris Giles, "Kenya's Empty Nets: How Cheap Chinese Fish Imports Have Hooked Buyers," *CNN*, April 18, 2018, https://edition.cnn.com/2018/04/16/africa/kenya-fish-china-imports-cheap-africa/index.html.

24. Mauricio Wendling Lopes (chief executive officer, MindQuest) in discussion with the author, June 6, 2018.

Chapter 5: It Always Starts with One Committed Leader

1. Manfred Kets de Vries, *Reflections on Character and Leadership: On the Couch with Manfred Kets de Vries* (Hoboken, NJ: Jossey-Bass, 2009), 211.

2. Anne-Titia Bové, Dorothee D'Herde, and Steven Swartz, "Sustainability's Deepening Imprint," McKinsey & Company, December 2017, Exhibit 4, https://www.mckinsey.com/business-functions/sustainability-and-resource-productivity/our-insights/sustainabilitys-deepening-imprint.

3. Greg Lavery (director, Lavery/Pennell) in discussion with the author, June 5, 2018.

4. Lavery/Pennell, *The New Industrial Model: Greater Profits, More Jobs and Reduced Environmental Impact* (February 2014), 16, http://laverypennell.com/wp-content/uploads/2014/03/New-Industrial-Model-report.pdf.

5. Beth Kowitt, "Climate Change Is about to Remake the Insurance Industry," *Fortune*, July 25, 2017, http://fortune.com/2017/07/25/climate-change-insurance-industry.

6. Michel Bande (senior executive vice president, Solvay) during presentation at ABIS conference, Brussels, Belgium, November 16, 2017.

7. Léon Wijnands (global head of sustainability, ING) during presentation at ABIS conference, Brussels, Belgium, November 15, 2017.

8. WhiteWave, *Corporate Social Responsibility Report 2014–2015* (2016), 40, http://www.whitewave.com/wp-content/uploads/2016/07/WhiteWave-CSR-2014_2015-Full-Report.pdf.

9. Sherif Hassane (director, Global Health Academic Partnerships, GSK) during presentation at ABIS conference, Brussels, Belgium, November 16, 2017.

10. "Sustainability Reporting," Sony, accessed July 10, 2018, https://www.sony.net/SonyInfo/csr_report/contribution.

11. SCG, "Employment of People with Disabilities," *Sustainability Report 2017, Ready to Deliver Sustainability* (Bangkok: SCG, 2018), 55, http://www.scg.com/en/05sustainability_development/03_sustainability_report.html.

12. Nitin Nohria and Michael Beer, "Cracking the Code of Change," *Harvard Business Review*, 2000, https://hbr.org/2000/05/cracking-the-code-of-change.

13. John P. Kotter, "Leading Change: Why Transformation Efforts Fail," *Harvard Business Review*, 2007, https://hbr.org/2007/01/leading-change-why-transformation-efforts-fail.

Chapter 6: Day-to-Day Problem-Solving Accelerates Change

1. Lan Anh, "Straw Mat Trade Village Is over 500 Years Old," *Vietnam Heritage* 2, no. 8 (2008), http://www.vietnamheritage.com.vn/pages/en/21418123940432-Straw-mat-trade-village-is-over-500-years-old.html.

2. Khanh Le, "Heart of Glass," *Vietnam Heritage* 2, no. 8 (2008), http://www.vietnamheritage.com.vn/pages/en/214181210807-Heart-of-Glass.html.

3. "Ho-Chunk/Winnebago," AAANative Arts, accessed June 19, 2018, https://www.aaanativearts.com/native-american-tribes-by-region/eastern-woodland-northeast-tribes/ho-chunk-indians.

4. David J. Wishart, ed., "Vision Quest," Encyclopedia of the Great Plains, accessed June 17, 2018, http://plainshumanities.unl.edu/encyclopedia/doc/egp.rel.051.

5. "Constitution of the Iroquois Nations," Indigenous People, accessed May 10, 2018, http://www.indigenouspeople.net/iroqcon.htm.

6. "Q+A: What Is Afganistan's Loya Jirga; What Does It Do?" Reuters, November 20, 2009, https://www.reuters.com/article/us-afghanistan-assembly-qa/qa-what-is-afghanistans-loya-jirga-what-does-it-do-idUSTRE5AJ18V20091120.

7. Steve Kerr, Dave Ulrich, and Ron Ashkenas, *The GE Workout: How to Implement GE's Revolutionary Method for Busting Bureaucracy & Attacking Organizational Problems* (New York: McGraw-Hill, 2002).

8. "CBI's Mutual Gains Approach to Negotiation," Consensus Building Institute, accessed May 5, 2018, https://www.cbi.org/article/mutual-gains-approach.

9. Trevor Martin (senior advisor, Galaxy Entertainment Group; former senior vice president human resources, Galaxy Entertainment Group) in discussion with the author, June 21, 2018.

10. "Ease of Doing Business Index," World Bank, accessed September 3, 2018, https://data.worldbank.org/indicator/ic.bus.ease.xq.

11. "Corruption Perceptions Index 2017," Transparency International, February 21, 2018, https://www.transparency.org/news/feature/corruption_perceptions_index_2017.

Chapter 7: Anchoring Sustainability into the DNA of Your Business

1. "Consumer-Goods' Brands That Demonstrate Commitment to Sustainability Outperform Those That Don't," Nielsen, October 12, 2015, http://www.nielsen.com/us/en/press-room/2015/consumer-goods-brands-that-demonstrate-commitment-to-sustainability-out-perform.html.

2. Audrey Choi, "How to Make a Profit While Making a Difference," TED@StateStreet video, November 2015, https://www.ted.com/talks/audrey_choi_how_to_make_a_profit_while_making_a_difference.

3. Chris McKnett, "The Investment Logic for Sustainability," TED@StateStreet video, November 2013, https://www.ted.com/talks/chris_mcknett_the_investment_logic_for_sustainability.

4. Christine Bader, "The Evolution of a Corporate Idealist," TED@NYC video, December 10, 2014, https://www.youtube.com/watch?v=jAh7YJFxgLg.

5. Harish Manwani, "Profit Is Not Always the Point," TED@BCG video, October 2013, https://www.ted.com/talks/harish_manwani_profit_s_not_always_the_point.

6. See United Nations Global Compact website, accessed September 9, 2018, https://www.unglobalcompact.org.

7. "Largest Casino Companies Worldwide in 2017, by Revenue (in Billion U.S. Dollars)," Statista, accessed July 15, 2018, https://www.statista.com/statistics/257531/leading-casino-companies-worldwide-by-revenue.

8. Galaxy Entertainment, *Q4 and Annual Results for the Period End December 31, 2017*, February 28, 2018, http://www.galaxyentertainment.com/uploads/investor/c098c7549f11a2a41f62821e548c126f8592e36c.pdf.

9. Trevor Martin (senior advisor, Galaxy Entertainment Group; former senior vice president human resources, Galaxy Entertainment Group) in discussion with the author, June 21, 2018.

10. "Founder's Philosophy," LUI Che Woo Prize, accessed July 18, 2018, http://www.luiprize.org/en/founder/founder-philosophy.

11. "Patagonia's Mission Statement," Patagonia, accessed June 24, 2018, http://www.patagonia.com/company-info.html.

12. "About the Prize," LUI Che Woo Prize, accessed July 18, 2018, http://www.luiprize.org/en/the-prize/about-the-prize.

13. Francis Ferdinand C. Cinco (former group human resources manager, East-West Seed Company) in discussion with the author, May 2, 2018.

14. "About Us," East-West Seed Company, accessed July 19, 2018, https://th.eastwestseed.com/aboutus/organization.

15. East-West Seed Company, *2017: Our Year in Review*, accessed July 19, 2018, https://th.eastwestseed.com/reports.

16. Mark Relova (group head, Learning and Employee Experience at East-West Seed Company) in discussion with the author, May 14, 2018.

17. Francis Ferdinand C. Cinco (former group human resources manager, East-West Seed Company) in discussion with the author, May 2, 2018.

18. Mark Relova (group head, Learning and Employee Experience at East-West Seed Company) in discussion with the author, May 14, 2018.

19. Mike Osorio (president of Organizational Change and Effectiveness at DFASS Group, and principal at Osorio Group LLC) in discussion with the author, May 2, 2018.

20. Leonard Greene, "Victoria's Secret Used Cotton Picked from Farms that Relied on Abused Children," *New York Post*, December 15, 2011, https://nypost.com/2011/12/15/victorias-secret-used-cotton-picked-from-farms-that-relied-on-abused-children.

21. Jason Burke and Saad Hammadi, "Bangladesh Textile Factory Fire Leaves More than 100 dead," *The Guardian*, November 25, 2012, https://www.theguardian.com/world/2012/nov/25/bangladesh-textile-factory-fire.

22. Angelica Mari, "Samsung Is Sued over Poor Working Conditions in Brazil," ZDNet, August 16, 2013, https://www.zdnet.com/article/samsung-is-sued-over-poor-working-conditions-in-brazil.

Chapter 8: Discovery, Value, and the Sharing of New Knowledge

1. Joe Haberman (managing partner, Global Markets at Heidrick & Struggles) in discussion with the author, June 8, 2018.

2. Everett M. Rogers, *Diffusion of Innovations* (New York: The Free Press, 1962), 174–77.

3. Nick Pennell (group operations director, Essentra PLC) in discussion with the author, June 19, 2018.

4. "Licensing Types," Creative Commons, accessed June 10, 2018, https://creativecommons.org/share-your-work/licensing-types-examples.

5. "CC Search," Creative Commons, accessed June 10, 2018, https://search.creativecommons.org.

6. LVMH, *LVMH Environmental Report 2017* (February 8, 2018), 6–8, https://r.lvmh-static.com/uploads/2018/04/lvmh_environment_2017en.pdf.

7. "Social & Environmental Responsibility," LVMH, accessed June 10, 2018, https://web-cache.googleusercontent.com/search?q=cache:_5nVueHxSNUJ:https://www.lvmh.com/categories/pillier-en/+&cd=1&hl=en&ct=clnk&gl=th&client=safari.

8. Ian Hardie (global vice president, Learning and Development, Sephora; former group executive development and learning director, LVMH) in discussions and e-mail exchanges with the author, July 25, 2018.

9. Sylvie Bénard (environment director, LVMH) in conversation with the author, September 11, 2018.

10. Peter McAteer and Michael Pino, *The Business Case for Creating a Corporate University* (Mechanicsburg, PA: Corporate University Xchange, 2011), 9.

11. Corporate University Research Ltd., *Corporate University Database*, Tortola, British Virgin Islands, accessed June 20, 2018, used with permission.

12. Ibid.

13. "DJSI World—Ticker W1SGI, " S&P Dow Jones Indices, accessed July 6, 2018, https://eu.spindices.com/indices/equity/dow-jones-sustainability-world-index.

14. Robert Eccles, Ioannis Ioannou, and George Serafeim, "Is Sustainability Now the Key to Corporate Success?" *The Guardian*, January 6, 2012, https://www.theguardian.com/sustainable-business/sustainability-key-corporate-success.

15. "Monthly Total Returns," PAX ESG Beta Quality Fund (PXWGX), PAX World Funds, accessed July 6, 2018, https://paxworld.com/funds/performance.

16. Kristian Heugh and Marc Fox, *ESG and the Sustainability of Competitive Advantage* (New York: Morgan Stanley, 2017), 2, https://www.morganstanley.com/im/publication/insights/investment-insights/ii_esgandthesustainabilityofcompetitiveadvantage_en.pdf.

17. Cambridge Institute for Sustainable Leadership, https://www.cisl.cam.ac.uk.

Chapter 9: Building Your Talent Plan

1. Richard Dictus (United Nations resident coordinator and United Nations Development Programme resident representative, Egypt) in discussion with the author, June 11, 2018.

2. Ibid.

3. Bill George, *Authentic Leadership* (Cambridge: Harvard Business School Publishing, 2003), 1–10.

4. Bill George, *Discover Your True North* (New York: John Wiley & Sons, 2015), 1–11.

5. "Big Business" (poll), Gallup, accessed July 20, 2018, https://news.gallup.com/poll/5248/big-business.aspx.

6. Edelman, *2018 Edelman Trust Barometer: The State of Trust in Business* (2018), 21, http://cms.edelman.com/sites/default/files/2018-02/2018_Edelman_Trust_Barometer_State_of_Business.pdf.

7. Dawn Denvir (global head of Learning and Development, The Nature Conservancy) in discussion with the author, June 19, 2018.

8. "The Dow Chemical Company," The Nature Conservancy, September 12, 2018, https://www.nature.org/en-us/about-us/who-we-are/how-we-work/working-with-companies/transforming-business-practices/dow-chemical-company.

9. Nitin Tikle (vice president, Strategic Sourcing, Mahindra & Mahindra) in discussion with the author, July 6, 2018.

10. Ibid.

Chapter 10: Strategies for Supporting an Evolving Business

1. C. Roland Christensen, David A. Garvin, and Ann Sweet, eds, *Education for Judgment: The Artistry of Discussion Leadership* (Boston: Harvard Business School Press, 1991).

2. "Teaching By the Case Method: Case Method in Practice," Harvard Business School, Christensen Center for Teaching & Learning, accessed July 15, 2018, https://www.hbs.edu/teaching/case-method/Pages/default.aspx.

Chapter 11: Key Areas for Training and Growth

1. "Top 10 CEOs Sent to Prison," *24/7 Wall St.* (blog), May 17, 2012, https://247wallst.com/special-report/2012/05/17/top-ten-ceos-sent-to-prison/2.

2. Patagonia, *Annual Benefit Corporation Report: Fiscal Year 2016* (2017), 22–23, http://www.societabenefit.net/wp-content/uploads/2016/11/Patagonia-2016.pdf.

3. Ibid., 22.

4. Ibid., 23.

5. Charles Duhugg and David Barboza, "In China, Human Costs Are Built into an iPad," *The New York Times*, January 25, 2012, https://www.nytimes.com/2012/01/26/business/ieconomy-apples-ipad-and-the-human-costs-for-workers-in-china.html?scp=8&sq=apple&st=cse.

6. Kraft Heinz, *Supply Chain Transparency and Labor Practices (Modern Slavery Statement)*, September 28, 2016, http://www.kraftheinzcompany.com/pdf/Supply_Chain_Transparency_and_Labor_Practices_Disclosures_FINALOct16.pdf.

7. Dow and The Nature Conservancy, *Working Together to Value Nature: 2016 Summary Report* (2017), 4–5, https://www.nature.org/content/dam/tnc/nature/en/documents/2016/-Dow-collaboration-report.pdf.

8. Ibid., 8.

9. See "GRI Standards," Global Reporting Initiative (GRI), https://www.globalreporting.org/standards.

10. Robert G. Eccles and Michael P. Krzus, *One Report: Integrated Reporting for a Sustainable Strategy* (New York: John Wiley & Sons, 2010).

11. Rebecca Hamilton (vice president, Research and Development and chief sustainability officer, W.S. Badger Company) in discussion with the author, July 3, 2018.

12. "Supporting the Community," Galaxy Entertainment, accessed July 15, 2018, http://www.galaxyentertainment.com/en/corp/supporting-the-community.

13. "Protecting Migrant Workers," Patagonia, accessed July 18, 2018, https://www.patagonia.com/protecting-migrant-workers.html.

14. Bobby Parmar, "Beyond the Bottom Line," TEDxCharlottesville video, January 8, 2016, https://www.youtube.com/watch?v=lOYe1fuWGdY.

15. Conrad Hackett and David McClendon, "Christians Remain World's Largest Religious Group, but They Are Declining in Europe," Pew Research Center, April 5, 2017, http://www.pewresearch.org/fact-tank/2017/04/05/christians-remain-worlds-largest-religious-group-but-they-are-declining-in-europe.

16. *The Silent Forest—Part 2*, documentary video directed by Gretchen Miller and Neil Trevithick, BBC World Service (2017), https://www.bbc.co.uk/programmes/w3csvnzl.

Chapter 13: Resources for Sustainability Champions

1. Nic Lutsey, Mikhail Grant, Sandra Wappelhorst, and Huan Zhou, *Power Play: How Governments Are Spurring the Electric Vehicle Industry*, International Council on Clean Transportation, May 15, 2015, https://www.theicct.org/publications/global-electric-vehicle-industry.

2. Imogen Calderwood, "16 Times Countries and Cities Have Banned Single-Use Plastics," *Global Citizen* (blog), April 25, 2018, https://www.globalcitizen.org/en/content/plastic-bans-around-the-world.

Afterword

1. "Last name: McAteer," Surname DB, accessed August 2, 2018, http://www.surnamedb.com/Surname/McAteer.

2. "United Nations Convention on the Law of the Sea of 10 December 1982: Overview and Full Text," United Nations, Division for Ocean Affairs and Law of the Sea (last updated March 28, 2018), accessed June 20, 2018, http://www.un.org/depts/los/convention_agreements/convention_overview_convention.htm.

3. Reg Watson, "Should We Ban Fishing on International Waters?" World Economic Forum, 19 February 2015, https://www.weforum.org/agenda/2015/02/should-we-ban-fishing-on-international-waters.

4. Jack Zenger, "Great Leaders Can Double Profits, Research Shows," *Forbes*, January 15, 2015.

5. Georges Desvaux and Sandrine Devillard, *Women Matter 2: Female Leadership, a Competitive Edge for the Future* (McKinsey & Company, 2008), https://www.mckinsey.com/~/media/McKinsey/Business%20Functions/Organization/Our%20Insights/Women%20matter/Women_matter_oct2008_english.ashx.

6. Georges Desvaux, Sandrine Devillard, and Pascal Baumgarten, *Women Matter: Gender Diversity, a Corporate Performance Driver* (McKinsey & Company, 2007), https://www.raeng.org.uk/publications/other/women-matter-oct-2007.

7. Adam Canwell and Euan Isles, *The Leadership Premium: How Companies Win the Confidence of Investors* (London: Deloitte, March 2012), https://www2.deloitte.com/content/dam/Deloitte/global/Documents/HumanCapital/dttl-hc-leadershippremium-8092013.pdf.

8. Michael C. Mankins and Eric Garton, *Time, Talent, Energy: Overcome Organizational Drag and Unleash Your Team's Productive Power* (Boston: Harvard Business Review Press, 2017).

9. Stephanie Vozza, "Why Employees at Google and Apple are More Productive," *Fast Company*, March 13, 2017, quote attributed to Michael Mankins, https://www.fastcompany.com/3068771/how-employees-at-apple-and-google-are-more-productive.

INDEX

PHOTO

PETER McATEER is managing director of SustainLearning Ltd. and serves as advisor to the board of directors for KPPM Global (Thailand). He formerly served as managing director for Harvard Business Publishing where he developed Harvard's e-learning and digital learning products. He previously served as director of learning services for the United Nations Development Program.

McAteer has served as adjunct faculty in human resource management at Columbia University's School of International and Public Affairs and has been guest speaker at universities around the world. He has authored and coauthored articles and commentaries in *Directors and Boards, the ASTD Journal, the Harvard Business Review*, the *European Business Forum, and Reuters Business Insights*. He has worked and travelled in more than fifty countries and calls Bangkok home.

www.pmcateer.com

Printed in the USA
CPSIA information can be obtained
at www.ICGtesting.com
JSHW021416230424
61724JS00001B/28